T0243386

THE SOUTHERN POETRY ANTHOLOGY

VOLUME IX

VIRGINIA

THE SOUTHERN POETRY ANTHOLOGY

VOLUME IX

VIRGINIA

William Wright, *Series Editor*

J. Bruce Fuller, Amy Wright, & Jesse Graves, *Volume Editors*

CONTENTS

Series Editor's Preface

Though this ninth volume of *The Southern Poetry Anthology* has been in production for a few years, the timing of its actual construction and publication could not have been better: J. Bruce Fuller, Director of Texas Review Press, as well as Jesse Graves and Amy Wright, all of whom I consider professional colleagues, collaborators, and friends, joined me to make this volume exceptional. The pleasure of working with such kind and focused colleagues is rare, and I owe much gratitude to them.

J. Bruce Fuller helped me clarify my vision for this multi-volume project. Through convivial conversations, he sculpted the first few drafts of this book. His leadership and tireless work have been crucial. He helped vivify this series.

Jesse Graves, one of the most celebrated and prominent poets and poetry scholars of the mountain South, took to the project with enthusiasm, good cheer, thoroughness.

Amy Wright, a Virginia native, had much to teach me about this landscape, evidenced in her beautiful introduction to this volume and her poetry within it. She filled the volume with light.

All helped me find poets I would not have found.

Of all volumes for which I have served as *The Southern Poetry Anthology* Series Editor, this one, centered on poets of Virginia, has been the most humbling. In full disclosure, I broke into a cold sweat of impostor syndrome when thinking about the state: (1) Since my teens, I have noticed that many great poets have called Virginia home, and (2), a disproportionately large number of these poets have influenced my own work, nurtured it with their own examples, been "silent mentors" to me for years.

My colleagues have helped me create a volume that demonstrates this vast array of Virginia poets, many new to me and from whom I will continue to learn.

William Wright
Dahlonega, GA

Introduction

It seems appropriate that the poets of Virginia cannot be conscripted into a single school or movement given the varied topography of the commonwealth. Five geologic regions define the landscape, including the Coastal Plain, Piedmont, Blue Ridge Mountains, Valley and Ridge, and Appalachian Plateau. Nearly six thousand feet of elevation differentiate the highest peak—Mount Rogers—from the sea-level Chesapeake Bay. Each province is marked by distinctive microclimates and plant hardiness zones, which are reflected in the points of view comprising this ninth volume of *The Southern Poetry Anthology*.

Among the images gathered here, you will find mountain bluebells as well as tidewater ducks and drakes. You will find Appalachian burial rites, red-clay Piedmont hills, and estuary-foraging Tundra Swans. The Roanoke Star features prominently, as does the Corcoran, the Coast Guard, the Nottoway River, Apple Orchard Mountain, and Natural Bridge. It is a tossup as to whether the appointed spokesperson should be The Urbilly, Michael Dowdy's coinage for a rural-urban character, or Leslie "Airplane" Payne, a crafter of life-size model planes that inspired him to rise, as Margaret Mackinnon describes, "toward some kingdom all his own." Yet even a highly dimensional individual cannot embody the reach of contemporary verse emerging from the commonwealth.

To appreciate it, we need to look back as well as forward, and many of the poets contained in these pages suggest we reckon with history. Let us open, then, with an acknowledgment to the Siouan-, Iroquoian-, and Algonquin-speaking people that first fished, farmed, and hunted the region. Through them, we glimpse the panoply initiated by the Cherokee, Chickahominy, Manahoac, Mattaponi, Monacan, Meherrin, Nansemond, Nottoway, Occaneechi, Pamunkey, Patawomeck, Powhatan, Rappahannock, Saponi, Totero, and Tutelo tribes. Their languages linger in Virginia's rivers and roads to texture the poems in this volume.

Their presence may even be the secret implied by N.V.M. González's poem published in *POETRY* Magazine in 1934:

VIRGINIA

You have a secret
but you are silent about it,
like the dawn that draws
its stealthy feet
upon the hills, and leaves
but the wetness on the grass
to tell of the mists that have settled and gone.

Language secrets people's origins. I like to imagine offering this poem, or another by one of the contributors to this collection, to read aloud and guess their regional relationships by accent. It takes a keen ear—good training for a poet—to distinguish the lilts and cadence created by those pockets of coast and valley, ridge and mountain.

Following the oral tradition of indigenous poetry, a long historical trajectory precedes this addition to the record of Virginia poetry. We cannot comprehend its reach without considering the palimpsest onto which it is inscribed—from the texts of Jamestown settlers like George Sandys who "Englished" Ovid's *Metamorphosis* in 1621 to Harlem Renaissance poets like Anne Spencer from Lynchburg, who were anthologized in 1922 in *The Book of American Negro Poetry*.

This volume's singularity is well suggested by five contributors who have won the Pulitzer Prize for Poetry: Rita Dove, Claudia Emerson, Forrest Gander, Henry Taylor, and Charles Wright. As if prompted by the same geography that creates adaptations between plant and animal species, these exemplars have each been shaped by and in turn, shaped their environments. The awarded *Thomas and Beulah*, *Late Wife*, *Be With*, *The Flying Change*, and *Black Zodiac* stand as discrete as a pipevine swallowtail from a red admiral from a hairstreak from a Luna moth from a viceroy, although all five poets and butterflies hold Virginia in common.

"The human ear is most sensitive / to the pitch of weeping," Gander writes in his contribution "from *Blue Ridge Log*." As if to explain what tuned that ear, Dove asks, "Why did history happen only on the outside?" The hardest questions are those the poets pose because they demand to be heard rather than answered. "History is a burning chariot," Wright responds in his poem of the same title, which Taylor underscores when he writes, "The life we live takes on...a shard of lore." Knowledge both rewards and stings, Emerson's speaker demonstrates in "Bee." So, "there you have it," she says to all of you prepared "to sting yourself" in its pursuit.

Such conversations extend throughout this volume, deepening our collective investigation into how to live and why. What does it mean to be human, much less Southern, Virginian, or provincial when Jim

Minick asks, "is there really a line / that separates us?" Or when Sappho Stanley adds, "Will 'woman' and / 'man' mean anything / in the future?" Can we not be more "Like the Trees in Alexandria," Zeina Azzam wonders in her poem, since:

> The soil we stand on is packed
> with the history of growth, the biology
> of perseverance—as fertile and deep
> as our affinities to each other.

And so, the poets gathered here express how different contexts, experiences, and landscapes distinguish what pains, isolates, joins, and nourishes us. In one of my last senior workshops at the University of Virginia, a dozen of us gathered around Rita Dove's kitchen table after she returned from her post as United States Poet Laureate. We were as drawn to her warmth as the crowds that surged in bookstores and auditoriums to hear her read during her appointment. The lesson that day was how to infuse a lyric persona with what individuates us. Her poem and others contained in this volume illustrate the influence that action can have.

Next year marks the centennial anniversary of the founding of The Poetry Society of Virginia, an occasion that will be attended by the current 20th Poet Laureate of Virginia, Luisa Igloria. Her included poem, "The Heart's Every Heave," reminds us that we advance by reflecting, and the lyric shines a useful lens across times and contexts. "If the future / is here," she asks, "whose face greets you / in the mirror as you collect / water in your hands"? It is a good question among others Igloria has been asking during her tenure as the ambassador of poetry in the commonwealth. Recognizing that the answer belongs as much to coming generations as to hers, she has been documenting the initiatives of young poets in the community on her website. I am moved by the advocacy of one eighth-grade poet at Tomahawk Middle School in Mosely, Virginia. Abigail Willis says, "for a social change, we must make people want to read poetry." Indeed, it is a worthwhile muse that prompts change, as are those that document struggle, integrate knowledge, texture language, and celebrate nuance, and there are ample reasons in the coming pages to want to read all of them.

—Amy Wright

April J. Asbury

Canning Time

When everything that blooms
is blown, when fruit swells,
heavy with sweetness,
labor is due.

Stand in steam and sweat,
trade heat of life for life: thin fingers
of green beans, pearls of white corn, yellow
chips of squash. Strain the black as blood
jelly, clots studded with seeds, save the mash
of peeled tomatoes. Let summer cling
to the windows until tears streak the fog,
until the sweat trickles under your hair
and streaks your aching back. Work fast,
in the scald and sweat—save all
against the Hunger Moon; the early gold
of walnut leaves already litters the ground.

Darnell Arnoult

The Gorilla Story

Around ten, the phone rang. We were all in bed. I was two.
"Joe," he heard the voice slur, "there's a fellow with a gorilla

down here. Says he'll pay a hundred bucks to anybody
who goes five minutes with his monkey and walks out

under his own steam." Daddy said, "Where is he?"
into the black receiver, heavy enough itself to be a weapon.

Between bed and the bazaar, he drank a fifth of liquor
and then had to pay fifty cents more to be foolish.

Daddy wore a coat and tie when he wasn't playing golf—
even to fight gorillas. The gorilla caught him

by the necktie. Dragged him through peanut hulls,
banana peels, slides of excrement, then tossed Daddy

to the back of the cage and rattled the bars
to scare onlookers and earn his pay. But daddy

came to and leaped onto the gorilla's back and grabbed
the bars just beyond all that hair and muscle. Pinned him

to his own cage. Daddy held on until he walked out under his own steam.
He held out his hand for the hundred, but the carney wasn't having it.

"You had an illegal hold on my gorilla!" the man barked.
"How," my daddy from that night until the day he died,

"can a man have an illegal hold on something with four hands?"
Forty years later, I met a boxing chimpanzee named Congo,

a champion in '57. He'd retired to Tarpon Springs. Someone wrote a book
about him, *The Gorilla Show*. I have this poem. He out lived Daddy

by at least twenty years. Congo never talked about that night in Martinsville,
ashamed to have been beaten. Not even to me. My daddy on the other hand

2

won years of telling this story. He taught me to tell it, that it's a story
worth believing, even with no proof but the story itself.

Learning Strategy at English Field

C.P.'s Outlaws versus the Martinsville Oilers.
Hot dogs and popcorn fill Friday night air
along with moths that flutter and flirt
with danger in the field lights.
Mothers ask questions of fathers
who talk to each other.
Their deep gravelly voices face the playing field—
they judge ball speed, weigh batting stance,
third baseman's charge, pitcher's windup, the balk,
short's scoop and fire to first.
They call for double plays, measure the power
of the catcher's legs, how fast his mask comes off.
Weaver, policeman, sander, insurance man,
mailman, doctor, lawyer, teacher,
foreman, yardman, fixer, preacher.
Their sons are scattered across a diamond
cupped in advertisements for WMVA, STP,
Blacky's Texaco, First Baptist Church, Red Man
Chew, Dixie Pig Pit-Cooked Bar-B-Q.
A fastball smacks the glove on third
then rockets to first—policeman to preacher.
A mother jumps on the concrete bleacher.
Claps and fidgets and does a hip walk in her seat.
She prays for a third out.

I am a girlfriend. A cheerleader. A rising senior.
I think I am listening and watching
to learn the game of baseball. If not for my boyfriend,
I would have no interest in the game.
An initiate spectator, I have not grasped
the mental energy of baseball:
telepathy between pitcher and catcher,
tension between the batter and pitcher,
pitcher and basemen, basemen and runner,
stealer and pitcher, catcher and batter.
SA-wing batter! Swing!
I only faintly appreciate the music of a hard ball
kissing the sweet spot of a wooden bat,

the dance of a runner in a pickle,
the warrior scrimmage as the third-base runner
goes for the steal and the catcher defends home.
I foolishly think I am learning baseball:
pass balls on third strikes, pop flies, fielder's choice,
fastballs, curveballs, spitballs, greaseballs,
high balls, low balls, inside, outside, bunts,
line drives, foul tips, steals, the sacrifice—
sacrifice fly, sacrifice bunt, sacrifice play on the runner.
So many sacrifices.
My boyfriend's mother shares her popcorn.
I clap when she claps. Yell when she yells.
Fidget when she fidgets. Smile when she smiles.
I watch her son, the third baseman.
He rests between batters, his right hip
shoved out to be a resting place
for the back of his gloved hand.
He spits absently and watches the pitcher approach the rubber.
He is cocky. He's also cute and a good kisser.
I forgive his arrogance for love. For his sake
I watch and learn and get my mind
around what I can in the little time I have left.
Come August he'll say no to college baseball.
I'll turn in my pompoms a year early.
I'll work half-days and he'll join the Marines.
The Cards will play the Braves in a three-game series.
Our honeymoon nights will be spent in Atlanta Stadium.
Our honeymoon days will be spent dodging rhinos
in his parents' Galaxy 500 at Lion Country Safari
and riding the roller coaster at Six Flags Over Georgia—
a preview of things to come.
I will throw up whatever I eat. I will lose before I gain.
By May I'll be a mother finishing senior English
and he'll make Lance Corporal and move us to Lejeune.
Our old paths will be unrecoverable
except through our son and daughter.

Fourteen years later, I shift my attention
from the memory of a third baseman
to the shortstop-gone-catcher
who, in the hesitation of play,
pushes out his right hip to make a resting place
for the back of his gloved hand.
He spits absently and pulls his mask over his face.
A girl somewhere in the stands

writes his name over and over in her notebook.
He squats as the pitcher addresses the rubber.
I am out of my seat as he pops up.
Out of his crouch, he flings off his mask,
backs up first.
Other players' fathers nod to me,
acknowledge a job well done.
Unlike the catcher's grandmother, I am forced out
of my element. I bridge the distance
between fidgeting mothers and voyeuristic fathers.
I am chastised by the blind tournament umpire,
my ex-mother-in-law in it right alongside me.
She shares her popcorn, watches and judges
her grandson—and me. Conspires in my strategy.
I am here, in the bleachers, willing a win
across distance only a mother can fathom.

Ode to the Dixie Pig—Business 220

God invented the bar-b-que
sandwich. It's a sin to eat it

without a dollop of coleslaw,
an anointment of Texas Pete.

Only vinegar-based passes
the pearly gates. God loves

take-out. This is His blessing:
a hog buried in a shallow grave

of smoldering ground, body cradled
by wet leaves covered in old tin

eating his last apple. Swab him in
vinegar and chilies,

a little brown sugar. Sop it on.
A towel made into a mop to bathe

his tangy flesh until it falls away.
Buns split and the rock slide

of potato salad tumbles onto Chinet.
God don't like doing dishes.

August

A china bowl filled with grain
and goldfinches glistens.
Flutters on the porch.

I nibble a biscuit.
Sip creamy coffee. Rock
out in the grassy yard.

In the hackberry
black and red beetles blanket
trunk and branch. Eat their names.

I see across the grass
what my husband told me.
Evidence of a bent blade.

It pie-slices the grass
and weeds pretending to be
grass—all disguised as lawn.

Picture him riding his mower
wearing the hat I pretend to hate.
His body muscled up and sun-warmed.

Picture me deadheading dry blossoms.
and heart-shaped leaves. How perfect a day.
Then turn to devour the imperfect world.

Artificer

The birdman conjures in recycled sheets and scraps
of old roofing tin and copper flashing. Wire. Magic

of argon, acetylene, oxygen, and flame. The flux.
What alchemy steps out from behind his shed's door

and walks to its place in the tall grass?
Lifelike, so sharp it can almost speak

in bird, in human, in metal languages, translate
the engineer into something godlike.

You there, maker, come out from behind the door
like your whooping crane, with its spread-wing

mating dance. Stand at water's edge
and be surprised by what you are made of.

Emma Aylor

Saltern

The history of the world according to salt is simple:
animals wore paths to salt licks; people followed.

And to clean water, too, and salt and water paths
became trails and later roads. We used to drive daily

routes 221 and 122 from one edge of the county
to the other through its forests in the dark.

Early spring green is the best time to establish a lick
for deer one hopes to track. Upright buds

of saucer and tulip magnolias like long flames;
some burst wide within the day, a rip.

Hunters may set up lick sites with cameras
to track the new antlers by June—the days and times

of their travels—which they plot on an aerial photo or map
to quilt grooves, herd paths: to wear in. To set up

near a creek crossing is often best. The kind of air
that can touch nothing touches salt and spreads it sometimes

on the road. That's how the mammal usually dies:
it comes to lick what's gathered on the asphalt. After it goes,

it will return each year. The rabbit my mother's car jolted
over, its body cracked under the wheelwell I sat above,

and we kept on into the dark of the hillbottom field
at the red mill nearly home—dark as deep as any dug hole.

I know we should have buried it
or licked its salt ourselves from the road.

An Appalachian ritual called for a plate holding salt and earth
to be placed on the chest of the deceased;

in a Roman rite, one settled grains
of salt on the eighth-day newborn's lips—to purify.

Apply and scatter a light coat of loose minerals.
There is no set amount. I mix them lightly

into the dirt with a rake or my boots.
To absolve. Once from the road a deer surged

its body clean over the car in front of us.
My mother has wondered twenty years

if the driver ever knew it happened. Sometimes we use
a whole bag and sometimes half. My father stored salt

and mineral licks as blocks in the wood-dust warehouse
of his farm and garden store. Hunters bought them

to lure deer sometimes, but more often farmers
for care of livestock: beef and dairy cattle, pigs, horses.

Flypaper spiraled yellow from the ceiling,
then less yellow for a crowded lace of bodies.

Over years, how many took a salt block—
ocher with mineral traces, and heavy—home

to their warm pasture of stock or loved animals to find it
gullied already by the red track of my mouth.

Hydronym

     1.
At the bald of Apple Orchard Mountain, red oaks
gnarled from winds; winter grasses; riven rocks fallen,
but these didn't *fall* from anywhere, my mother says,
it's just the skeleton of the mountain
collapsing on itself. The mist of the bent
valleys collects—water in the air, rivers hard to see
for all the hill shroud. Nothing is clean, nothing low.

2.

The man said, *I had a ghost to haunt me once.*

I went down the next morning
        a little before day, and she
went down stairs. It sounded like someone rolling marbles
                down the stairs. When he moved house he was sure
his feet crossed creek.
                    Little splashed at the toe.
She couldn't come across a stream of water   no bother

after crossing   she left alone

        at bottom   of dry slope   she pulls black thread from her
eyes.

                         she folds salt between her hands.

3.

When the salt melts, it will rain soon.
I think of moving home by earth, not air. West to east
the land crumples, smooths, then rises
tender bread. The rivers get familiar.
The rivers' sopped talk. When corn twists, rain is coming.

From my grandfather's abandoned home I can see the James:
in summer through easy leaves. In winter cut. Always rust
brushed at its banks. When distant noises are heard plainly
in the morning, there is rain before night. Can a ghost cross
the water when it's spread all through the air

4.

One   sprayed hairspray in the closed
bathroom   came in by the glass knob

Another trailed its feet   on floorboards upstairs
Each one of us in the basement   listening

Every photograph in my father's office   propped
in places of honor   knocked facedown over

All over the yard the slabstones   one for each
Touch of the heel   Face in night window

One strung her hair parallel   to the fenceline
      She couldn't cross the stream of water

Zeina Azzam

Like the Trees in Alexandria

> *"Forests aren't simply collections of trees; they're complex systems... [that] connect trees and allow them to communicate... and this makes the forest resilient."*
>
> —Ecologist Suzanne Simard

The soil we stand on is packed
with the history of growth, the biology
of perseverance—as fertile and deep
as our affinities to each other.
This is where we start.

It took us thousands of years
to understand the community of trees
in a forest, to listen to the way roots intertwine,
communicate in safety underground.
This is our language, too—

of carbon and nitrogen and phosphorus
as we construct infinite, unseen pathways
to share nutrients and water, stories
and poetry and songs.
These are our common roots.

We are the trees of the forest, leafy
and floral, coniferous, with flashy crowns
or simple beauty. So many shades
of green and brown. Hues of loveliness.
This diversity is our touchstone.

Cypress, juniper, and palm, jasmine
and jacaranda, many have traveled the world
as flying seeds to land and re-gather
and celebrate our homecoming.
This is who we are.

Our root systems teach us to behave as a single
organism, to uplift all branches, young and old,
she and he and they, watering and nourishing

each other, safeguarding saplings against injustice.
This is our present and our legacy.

We are the trees in Alexandria's forest.

A Language for Colors

Asfar she would say
pointing at a yellow tulip.

And the color of grass?

Akhdar.

My young daughter had mastered
not only the colors
but also the throaty KH,
two letters in English
that equal one in Arabic.

I would tell her it's the same sound
as in khamseh, khubez, sabanekh—
five, bread, spinach

and my favorite name
Khaled, Immortal.

I once confessed to a friend wistfully
that I would not name my son Khaled
because Americans couldn't pronounce it.
Now I wonder about such wisdom:
even my eight-year-old
could constrict her throat muscles the right way
to say Khaled—

immortal like an ancient olive tree,
a flame that never abates,
a mother's love.

This spring, I saw a patch
of double hybrid tulips,
asfar tinged with akhdar,
and thought of my daughter's

satisfied grin at learning those words
thousands of miles away
from her grandparents' home
in Palestine.

Here we are, hybrid Americans
living between two languages
and speaking in colors,
splendid flowers in a distant field.

A Grammar for Fleeing

*You know, when an emigrant needs something to hold on to, a spider web looks
like a wooden beam.* –Rafik Schami, Damascus Nights

Hudood, the word for border,
looms in her mind's vocabulary
like a passive voice, a noun for longing.
Maybe the undulating line runs in water
or in sand, splays on the imagined cover
of a passport, map for a new home.
She has vowed to cross it, daughter on her hip,
two legs doggedly moving apace,
two legs suspended, bare.
She plans to learn the other side
like a foreign language:
first the stones as single utterances,
then the houses and hills, sentences.
The scenes will warm in the light of the sun.
Now it is dark and the little girl
is ensconced in her arms, eyes closed,
but a lulling breeze could spell betrayal
if they aren't careful. She reaches
between her breasts for the pendant
inscribed with *amal*, hope, rubs it
like a magic lamp. The din of conversation
starts to rise as light gathers at the horizon,
where the singular message of true East
has grounded her since childhood.
Lay low, look west, wait for the boat.
She understands the grammar for fleeing,
unspoken rules that decide how
the journey will end, when words

like *harb*, war, and *joo`*, hunger,
might ebb and not flow.
Her toddler wakes asking for water
as the sea responds with crashing waves.

A Refugee Grows Old

For my mother

She is surprised by the pink cyclamen
in the pot, examines the foreign

petals, upswept as if reaching toward
another place. Her own journey seems muted now,

details as far away as her childhood in Palestine.
Where in one scenario she would have lived

in the same place until great grandchildren
played around the lemon tree that defined

her family's house in scent and space.
Where in the real scenario

she fled for her life with a husband and baby,
in her pocket a key that rusted over the years.

Her memories are like henna on a hand,
splendid arabesques fading each day

until gone. She has covered so many miles
by boat, plane, car, on foot, measured

by oceans and clouds, gas fumes,
tattered flags left behind, driver's licenses,

rental agreements, goodbyes to friends and family,
a lifetime unanchored, cleaved.

She continues to worry that someone
is plotting to take away her home

while slowly hunching over, a downswept
bent flower, weighed down by hallucinations.

She knows some things never leave you
so you have to leave them yourself, takes

small steps away
looking for some peace.

To Bring Justice Near

*On the commemoration of the lynching of Joseph McCoy in
Alexandria, Virginia, on April 23, 1897*

A Black man was lynched in our city, *here*,
where a white mob savagely had its way.
We must face history, bring justice near.

He lived on Alfred Street, age eighteen years,
grew up when harsh Jim Crow laws ruled the day.
A Black man was lynched in our city, *here*.

Together let's say his name, bare our tears.
We lift up Joseph McCoy, and we pray:
We must face history, bring justice near.

The trauma from racial hate is severe,
remains till *now*, unless we change our ways.
A Black man was lynched in our city, *here*.

No one was tried for his murder; it's clear
that this son of our city was betrayed.
We must face history, bring justice near.

Let's educate our youth, open eyes, ears,
so inhumanity is *not* replayed.
A Black man was lynched in our city, *here*.
We must face history, bring justice near.

Jeff Bagato

Hold This Moment in Stone

Chits and snares,
chances receding
into yesterday's twilight;
time travel cannot return the past;
errors must remain
errors

A dig peels back the days,
one by one—
increments,
grains of sand,
margins of retreat

Sifting the bones and shards,
a kind of guessing, a leap
of faith that an ancestor died here,
that this pile of sand
or soil conceals her
hearth and home,

and worldly goods
from eyes and more eyes:
foul children peeping through a keyhole—
this doorway
in time

Firelight parts the gloom;
there she stands,
a drink at lips
and a babe in arms,
stew pot heating above
the flames

Icons and pottery new made,
newly invested
with meaning and power;

meaning, that is, strength
to survive
this moment
in the light

Faith is for the present
and not for gone days
or a future
that can be excavated only
by tumbling
into death

Witness these various ruins:
columns that held up the law;
domes that sheltered
councils of war
and welfare;

walls
to hold these people
to their daily bread;
watchtowers from which to mark
those hoards of doom
for an arrow
or a sword;

and temples,
tombs for gods who also died here,
or sometimes changed into other gods
as one alphabet overtakes
another

This brick—
a road, a gate,
a headstone now—
though earth has swallowed
its true
meaning, too

George Bandy

ash borne

ash borne
and rain speckled,
steeped in mud and cold
we refuse to breathe
though breath comes
in haunted gasps—
we clutch our shoulders
and dare the living
to follow

Christina Beasley

Meditation on Hunting Season

The deer infiltrate our suburbs.
                Invade, soft and wide-eyed.

The rifle's muzzle, slight in my palms
          and cold in autumn.
                    The nearby beast body
       creaks, shifts and rustles the leaves.
       Destroys flowerbeds with its hunger,
                  snout deep in the daffodils.

This moment, overwhelmed with the possible—
              bolt action of a gun,
                  bolt action of a stag—
if I give too much headspace, the gun misfires.

The nipple of a firearm
              is near its percussion cap.
Its explosions, the beating of a heart.

              A weapon lives like an animal
              and corrodes like an animal.

Rate of fire is prized over accuracy
              and nature requires a blaze.

The energy of a cosmos can be condensed
          into a metal pin the size of an eyelash.

I've learned to cradle it in my hands—

to hold death in my hands—

        and I muzzle it,
                unmuzzle it.

Ladybug Hit-and-Run

On Skyline Drive, the Shenandoah Valley

Despair knocks on my small intestine
like a mortar   as the ladybugs explode
        against the windshield.

Pestled paste of parts
        spread slender on the glass.

Luck wasted on the asphalt,
world blurring by like a wet dream,
        immense and joyous.

For some, these abstractions are
everything.   I've always skipped too fast

        to scoop them up.

John Berry

Blackbirds

It began with the din of blackbirds
palavering in some nearby trees.
A crease of light unfolding under clouds
inciting them to animated conversation.
I loaded my bag, some books, my fiddle
kissed my wife, patted the dogs
and said goodbye. I crossed
the Cacapon River at Yellow Spring,
ran beside it to Wardensville, and climbed
the grade to Corridor H.
Near Mt. Storm I thought of bears.
Two minutes later, if that, black fur
and a red flag of blood waving
from the shoulder. Near Thomas
I noticed the wind was high. I decided
I should pay attention to the trees;
their breaking and falling. Two blind hills later
and a top was down. Men were cutting
and moving it away. Coming down from Parsons
where the feet of a bridge would one day
straighten the passage to Elkins
I thought   *if I could only forgive myself*
            the grey soot of doing and being alive
            everything would be ok.
I thought about the harmonics of bridges
how without the song that wanted singing
in the cement and steel of their bones
they would surely fall, which brought me back
to the din of blackbirds cracking jokes
with the sun, their considerable weight
in the branches of some nearby trees
hardly a burden.

For Dave

I don't know why
we never spoke of God.

Except that Time
is an old cellar door

and the shelves and dusty jars
of peaches and beans

will, eventually
disappear.

David Black

Dooley and the Hawk

A pair of redtails nested
near my garden this spring,
bold enough either would rest
in my hammock tree
and watch me with indifferent eye.

At such times they reminded me
of a falconer friend who took his bird
north across the border. On the return,
a guard ordered the hawk be freed,
so Dooley loosened the jesses
and watched him alight
in a tree some hundred yards away.

Imagine then that Dooley crossed the frontier,
stood in the highway with extended arm,
and the hawk flew back to perch and hood.

Imagine, too, that moment's uncommon strife:
the man bound by laws and vexed by doubts—
the hawk that far away,
yet so free he chose to return.

The Farm Boy's First Hunt

As a thin alder limb whips across his eye,
he knows it's gone, that more than tears run
down his face, that his brother striding
through the thicket ahead of him
was thinking only of the buck they've stalked
since dawn and, like the keen switch,
meant him no harm.

This is the land of hog slaughters and chickens

running about without their heads,
savage wounds, broken bones, and nine-fingered men,
of women tough as cast-iron skillets
and home births gone awry.

It's a lesson learned early that we patch
what we can and die if we must,
that we are shaped by mishap and time
into gnarled, shortened versions of ourselves,
creaky in the knees and stove up in the back,

and, truth be told, as able see the future
with one eye as with two.

Sleepers

A *sleeper*, they used to call it—
four passes with the giant round saw
and you had a crosstie, 7 inches by 9 of white oak—
at two hundred pounds nearly twice my weight
and ready to break finger or toe—

like coffin lids, those leftover slabs,
their new-sawn faces turning gold and brown
as my own in the hot Virginia sun,
drying toward the winter and the woodsaw

and on the day of that chore
I turned over a good, thick one
looking for the balance point

and roused a three-foot copperhead,
gold and brown like the wood,
disdaining the shoe it muscled across,

each rib distinct as a needle stitching leather,
heavy on my foot as a crosstie.

Terry Hall Bodine

Influenza 1918

Ineluctable as water seeping
into our cellar whenever the New River
rose out of its bed, so did influenza

flood our house that wet October,
its dank chill rattling in the chest
like coal in an empty scuttle. Cots

were rigged in the front room
when we all took sick—Alice, Nora,
Daddy, me—curtains wheezing

in windows, bedsheets wilted,
limp pillows rusted with spittle.
Mustard plasters loosened lungs pasted

with phlegm. Breaths seized. Fresh waves
of fever crested in sweat, Mama
there to ease me up for air

through days drowned dark inside
blank drawn shades, willing my
hesitant wade toward reprieve—

a cool cloth, a tin cup, a spoon.
When at last I surfaced—Daddy bathing
Nora, Alice quiet in sleep—only then did

Mama go under, young tree with its
roots washed loose, and we, like wrung-out
kitchen rags, too weak to drag her home.

Tara Bray

Owl Prayer

The daughter refused to get out of the car.
She did not want to come out so early in search
of an owl. I had heard there was a nest in the wetlands.
We went first to our usual blind and like a miracle,
like it had been waiting just for us, it rose up,
our first barred owl, in flight,
its muscled wings spread, its blunt profile a shock.
It landed on a branch and my girl kept saying, *Mama*
it's looking at us. Mama I am so happy for you.
You prayed for this. What kind of mother prays
for such before a child? There is a touch of shame

to this story, the way I kept quiet, wanting her to believe,
not that a mother might muster up grandeur
by asking out loud for those feathered shoulders,
the marbled stare, but that a god might hear,
plant a little sighting out of love.
I withheld that I'd prayed for the end of illness
repeatedly, for my body to hold firm, only to watch it ruin
itself a little more. Forgive me. So I let her revel
in the world's rightness at the end of a tough winter,
and I let myself feel the relief,
in the name of the mother, the daughter & and the holy spirit,
our gazes all converging in the trees,
in this fractured lineage of belief.

Bird on Knee

There was a man who filmed
a wild bird perched lightly
on his knee, an eastern phoebe,
and how I wish it had been me
to receive a little sign
the tide might turn, shift.
Think my rod, my staff, the craft
of conjuring a little belief,
a field of grass, a clear horizon line.
Goodness is not the key,
but comfort and small things
that land softly, stun the breath,
let you have a thrill just long enough
where the knee quivers,
and a bird shifts accordingly.

Robert Brickhouse

Crossing the Inlet

for W.L. McL.

Winter stars and ice on the river.
A dear friend who lived back in the mountains
a notorious tale-teller who'd traveled the world
once led me down a narrow trail past bluffs
to chain his pasture gate flapped open in snow.
The scene, wind whip through denim and boot crunch
inspired him to dream yet again
another wild story among all those soft-spoken
through years by lantern light on his lane.

On an arm of some far northern sea
where he said he'd once stayed for a while
he often skated across by starlight on glaze
vastly thicker than this forming now.
Dark all around, below.
A few lights a mile and more off
on the little houses on the frozen spit.
Each night he glided in arcs in joy on the ice, under Orion
a scarf across his beard and flying.

On the night he told of he thought he heard
through a crazy wind off the open ocean
a strange cacophony of faint cries, among thunder
and ice crack. In cold so bitter, he said.
No boat could venture out there. No ice-fishers from the village.
Curious, helpful by nature, he swirled seaward
to the thinning reaches of ice as far as he dared go.
Heard shrieks and wails such as I never wanted to hear.
He grabbed my arm as the path turned perilous.
*I flicked on this miner's light I'd rigged
on my cap, swept it to all the commotion.
On out was a great flock of sea birds.
They'd stayed too late seeking one last bite
in their quest for herring. Feet snap-frozen now.
They were screaming and flapping, furious to escape.*

Then in my lamp's beam I saw what the gulls already knew.
At the edge of the dark, rows of bright yellow eyes.
Foxes were gathering. Waiting for firm freeze.

On our path the stars were thrown close.
His own eyes watched sharp.
I think he believed that his outrageous stories
helped open our hearts to the world.
Back at his cabin, by a crackling fire
he poured me a shot of some bitter liquor
he said they drink in that north country.
It's supposed to be good for you, made
with a secret recipe from wildflowers.

Days at the Store

in memory of James Robinson, mountain man

Sun and shadows climb red-clay hillside,
so I see when I go back into that country.
Apple trees bloom there.
The creek that ran beside his shack
wanders down through pines,
cold water shining like broken glass until
it turns cloudy in the weeds beside the road.
Trucks wild as any winter wind rushed right at him
when he crossed "to get a few things."
I'd see him coming with his empty onion sack.
Oh, hell, got to put up with James for a while.
He smelled like a charred oak log in that old army coat,
leaning there against a post, guzzling milk
from a cardboard carton, scowling at me,
smearing the counter with grime
wherever he placed a hand.
For weeks he'd have a sick eye
that streaked tears through his grizzled beard.
Need bread, some sausage, pack of Camels, rice.
Spring of the year, where's your garden seed?
Scratch feed too high to be wasting on no fox.
Always wanted coffee. Now no coffee on his stove.

He'd whoop, jabber, hang around.
Follow me if I turned my back,

went to dust a shelf, unpack a box.
Can of snaps. Corn meal. Nice afternoon.
Owls hootin' all last night.
Out-of-state cars would honk at the pump,
wheel off when he bounded out to help
in moth-chewed cap, boot-laces dragging.
Once a month a lady from town
came to pay off his bill with a government check,
add extra from her purse if he needed gloves, an ax handle.
Neighbors patched his roof, cleaned his spring.
Each week I'd have to hold him to what he could afford.
You just got radio batteries, James.
Make up your mind. I don't have all day.
He'd look down, frown.
Some lamp oil, I reckon.

The joke, the truth:
one thing I did have
trying "back to the land" was time.
And together we each could lose
for a while our loneliness.
How those children? They like candy,
I see them eyeing that candy.
They like school?
I can spell my name but I can't write it.

In our own strange school
he taught with all seriousness.
The cat slept in the treetop.
I was picking apples but then I look for zing-zang.
He made me learn the right questions.
Was the cat watching for the fox?
Do you see any good berries up the hollow?
The delirious laugh would start low in his throat.
No-o-o sir, I don't touch that 'Shady' wine.
Then he'd flop on the feed bags,
observe for a while, nibble crackers.
When the spirit moved him, in chill
he'd button his coat, pull on that watch cap.
Look for his stick, his pack, his kerosene can.
Slip off, class dismissed.
Cross the highway, disappear back into his woods.
Some years later, one of those semis
roaring to Carolina
finally struck him by the roadside.

Up on his mountain he had a garden,
sometimes some chickens.
Owls, a cold stream, the wind.
Fog rising. Smell like fall.
A rusted tin heater, a frying pan.
A coffee pot, a lantern, a dying radio.
Yessir, could be right nice day.
A heap of old cans
hauled from the store.
A stack of fresh firewood
cut by better men than I.

Candace Butler

Still Life

after Ruysch

I want the silk of blueberries
without the softening centers;
I want all the shades of dusk in one small fruit.

I want the cobalt salamander
uncovered from the shadows,
I want to see the small steel specks along its back.

I want the leafy vine of cantaloupe
haloing the citron melon;
I want the maze of rind, the subtle green.

I want the cerulean fringe of chicory
floating in the air, highlighted hue;
I want a ray of light through this dark space.

I want the chubby blush of peaches
laying leisurely in stacks;
I want them forever framed by fine-toothed leaves.

I want the partitioned pomegranate
always sliced at its alzarin prime;
I want the rosy seeds, the film of white.

And I want the horsehair nest
before the fragile, soft eggs hatch;
I want the fear of breaking at every touch.

White Wire

Fence my eyes with chicken wire;
call me your foiled bride.
the pale pink darnings of yestercade are nothing more
than a forgotten study on a dusty floor.
the white lace train hocks over
the mountain, hunching its back against the cold.
the woodstove of my childhood will
asphyxiate me yet.

The only color I'll know now is dried flowers
tied with ribbon in a closet in a shoebox in the snow.
My reed neck in biplicity,
my domed cathedral of a throat
lying dormant like hornets in a nest of spit—
who tells them to hum the score you wrote for me?

The Kiss

the points at which we bend,
the wrist, elbow, index,
dancing
the points of all those rectangles,
gold streams run past his neck,
past points of jaw and cheek and nose,
past hands firm with intent
to press soft lips to skin—
a sigh of the west wind,

sky full of golden flecks
a wide and painted meadow
reds, greens, and ultraviolets
against his gold and monochrome,
with lips still touching petal skin—
years of living leave the mind

knees buried in soft grass
toes curled, eyes closed, hair

in circles down her back,
trickling past her calves,
past flowers blooming 'round
to frame her orchid cheeks,
that skin to feel soft lips,
a primavera pink.

falling on the cliff's patched thigh,
forelsket fresh in the breeze
now rippling up her side
over fabric so delicate, so free
oh! to recall the feeling first
and these small moments last.

Ben E. Campbell

Left to Smolder

Here soil's swell, bored ground abound to rupture.
Earth spilled Milesian dark. Sieged father's father's land.
But blameless rusts the plough in this scene to sewn invasion.
Bees swarm their hollowed home in a clannish-crazed defense.
My father flanking hive, we two eye their dance at door,
hole slimmed a quarter crater, ants skirting loch-like edge.
In hand he holds dual swords—coned paper wick, flick lighter.
And I, seemed ocean's length apart, grip can of kerosene.

Silence. So little shared of sound, words spared sacred as a stinger.
Talk the devil's ruse that will still a hand to idle.
Yet periled to the pull, thoughts drone a young boy's mind.
Why here? I want to ask in a wait of walk-to nod.
Who made home this hump of hill down the Rappahannock's stream,
trading Scotland's rocky shores for a field of Old Dominion?
Alba singed to blank by "what's lost is not what's left",
no fight for our own line like the flurry here before us.
Little do I know just how little do we know.
Names and places Gaelic graced buried still beneath some ground.
What is known? The whos and whys gave long ago to LIVE,
the remnant of our hive lost amid the working struggle.

Eyes adjusting to the now, I swat path to hand off fuel.
He shakes douse to drown the den then passes lighted torch,
newsprint stricken by the flame as the Seanachaidh to clearance.
I fling it flashing onto mound with a hard, resounding *whoosh!*
Before us drunken forms wisp as fairies on the flee,
each fighting to stave off what as slayer I'm to reap:
That death is better served when it's swift and wholly soundless,
no trail by root to trace that which smolders from afar.

Soup Bean Supper

One cannot fill a poor
man's bowl by the
harvest of coke and cinder.
Want to feed a ravaged body?
Ladle soup beans over
corn bread so he may
dredge a crumbled mound,
auger hunger just as Grandpa did
by heft of force-bent spoon.
Our last supper I recall
he gorged on mess'a beans,
sharing praise for lifelong bounty
through chomp and singsong slurp.
Father who art in Heaven,
he gave thanks for seasoned kettle,
for souls called gathered 'round,
for light that coal mines fueled
that he may read a diner's work.
Let sustenance rain like
manna on yon hill,
over haunting conjured face,
stored rasp of hard-drawn breath.
No vessel fills his table end.
Only grit of grainy bean,
the breaking time-staled bread.
These customs proxy remnants
feeding hunger left by void.

John Casteen

Incomplete Stranger

October evening, in pasture at Appalachia's slender feet:
        the tufted sprays of little bluestem that flicker
like votives on a hill full of early fall snow. Skaty
        night sounds of raccoon, leaf litter. To the east,
a floodplain, reeds. To the west, starlit beneath the new
        new moon: old dogs' teeth of the Blue Ridge.

Before me, bathed in starlight, the Rockfish River courses
        from nowhere to nowhere else, like a vein
of the landscape's earthly body. Marl-encumbered.
        Leaf-mottled. Sinuous. And my favorite fine
distinctions: hunger & appetite, delicate & fragile, secret
        & private. The clouds and hills are speaking

in their own tongues again: opaque blue-black veil
        of evening, opaque lacunae of the past, the past.
One durable memory: the crisp, sharp, nothing-
        scent of cold she finds in my hair with her face
and slim fingers. Big medicine. The needle ice that springs
        up from the loam and shale. The hem of the ginkgo's

saffron dress of dropped, fanned leaves, draped luminous
        over green swards of lawn. A happiness like children's.

        [sometimes it's best to take a thing too far sometimes
                it's not an ending   just an end]

Dining Alone

Manger seul, yes. Perhaps at the bar,
straight-spined and right in your mind as rain,
or a deuce of your own, off to one side.
No one really minds your strange assemblage
of small orders, dish-calm and many, supper

for one made of spare parts, possibilities.
You are better than nothing, of course.
You mean conversation, a tip, a curious blip.
Do they wonder what's gone off the rails
that you're here with no one, that no one

lives for your company? No one who loves
nothing more than the touch of your gaze
across a set table, the badinage of others,
a meal on its composed way, the kitchen
humming, your name on the tip of her tongue?

For the Mountain Laurel

Here's what to admire: how it thrives
on adversity, accepts its condition of want,
and greens. Makes a limber bark, makes bright
ecliptic little coronated flowers. And speaks
in the vernacular register: a watershed.
In downpours, a verdant shelter: sheds water.
Canny scantling. It's good at what it's good at.
I'm trying hard to clear my head, to think
without language, to remember that whole life
before the adjective. Don't forget: the shadow moves
more than you move, and intends less. Overhead,
contrails sinter where jets just passed, just ice
windblown like seed where stars are what belongs.

My Time Among the Swells

In the tacit light of a jejune June evening,
swallows flit and curl, the little frogs clicking
desire at one another in the cattails. Gabardines
and high cheekbones assess their own
and only tender merits. Contrasty waiters pass
superior comestibles; the crowd shifts comfortably
from foot to foot. God look kindly on this man
and this woman, for richer or for less rich, till
death, et cetera. Fireflies light like sparks.
The gaze of the Lord, straight as a gun-barrel,
so we imagine. But my God is a lonesome
and melancholy God; just above my ankles,
my creases' crisp breaks correct themselves.
Have another drink. You'll like yourself more.
O first among equals, delible as memory,
indelible as cloud: imagine an ideal world,
its people's lives like ours, mannered, but more
spontaneous, and fuller of delight. Marriage material
out on the stroll, because, hey, you never know.
For reasons known only to themselves, couples splinter
off into bad musical dusk; someone tells a joke,
softly, someone laughs a little too long. A trickle
of voices threads its way along the stair. Sleek words.
Indifference is what the world says, and loud
in its enormous voice; in full throat, a barred owl
calls its audibles. In the poem that's happening now:
and now: I am impeccable, gleaming. I understand
everything, tonight. Abstraction is what's here.
Our thoughts are behaviors; they continue in our absence.
Imagined, like the future, and over-toned the orange
of midsummer, a lot depending on a lot, the drawn thrum
of evening's bees, alive and in that golden hour....

Bird-Teasing After the Hurricane

Once late-summer storms blow past and leave
high pressure alone in their wake, cerulean skies
and bright, whippy wind, things start to dry
from the top down; they glisten, and I
in my kingly leisure lie among the maidenhair ferns
low in the woods by the once-parched creek. Imagine
how I appear to them, those black and turkey
vultures who circle like a posse and endingly sink
as they ponder me, naked as the day I was born,
as dead and good as dead can get, like a morsel
from heaven, six foot one and a buck eighty-five
of solid wish fulfillment, a spread picnic of carrion.
They clasp their wings in gratitude, ah,
their good fortune knows no limit, me as meat
on the ground, lungs full of water and nothing
behind my face, my eyes open to the sky
they circumscribe. See how they acknowledge our grief
with hunger, the best sauce; see how the red blisters
of their heads turn, turn, fixing on certainties
laid out for them like supper without a voice...
In my mind, Emmylou Harris is singing
with Gram Parsons; they're working through
that Louvin Brothers song about the way
the true heart's called back home before
the scoundrel finds his faith, the father making right
what ailed his child. All the jokes we understand
are about misfortune; all the ones we don't
are about us. The birds drop still, their circuits
shrinking, fix on me like I'm what's on t.v., then spot
my pulse. Then a sudden ruckus, frenzy,
terror, wheeling away, a wild man screaming poems
at the gleaners of misfortune, *I ain't dead yet motherfuckers*,
hot-blooded as I ever was, quick as Clint Eastwood,
howling at the birds and world for everything I'm worth.

Michael Chitwood

The Great Wagon Road, or How History Knocked the Professor Cold, or a Storyteller's Story, or Why Appalachians Are a Mountains and a People

Scottish, by way of Ulster, Philadelphia,
the Valley of the Shenandoah,

generous, clannish, violent, kind-hearted,
they walked in (the Germans rode)

and stayed mostly out of county records
and the backs of Bibles, unlettered.

Their only correspondence with me,
son of their children's children's great grandchildren,

is this ditch, these nearly healed wheel cuts,
the line they traced in the earth.

*

Locally, it took its name from where it was going,
the potent away-from-here, the better place,

the how-it-could-be, not wintering on beans,
the infant not dead with the flux,

the ground not snagged with roots
that sang from the plow's cut and welted the shins.

Yonder. Chewed with scratch biscuits,
smoked in the porch shade,

something to be believed
when believing was the only solace.

*

"Fortunately, only Single Brothers

made this trip. This trail

at times is impassable and these folk
are wild, unpredictable.

Unlike our brethren,
they came not seeking but fleeing,

the almshouse, the sheriff,
a shamed woman or her brothers.

We sought the freedom to worship.
They worshipped freedom from seeking."

*

"I don't know now, though I knew...."
Her palsied hand goes to her forehead

as if to draw memory with a touch.
My past grows dim,

illiterate, abandoned,
free for the taking.

*

A boy of four, he killed
one of the King's overlords

for casting a desirous eye on his mother,
and stowed away to sail the whale road.

Saving the crew and cargo from storm,
he was rewarded in Philadelphia

with a seventeen-hand stallion
and rode out of the city stench

to the Blue Ridge which reminded him of home.
There he killed and married Cherokee,

fathered seven sons and seven daughters,
coaxed Highland pipes from fiddle's catgut,

distilled moonlight, slaughtered hogs,
lost fingers in sawmills,

hoed, suckered, topped and primed tobacco,
discarded washing machines in creekbeds,

learned to read the Bible, believe obituaries
and recite where he was and what he was doing

when the first Ford, radio, television
and news of JFK's death arrived.

He put on a tie, conditioned the air
and forgot the song of the whippoorwill.

*

"There is no history, but histories."
His shoes aren't right for this rough ground.

The sapling branches whip his back
as he backs into where we're going.

Educated, tenured, he hopes to publish
a study of The Great Wagon Road.

"Until documented the facts are in flux."
He is lecturing backward into the understory

where a honeysuckle vine catches his heel.
He barks his bald spot on a sweet gum

and is silenced into the fact of himself.
Out cold, he's received his dissertation's introduction.

*

Count Casimir Pulaski, Bishop
Francis Asbury, Lorenzo Dow,

the Moravian Single Brother who wrote
"We had to watch our horses closely...."

They crossed Maggodee, Blackwater,
and Pigg, scribbled down some thoughts

that I'm stealing outright,
keeping an eye on their horses, too.

Warrior's Trace, gospel road, going now
into sumac, scrub pine and books.

I take your dirt in my hand.
I take your dirt in my hand and move on.

Virginia Opossum

> *"hath an head like a swine,*
> *tail like a rat,*
> *of the bigness of a cat"*
> —*John Smith*

The dog charged
and it did what they do—
it died.
It's a trick maybe we should learn,
faint rather than fight.
It's served them well,
a fossil mammal, North American marsupial:
they survive, nocturnal,
and will eat anything, fruit or rotting meat.
But this one was ambling in daylight
which made me think something was wrong.
After I got the dog inside,
the scruffy little Jesus didn't resurrect.
Thirty minutes, it was still dead.
The dog was going nuts.
Finally, gloved, I lifted it by its thick bare tail,
a five-pound history lesson, colonists, Powhatan,
like us, grubber, mongrel,
and took it into the woods and tucked it in the fallen leaves.
Did it rise, return to its omnivore ways?
I don't know, but history says yes.
It was gone the next day.

Kathy Davis

Undone

Borage leaves for courage, heart,
but I harvest just the blossoms, layer them

in plastic clamshells. Squint, they're blue
sky in a box. The black anthers,

a murder of crows. Bones sometimes
surface in the compost. A sheep's skull

over the greenhouse door. The farmer
down the road never mucked his stalls,

left ewes, lambs to rot where they fell. *Garden,*
I thought when he died. Took a shovel

to the rich dark mix, hauled it and his
abandoned collie home. The flower

tastes like cucumber. Watery, bland. Pleasure
mostly in the color. Each day, nosing the path

back to the old man's, the collie sits at the end
of her undone chain. The way—out of longing,
duty, habit—I've worried my own dead.
Time and worms and heat have worked

the stench from the manure. My hands
gentle, the dog cowers, still anticipating blows.

Eve: After the Fall

The stone has fallen from the bee box,
the hive is loosed,
                    the music started,

& a child wearing glitter
in her hair, a sprinkle of barrettes,
sequins on her slippers,
whirls in bright hands-over-head abandon.

The gods had covered their ears to me
& cried, *Enough.*

So much drudgery & drivel to suffer through alone.

But then one day my dryer lint
                              was the palest lavender.

I molded it with glue into a tiny man.

Hands shaping hands, flesh sculpting flesh,
we were somewhere between
                          beautiful & ugly
when he first drew breath.

R. H. W. Dillard

Fragments of an Autobiography: The Early Years

Who is this happy infant
in the white snow suit
tottering toward us?

Domine, whence cometh our help?

Which shall it be,
comforted or comforting,
alibi or lullaby?

True, an elephant divided
into fingertips
becomes an incomprehensible presence.

Nevertheless.

An unbound ovary,
once the tied tongue loosened,
babble, prophetic ruin,
one long letter,
perhaps an ā.

Only then the necessary steps taken.

Rain in a dark doorway,
ivory clicking. Hush.

Night.

Brotherhood may be lost
in three days.

This little piggy and that.

Clean sheets. Clean sheets.

Up and down the boulevard, alarm

alert, earth's crust in minor motion,
a plague of frog,
another day, aperch on a stone wall,
an unexpected punch in the flank,
misericorde.

Too much, too much to bear
away, the slight thief wept.

Crow with the cock, a doodle do.

Kriegsprache on the shrill short wave,
Martians in New Jersey,
blue turtle, cracked nerves,
tightning of the chest,
numbling of the fingers,
the circling airplane, so low on gas,
"Oh, the dayes that wee haue seene,"
ankle deep in agony.

Fire truck slams flat the gray coupe,
bomber in mud bank, that file of staring cars,
burning house flares across the wide Ohio,
stone, bronze, iron, steel,
titanium bonds with bone,
blazing o'er the ocean, bonny ocean,
as the bell went down.

Ann, her lopped arm, gripped stump,
Such a little dance, round around,
Lordy, Lordy,
Misericordia,
Step, hop, step, hop,
Wolf at the third pig's door.

Truth a feature of fact,
often undisturbed
or disturbing,
How doth the brain
Both hop and skip.

A terrible time is come upon us,
a time of cruelty, two sisters
hold hands and sing carols
by the red hot wood stove,

seven times hot, Christmas
wood ashing iron.

Stacked, piled, unruly,
first the sprinkle, douse
holy water, then the fire,
cornet, flute, harpe, sackbut,
psalterie, and dulcimer,
and all kindes of musicke,
warm wind, why was
the smoke so black?

Is that what you remember most,
fat smell, wind suck,
and, of course,
crackle and char?

The fourth man?

Domine, it is so difficult
to remember:
the sheep like falling
rain on Glencoe steeps,
spear thrust in the side,
rush of water and blood,
vinegar, bullets
hollow pointed,
stones from their graves
still in my pocket, sparkling
rat-a-tat from the stairs,
cardboard bomber,
sprung wood.

Quo vadis, Domine?

Wee, wee, wee,
all the way home.

Words and shadows.

A stag clear of velvet
lowers his racked head
to lap.

Raven

Edgar, they are still telling lies about you,
Old calumnies, scornful, never-ending,
(The drink, the dope), humdrum, lollygags,
Starved your mother-in-law to death
Though fully known Mrs. Clemm alive
And well when they did you in in Baltimore,
Suppose some solace in that you're not
The only one they victimize these days,
All those lies, caw caw cacophony,
Smear the air like mustered crows,
Is that what it all amounts to, crowbait,
Glassy eyes, those "windows to the soul"
Cracked by hungry beaks, midday
Snack? better to lie there in Baltimore
Than to have to put up with lies, more lies,
Lies within lies, and "all within the *Spirit Divine*."

Walking Home from the Raleigh Court Branch Library

I reach the first real page
Of John H. Watson's reminiscences
Who took his degree in 1878.
The year is 1949, and I have only
A mile to go. I am walking home.

Sometimes today I want to loosen out
Like a large flag, possibly orange,
In an early April wind, and do.
But more often I remember
Walking home where I can really settle in.

Surprises

We cannot stay among the ruins.
–R. W. Emerson

The sudden edge of a bell
Or a knock. You answer,
If at all, touching wood.

You touch wood, and you answer.
It is like turning a page.
It is a mailman or a boy.
It is the undertaker.
It is Cyndy whom you haven't seen for months
Or Cronan who was just by yesterday.
It is a pirate with somebody on his shoulder,
Someone you know.

The day dazzles, dances,
The light splashing in like rain.
There are twelve policemen at your door.
There are two men with a cow
Or one man with an eye like a radish.

There is no one at the door at all.

No point in going back to bed.
The day is torn open like an envelope.
It is as open as the door.
You are opening like a door,
Steadying like a zeppelin in the air.
You take on edges. You expand.

Something has come to call
And found you in. And now
You must go calling on the day.

Rita Dove

Declaration of Interdependence

Hooknose, Canada Goose, slit-eyed Toucan.

       Porch monkey, baboon, trash-talking magpie.
I cover my head in adoration, just as you doff your hat.
       Do not rub my head. Don't even think about it.
I bob as I chant, I pray as I breathe. Does that disgust you?
       I shout to the Lord, dance out my joy. Does that amuse
you?
To my knowledge I have never terminated a deity.
       Last time I looked, I did not have a tail.
Business is not "in" my blood. I attended university. I
studied.
       I am a trained athlete. Nothing I do on the court is
         natural.
Matzo is not a culinary delicacy: There wasn't a menu.
       Fried chicken will kill you just as easy as the
Colonel.
You buy tickets to hear me crack jokes about my tribe. Are you
       uncomfortable yet?
       Suddenly you're walking up the same street
I'm walking down.
       Are you frightened yet?
You laugh, and forget. I laugh, and remember.
       I laugh to forget, and the thorn deepens.
Excuse me, but what do vermin actually look like?
       Raccoons are intelligent, curious, and highly
industrious.
I am not the problem or even
 a problem. Problems have provenance;
someone
created them.
       I'm neither exotic nor particularly earthy. I was
a child
         once; I
       belonged to someone.
No, I do not know how to play the violin.
       Sorry, I'm tone-deaf. No rhythm here.

Bagel-dog, Bronx Indian, Beastie Boy.
        Buckwheat, Burr Head, banjo lips.
I have never even seen a well.
        So is that
 a poplar?
Do not talk about my mother.
        Do not talk about my mother.

Michael Dowdy

The Urbilly's Field Guide

Wind deep into the wet valley: town of twelve mountains, sudden weather, penumbral springs, the New River cutting your way into the country.

Follow its fork and bend, stone-braced and boulder-steep. Outside its gauge a dark-graded future: roads when you think of crowds.

Telescope down: the city's a furnace of glass, spa of traffic, gorge of shoulders, the outbreak of kings. Your will to the land: in snow a drop of gas.

Reckon the past again, pursuing nest and pillar forge, Virginia morning swinging pine-green against your now. The high passes unpack a hawk's reason.

Case the trail of sulfur and coal, touch the leaves, read the rock, the air, the faces in chalk, remove the strong for the good and fair. Here, friends hard and dear iron you out.

The maps back are small lights: when fighting the tall station clock, when you bring to the precipice your first wish, when the river white and fierce calls you down.

The Urbilly's Family Tree, as Seen Through Binoculars

       Smudged along the lower ridge
       a copse of knobby hardwoods

withers in coils of cold wind.
Squint past the blind curve scribbled

       in cut banks of brush, just there,
       where fog-coated sycamores

unfurl scrolls of icy bark,
where taillights trickle beyond

Oblivion, Virginia,
where calm haunts the revenant.

Laurel hells strangle hearth and flue.
Even springs zigzag uphill.

No good here my wistful words.
Those provenance jackets veil

my sparrow chest and stuffed gut.
Here, where decades stretch threadbare,

my grave dark eyes, sockets deep
as karst caves, skitter and rest.

A tongue rhododendron tied
slips loose; restless legs snap to.

My sneakers swoosh in hoarfrost,
scything kin from the harvest

of time, stutterers who hauled
fieldstone, sunk wells, and raised beams

right about there. You have to
cock your head just so, just there,

where clouds lung the mountains' ribs.
Where trunks bend and crack the last

inky leaves bear down, hold outs
against the thieving north winds.

Hilda Downer

Clothespins

Not every girl looks
this glamorous out of the shower—one
clothespin clinches my robe
with the lost tie.
Another repairs a worn-out shower cap;
it sticks out on the side,
cartoonish as a Dagwood ponytail.

Clothespins organize letters and bills
(in line to be the next to go),
keep bags of flour and cornmeal tight-lipped,
and hold cereal bags to soothe them quiet.

Paper clips do not have such wooden wings.

Of winter laundry, jeans frozen stiff as new ones
until my mother surrendered to lines
across the living room
to duck under or fight with shirts.
I would quickly tear away my underwear
when a car pulled up.

From the yard sale of all her belongings,
I kept my mother's clothespins.
I had no need for them.

I already had enough
to share when I extended a clothesline
across the backdrop of your cityscape.
Not used to hanging out clothes,
you began to report
each time the wind patted
your sheets and towels dry.

Positioned as a sundial,
laundry sets its timer
to be brought in
by the shadows of its alphabet.

I painted clothespins

into exotic animals
to hold a young son's attention
and keep him nearby.
Just as he started to wander,
he would run back to laugh
as I pulled out a hippopotamus
or alligator to chomp down
on a wet sock wriggling to escape.

When I was a child, my mother's
straight clothespins were my first models,
practice for making my own clothes.
As she cut quilt pieces,
scraps themselves,
I gathered her scraps off the floor.
A scrap tied around the bodice of a clothespin
fashioned an elegant prom gown.
A scrap goes a long way.
A man survived death camp by a scrap.
After dishing out the last portion to others,
he licked the spoon.

A clothespin is just a scrap of wood.

Oiled by fingers skillful across piano keys,
my mother's clothespins
absorbed some of her music
as they rattle in her coffee tin.

Buttons

I cannot guess the number of buttons
in the huge Vaseline jar.
A kaleidoscope of variety and color
slinks a waterfall over my fingers
into a lake across the table.
Culled from flour-sack dresses,
infant clothes, and military jackets,
some are big as a doll's plate;
others, so tiny and delicate
that their white is transparent.
Among my favorites are the black ones
centered with clear rhinestones
like stars floating on a cup of night.
I position them as the Big Dipper.
One, elongated and made of wood,

is shaped like a lozenge for a barn.
Anchors and sailboats in relief,
metal holds rank over all
but cannot recite ocean waves
as the Mother of Pearl, wafer thin,
with its curvaceous tan hues.

Each button is cool and smooth
as a worry stone.
I can feel them there—
the touch of my mother, aunts, and uncles,
their small fingers fumbling buttons
starting at the top of the shirt
until one side is longer at the bottom.

My grandmother never seemed to smile.
She did not sing or pick guitar
while the family played music on the porch.
For perfume, she dabbed vanilla behind her ear.
She wore no jewelry—
no diamonds or gems
brilliant in a blue velvet-lined box.
Even this button collection was utilitarian,
to save money
when sewing new clothes.
She collected what was necessary
to can or dry for the winter—
no time for gluttonous collections
of vintage dresses, hats, jewelry, rocks,
depression glass, and old books
that I must now purge.

When the buttons pour out,
some roll off the table and bounce
out of sight.
I put the rest back into the jar—
an hourglass starting over again
with fewer seconds left to use.

Dark Pearl

My son, out of breath, explains an injured deer
charged at him
about a fourth of a mile down the driveway.
I watch him run back with the rifle,
wondering if he has ear protection.

Not even the ruffled moss of upturned stones
knows how far the buck clamored
with two legs, badly torn and broken.

When he steps onto the porch where I wait,
the merciful shot still rings.
Mom, I've never had anything
look at me that way
when I pointed the gun–that dark eye.

My son grills the tenderloins.
I don't understand why animals have to eat animals
or why anything has to feel such pain.
He mocks me as he flips the venison,
What kind of hippie shit is this?

As a child,
he drew our rustic house—
but with a purple chimney and orange roof
to mislead a dragon.
What if the dragon found our house anyway?
I still doubt some of my mothering impulses.
Then, I would just punch him in the nose!
was his brave ghost dance
against a nuclear world.

Ear infections muffled his hearing
as though underwater.
A toddler, he looked back at me
from the wagon
pulled to surgery for ear tubes.
Then, in high school, he and friends
jumped off a bridge for fun,
and the hard slap of the lake
burst his eardrum.
Yet, he became a professional musician.

I don't understand pain.
I understand death more
as new generations benefit from adaptation
to a changing environment.
Still, the story of a burnt hand
should suffice as enough warning of fire
without the overkill of pain.

In that old Prell shampoo commercial,
a pearl dropped

into the emerald ocean of a bottle;
plunged so slow and luxurious
that it gathered all time with it.

The negative of that white pearl
is the dark eye of the deer,
the dark eyes of our sisters and brothers
taken from life by the use of guns.

I touch a cold hoof.
Nothing.
I can feel the deer feel nothing.
Yet, the scream of pain must go somewhere—
dark pearl to sink and resurface
in the ocean of my son's mind.

Angie Dribben

When the bough does not break

Wild dogwoods bend toward light come March.
Needing to make it beyond broadness of maple
and oak for sun, some bow as early as when trunk
pushes past soil. They crawl belly down, their gray
scales against earth. Spray ivory blooms like crosses,

two long petals, two short. I count the crooks,
reassuring myself that I am like dogwood,
arced not because I am broken but because I
find light. That I too am valuable for making
tools of purpose—loom shuttle, arrow, helve

shaped for holding. A curved spine withstands the shade
as long as it takes. The man walking with me reaches
towards blooms creamed and splayed open, swears
we will never starve. The one thing he recalls of Boy
Scouts is how to make broth from dogwood branches.

Taking what I know about men into consideration,

I wonder if what he means is, he will never
starve, and what he meant to say was bones.
Like it is my bones he sucks clean if he ever feels hunger.

I consider what I know about this man

who calls all clusters of trees orchard, meaning peach
cobblers and pear preserves, as in a family
fed. He names every gravestone loss and shines a flashlight
into the night's sky certain someone somewhere sees a star.

He strokes my humping ribs. Calls them graceful, the way
my body moves like dogwood boughs torqueing to the sun.

Claudia Emerson

Bee

When Claude says blessed is he who has seen
and believes, you know he is about to tell the one
about bees. His father told him which kind

of sting was worst, but you have to see some things
for yourself, and when you ask how on earth
do you catch a bee to see anything, he tells how

you hunker down next to a sweet potato blossom
and watch until one lands on the ruffled cuff

and then ambles down into the sweeter sleeve.
You lean over and pinch the blossom shut,
and there you have it, ready to sting yourself

so you can decide on your own, and he wants
for you not to doubt this: even more blessed,
you will be, you have heard—and not seen.

J. Indigo Eriksen

Clint

at sixteen I walked in a river
to give god a chance.

the night before I'd gone to prom
with a boy cajoled into accompanying me,

there are many stories there. at thirty
he and I became lovers, but at sixteen

I tore my vintage dress, found for $52 in the backroom
of a thrift store, on the edge of his blue car, some sort

of a classic. that car would later turn
mangled, a combination of too fast alcohol and

night roads. last night I found the photograph,
tuxedo on a country boy with his arms politely around

a riverless girl bound in tinsel and crepe de chine. it wasn't
until the spanish-speaking mountains that I found god living in my bones.

Latorial Faison

Mama Was a Negro Spiritual

She was a goodnight prayer, a moon that shined down
through my bedroom window. She was the alphabet,

a Sunday School verse, a third Sunday gospel song to rehearse,
a mostly misunderstood exchange of power, responsibility & command.

She was a black '73 Ford LTD, a Nottoway River crossing,
a house filled with too many other folk's children,

an orphan that life & death left behind to find, to give, some joy.
She was a funeral going, everybody in Southampton County

knowing, bad manner destroying pillar of strength.
She was a Friday evening ride to town, a Saturday morning

cleaning, a Sunday go-to-meeting kind of human being.
She laughed louder than Jim Crow's law & cried softer

than God's peace. She was the secret I never told, the carrying
of some other man & woman's burden.

She was rare, uncut, Black & picked up, ripped from some earthen
mine, placed beneath a sharecropper's kind to bear witness,
to bear it all deep down inside. She was a black hearse,
a deaf man walking, a raising & waving of tired hands.

She was thunder, she was lightening, a heavy rain that fell in spring.
She was a third grade education, small-town syndication.

Her house a good book & she the words penned fervently, permanently
on all its pages. She was a Ridley Road scholar, a kitchen

Where cooking got done & well. She was Ms. Shirley, the lunch lady,
the bus driver, Sammy's wife, giver of too much self.

Mama was a Negro spiritual, a hymn hummed from inside a Baptist
Hymnal, in an old rocking chair from a corner of our living room.

She was a wisdom no man could whistle, a fancy no woman could fake,
a journey none living in the now could take.

She was an old-fashioned lyric—
everybody could lift their voice and sing.

Mama Sang the Blues

I.

Mama's bottle tested illusion. Therein was a holy
Water from an ancient river that healed the sick,

Raised the dead. She sipped small sips with her Black
Lips, hummed hymns between soprano & contralto

Like Mahalia Jackson. Tell the angels I'm on my way,
She'd sing, toe tapping, head rocking, hardworking,

Poor & saved. Bittersweet like a one-room school,
She came together like an old Negro textbook—

Missing pages yet heaven sent. The god of white evil
Couldn't have created a strong, Black woman like this.

Like a daystar, she appeared in indigo skies, orphaned
& unknown. From a dying womb to a tenant room,

She came like a blonde-haired, blue-eyed baby Jesus
In a brown-skinned country; it didn't make no sense.
The poison she picked—a balm that chased all evil,
From lying white tongues to the lynching of Black sons.

Mama grew stronger than Samson on Friday nights
Every time she stole away to grab ounces of her

Humanity back. It was a happy sadness that dealt in
Pain. For when white folk got your tongue, you

Can't tell nobody but Jesus & when Jesus got you
Singing like Mahalia, you can't trust nobody but God.

II.

Mama was serious about her religion, the Baptist
Church down the dirt road & choir rehearsals on

Thursday nights. With songbooks, hand-written
Notes & a third grade education, she impressed

Her own self. Standing in the choir on the promises
Of God, all robed & righteous, she was worth more

Than white women. Her voice, like a whippoorwill,
Could whistle a song all through a night, all through

The struggle. When she sang from her darkness,
I knew she was light. Mama was a voice of dark brown

Reason—calling out to god, crying out for freedom.
I listened with everything that had ever come between us.

Mama sculpted me into me with a melody she hummed
Through all kinds of hell. She was a nuance, a renaissance

Inhaling & impaling grief, exhaling peace of mind, a piece
Of mine. She was a professor of arts & letters & god

Quilting me with all the pieces she was. Like every strong
Black woman who ever was a warrior, whoever came

Before her, she came bringing gifts, bequeathing songs.
They came, she came & I, too, have come to raise the dead.

Forrest Gander

from *Blue Ridge Log*

–for Mark Craver, Virginia poet & raconteur

I'm home at last

like they say, and
the phone call's for me.

The human ear is most sensitive
to the pitch of weeping. Our son's cello

remains unpracticed in the corner: let it.
You stand at the counter chaffing bay leaf

into a bowl. Eyes reading my face.

Mums you placed in a vase last week
as I left for Mexico wilt by the window.

Our mutual friend, the stranger

on the phone tells me, suddenly
died, who despite every determination

to go on living was waylaid by the sheer
organic ineptitude of the body.

On the refrigerator behind us, a photograph
of our son as a baby

balanced on that same friend's outsized palm,
their eyes locked in mutual thrall.

Beneath my solar plexus the present
and past circle the last chair

and the music stops.

Moving Around for the Light: a Madrigal

–for Lucas Foglia & Utopia, Virginia

The natural order of things.
      Sugar-bushing. Some
            things we do would gross people out

because they just don't know. Always was
      baffled by the connections in life. It's
            moving around for the light. I thought,

that plant's growing before my eyes, it's insane.
      What the news media don't want you
            to know. All the wild edible plants,

for instance. Getting on good here, blacks
      and white. No fossil-fuel based technology. I've
            eaten owl. Wing muscles and leg muscles,

that's the only meat on him.
      So much roadkill—beavers,
            otters, deer, raccoon.

We cook them up, preserve
      the hide instead of slashing it. Got it
            laid out real clear.

A lot can be done with duct tape. A bucket
      of honey between May and August. Who
            controls oil controls the world.

It's a lawyer's racket, but they don't go
      by law. That's the truth and people don't even
            know it. Want to find my bearings in

what's real. Started an anarchist collective with
      thirteen others. Like myself, independent people.
            Mountains seem to draw folks who want to live

in wilderness. The biggest problems come from being
      disconnected. I did really well in school, but
            I didn't like it. How do you sustain yourself day to day?

Take five milk goats and a sack of sweet potatoes.
              A grist mill, a harness shop. Most people
                            independent enough to live out here like this,

they're too independent to listen to each other.
              Feed somebody lunch and they cut your wood
                            all year—that works. Until

the kids are grown, don't want to
              bring others in. On account of influence.
                            Some things we do would gross people out

because they don't know.
              Where do you think you come by your pattern
                            for your ax handle? Take your old ax handle

and lay it on there. Nobody comes in,
              nobody leaves. We'll mind ourselves, let us alone.
                            They wear people out so they say, I'll

just pay the fine. That's the truth
              and people don't even know it. I was on her windshield
                            20 or 30 feet and then she hit the brakes

and I flew into a telephone pole.
              Heard a lot of stories about people's
                            lives. Who needs a house and how much

tin? We're different, you can't treat us the same. Garlic,
              pumpkin, onions, squirrel. And they
                            come to learn to make sorghum. Those that

have enough guts to live off the land, they are
              independent people like myself.
                            But I lived in community. Lived with the Amish.

With them, wood-cutting isn't cutting wood,
              wood's a by-product. That's why you can't
                            use chainsaws. Can't talk to someone

over a chainsaw. Want to move
              in a way that's more connected. See
                            the cause and effect in my life.

Right at the start of my senior year. A natural
            progression from activism and travel. How do you
                        sustain yourself day to day?

And they come to learn to make sorghum.
            What the news media don't want you
                        to know. Those dogs, they're rabbit dogs. Like

to lose that feeling of being a foreigner and find
            a sense of being at home. Out
                        felling trees alone on a windy day. Took my eyes

off it for 3 seconds, a big gust of wind came up
            and blew it down on me. My first thought
                        was Oh shit I don't have insurance,

which is a really funny thought, considering.
            Let's get this process right.
                        I'm not quitting unless I feel

in my heart I'm going to quit.
            That's the difference between me and other people.
                        Blue heron is good, tastes good.

Ever eat a blue heron?
            Supervisor said there's no common law
                        in Virginia. We don't know how fast it's going

to happen. Food's going to be
            number one. Next is going to be
                        ammo. We figure we'll end up feeding

a lot of outsiders. Took my eye off it for 3 seconds.
            First thought was Oh shit. It's
                        a right, it's always been a right.

The difference between me and other people.
            We care for ourselves, let us alone.
                        I've got it laid out real clear.

Biggest problems come from being
            disconnected. Beavers, otters, deer, raccoon. I've
                        eaten owl. Hard to feed yourself for a year.

Milk goats are the most valuable thing
                you can have. Banks go down, people can't get
                        money, they'll see what they need.

Food's number one. And next
                is going to be ammo. If bad goes to worse,
                        we'll post a man to keep out strangers.

Working to get that other doctor to move here. Like
                in Vietnam killing those women and kids, that's
                        not the American mindset but

I think it might come to such. Tanning
                hides. Fire without matches. When
                        others won't, we'll make it. Take

five milk goats and a sack of sweet
                potatoes, you can go anywhere. The
                        natural order of things is when

a species gets dominant over its niche. I'm always
                baffled by the connections. That plant's
                        growing before my eyes, it's—.

Instantly felt comfortable here.
                Skinned my first raccoon and it looked
                        so much like a fetus I cried.

Don't know how fast it's going to happen or
                if it'll happen, but if it doesn't happen,
                        we're not hurting either way.

Grew up using a bow and
                arrow to shoot rabbits. Need to be around
                        like-minded people. So I can see

the cause and effect in my life.
                They're really strong personalities.
                        I have a strong personality too.

Nobody comes in, nobody leaves. Ever
                eat a blue heron?
                        Natural order of things.

Wing muscles and leg
      muscles. That's the only meat on him.
            Where do you think you come by your pattern?

Let's get this process right.
      Want to find my bearings in what's real.
            Move in a way that's more connected.

Matthew Gilbert

Still-Life: Home Living

Pine branches iced over, siskin wings rasping at the windows at sunrise.
Winds whistling beneath the door, advising a house to congest her airways.
Light pours through the rimed glass, huddling on wooden floor around one mattress
smothered with children blanketed four feet from a furnace full of ash.

No one knows names or faces. Each brush stroke tells stories of that open cold.

A mother stands jacketed, rubbing her hands together for warmth
           over an open oven door.
Here, a tiny boy, who stutters to say th- or f-, searches for meaning in shadows,
toe sticking out of a sock worn-down because the good socks are for school.

Only the empty chair comforts his aching stomach, for an empty table chair
means missing boots tracking snow through the house at his father's return.

*   *   *

In late November, plastic seals all the windows to cut down on electric.
On a few occasions, I tiptoed to hold sheets of it against the frames so my mother could staple
           them in case the power shut off.
She would cut a hole at my height and seal it with transparent tape because I liked watching.

I wanted to watch the roads, watch the neighbor's dog scurry across the creek bridge and toss
snow into the air, because we couldn't have a dog. Dogs meant another mouth to feed.

Some mornings, my mother would make *drop biscuits*. Once, I raised the spoon and slammed
dough into a big splat, causing the pan to fall. She sent me to my room.
Later, she emptied the pan, gave us each two biscuits and ate one because she said she wasn't
that hungry. We had bologna sandwiches for dinner.

*   *   *

No one came to visit in the blizzard of '96. Feathers of snow
           tumbled from the branches and piled twelve-inches tall on our ruined
concrete porch and concealed the rubble of a demolished spring.

My mother scooped winter into a large metal bowl. *Only the top layers are clean*

for creaming, she would say. She mixed ice with hydrated milk and sugar. Then
we'd all gather in the floor with our treats and watched one of ten movies we owned.

*   *   *

Left alone in the kitchen when my sister was born, I tried to play cook with the cornbread.
Fear surrendered to blind confidence and I felt the sting of the grate.

My mother poulticed potato peels to the blain and yelled because I didn't want to wait.
It was the raw fire of her care that left a mark beneath my skin.

The kitchen table became shelter when my mother cooked. Table too tall, chairs stretching from
        the floor, threatening me with splinters if I dared move.
I learned to deconstruct the world around me for future exploration. I measured the oven,
skillets, whisks, counted the times my mother stopped to add breadcrumbs to bulk up the side
mashed potatoes or soups so they would stick to our stomachs.

No room in the house spoke more.

*   *   *

By December, we were driven downstairs by the frost. Draft of cold air blowing through the
        broken glass.
Bedrooms emptied of all but the wooden paneling on the walls,
        plastic over windows, a dead crow
where the crib had set, and my mother had sworn she heard talking.

I grew fearful of climbing the stairs and staring into the empty closets.
Our most important treasures were boxed and sent to my grandmother's.

The vastness of that house grew large and overwhelming, the warmth became subtle

Here, a man who stuttered to say thank you or forgive me searches for meaning in shadows,
conjuring the past for ghosts.

Observation of Autumn Burning

When the county bans backyard fires
because the season is too dry, dreams
ignite for a small boy rummaging to heap
scarred leaves so he can reattach the branches.

His mother sends him outside for quietness,

73

but the house cannot contain the rage
flooding out the kitchen window,
his father drunk on threats, a taste

too acetous to swallow. If it were spring,
his mother would take him up the mountain;
they would pick nightshade and self-heals
from the trail, just as grandmother had taught,

because finding your way home means
uprooting yourself from thick clay
before you shrivel in thirst; however, the climb
tells the world know you'll make it—you'll bloom.

But for a child color imparts truth, and he picks
out each leaf based on its shape, not knowing for certain
the sharpness of each spine until he starts
to bleed.

Silence begets the cold crackle of leaves—
The child's hands struggle to piece the tree back
together in vain, seeking that warmth of spring
heat flickering on his face again.

Dry fire weaves itself a coiled serpent,
umber and feverish gold. If you listen,
you may catch the hiss of cracked leaves
rustling across a burning yard.

Homecoming

Now they have bridged the road and walking path
Where so many of us learned to play hopscotch
And staked a *no loitering* sign so teenagers
Won't hang around Simmons old deli anymore
When they don't want to go home.

Kudzu creeps along the railroad tracks of childhood memories:
Off-beaten path leading down the Clinch River, petals
Of floating lettuce gobbled by a brood of ducklings,
And drooping, tangled vines where lovers met to etch
Their dreams in pocket-knife words on the willow trunk.

During hunting season, my father hung a buck
By the rafters of our basement as he skinned it.
I held its shoulders steady, stickiness of muscle
gluing flesh to body as he ripped away the fur.
As the last bit was released, his friends cheered.

There are too many names to remember, even
When everyone knows so-and-so's grandson
Kissed a boy under the bleachers during half-time.
The church prayed for his salvation and off-duty cops Baptized him
in his own blood, left him shaking with pleas to God

On the riverbank. I remember our neighbor sketching
The outline of his body with a stick in the dirt
Before smashing a turtle's head with a sharp stone.
He smeared its blood across my face when I wept—
Perhaps, that's why I never learned to shoot or wanted to.

I wonder how many return to those moments
On their drive past those collapsing monuments:
It's pouring down rain. Could they pick up the shell—
Sky lighting up and body shaking like thunder—
And toss its corpse in the upsurge river waves?

Charles Gillispie

The Afterlife

According to tradition,
when a horse dies
in the country a child
in the city loses a tooth.

Whatever the child says
the next day
will be painfully true
and drive his parents apart

as if the gap in his teeth
were a gate left open
that allowed the dead horse
to slip through a meadow and run free.

Leah Naomi Green

The Age of Affection

Thank you, moon, for following
across the pond

while I walked,
for bringing me

to the shore
to say goodnight.

The affection
of your speech

is inside me.
That is exactly where I want it.

Has anyone I've loved
ever been

anywhere else?
You followed over the field too,

and inside the house,
though the grass

did not reflect you,
or the milky way rising,

as I can sometimes witness
even from inside it.

The More Extravagant Feast

The buck is thawing a halo on the frosted ground,
shot in our field predawn.

Last night we pulled a float in the Christmas parade.
It was lit by a thousand tiny lights.

My daughter rode in my lap and was thrilled
when the float followed us. Ours is a small town.

Everyone was there. And their faces,
not seeing ours, fixed behind us, were an open sea,

a compound sea of seas that parted
under our gaze. And Santa was bright,

though my daughter shied from the noise of him.
She studied the red and white fur of his suit.

She woke this morning when the rifle fired outside.
I lifted her to see the sunrise

and her father, kneeling above the buck's body
in the middle distance. She asked if they would be cold.

I brought him gloves and warm water, knelt with him
in the spare light by the buck, who steamed, whose liver

and heart, kept so long dark,
spilled onto the winter grass,

whose open eyes saw none of it, realized
nothing of my husband's knife

slicing open his abdomen, his rectum. The puncture
of his diaphragm startled me more than the gunshot,

opening a cavern of deep blood that poured
over his white belly. I did not

understand the offering, but loved it,
the fur red, white, incoherent. Somehow cleaner.

When I come back in, she asks me to draw a picture
of her father on the hill. I pick her up—the miracle

of her lungs that grew inside me,
kept long dark—her working heart

let out into the rounder world,
the more extravagant feast. The miracle

of her dad on the hill as we draw him
in his big coat, warm. Afterward,

how he and I hold each other
differently, feeling

the collections of muscles
and organs held

somehow together. The miracle
of bodies, formed whole like fruits,

skins unruptured and
containing the world.

Jacob Have I Loved

I.
I think I lost the genetic lottery,
my cousin told me

in one of the last conversations
we had. He was thirty-three,

our parents, twins. We were living
again the few good stories.

*Tell me the one
about Esau.*

II.
*Tell me about God hating him.
I want it to be a problem*

of translation: language or time.
I have never met an Esau,

and what chance
does a born person have,

though we name them all Jacob?
Tell me my own daughter

doesn't wonder
if she's naked.

She is running through the yard
explaining something to her sister.

I want to keep her
from hiding

in the understory
as Eve did

with Adam, children
believing they could

disappear
from God.

III.
The absurdity of hiding anywhere:
I want to show her

how to hold her fear
like a child of her own

how to ask it, between sobs,
where it hurts.

IV.
Can I hold you when you're born?
my daughter asks. She is sitting on my lap.

We're sorting photos of my cousin,
every one in time,

collapsed. Not a good shot
at any age.

I hold up the best, a young man,
to take a picture

of the picture for the obituary.
I orbit it for some time,

trying to remove my body
from the light,

believing the shadow on his face
is from me.

V.
I've tried to remove my body.
How afraid have I been

of being found in it,
unblessed?

There is no reason for beauty,
no metric

that holds—
a blessing

in itself.
How we look

to one another.
Don't you have

even one blessing
left for me?

VI.
The shadow is in the photo,
on him, in the room

where he stood without me,
before I was born.

VII.
In our yard it's getting dark;
shadows are blessings

that diffuse all the glare
from the heavens.

In the cool of the evening
they heard God

walking around in the garden:
Where are you?

My daughter's face is a clean window.
No glare to mirror

or ask if I am naked,
if she is Jacob—

only this reflection
in one another's eyes.

The Transitive Property of Song

> *Birds Sing to Their Eggs, and This Song Might Help Their Babies Survive Climate Change*
> —Headline, Smithsonian *magazine*

Of course they sing—
we have given them
no other verb.

And because *sing* is what I do
to my girl in the dark rocking chair,
I call it the same;
I conceive of myself: *gentle*
as the wren, *master*
of my singing, signals borne through
my body, the bird's,
every loving thing
just converting nouns to verbs
for survival—*air* into *breathe*,
sunlight to *grow*, infinite grammars
I can't make or know.

Some *things*
are verbs, you'll learn: *fire* and *flood*,
yield and *smile*. I teach you,
never knowing I do:
You will make it

if they like you.
You are listening.
Let us imagine it then

as song,
harmony nested in the dark
humming *live, live, live:*
intransitive. I am humming.
I am hummed. Singing
is happening. Song is
being sung.

Origin Story

> "What is dying is the willingness to be in denial."
> —angel Kyodo williams

The heron flew away
and I wanted to tell someone

how long it stayed,
how close I got,

how much I missed it
even as it stood

to watch me,
large-eyed animal

that I am, terrible
at believing what I can't see.

You see fire in the home
where we live: the world

in cardiac arrest.
A *heart attack*

is not the onset I want to say
to someone, it's the flare.

It illuminates what's already here:
the forests

illuminated, the earth
lit as an origin story.

Here you are,
I say instead,

aloud, surprised
at how close

I've been holding you
in the dark.

Flame yields
no new landscape.

It bares the contours
like a map

so we can see
where we've been all along,

can see one another
as we walk, and say,

for once, nothing
at the fire's steady flight,

like a heron
lifting in loud beats,

our silent mouths open
as if to give it a tunnel.

Lucy Fowlkes Griffith

Why I always close the porch door

On occasion, Bernard's brothers drop in to Elm Hall.
Uncle Matt and Uncle Ludd, every kind of scruffy, like
two Davey Crocketts, lean on the porch rail.
They're full of hunting tales, bears and bucks. They
smell of whiskey and wet dogs.

A far cry from the gentlemanly figure cut by baby brother.
Bernard hangs back on their visits, watches.
My mother invites them in for Spam sandwiches, iced tea.
As he steps inside, Ludd booms
Laura Jane, you've got a snake in this house!

Horrified, she asks how he knows.
I smell it, it's a big one! Bernard, gimme that cane a yours!
Ludd pokes under the day bed in the wide hallway
between the front porch and the back porch,
My favorite nap spot. Beneath a wash-faded quilt

hang pale blue ruffles. Hooked by the cane handle—
a rat snake as big as his arm
writhes out from under the bed,
dark as midnight, pale on its belly.
Ludd flips it out the back door,

hands back the cane.
We stare at him as if he conjured it.
I start napping upstairs.

Just One More Thing

Besides banking runs for families with no cars
Bernard offers secretarial services free of charge
for those unable to read.

At a white wicker table on the porch of the hotel,
he arrives with a stack of envelopes,
an assortment of stationery.

Like my father, like me,
he loves a fine fountain pen.
His penmanship so old world—

grand and flowy as the Bill of Rights.
This Saturday, Nat comes to the table.
Wearing his go-to-town clothes,

dungarees starched and pressed,
a t-shirt blinding white with bluing.
His cap crumples in his fist.

Mister Wilson, my gal, Maisy, is down Georgia-way.
I need her not to give up on me.
Bernard takes dictation in the morning sun.

How high the corn, how we need rain with no hail,
how close Nat's savings are to a bus ticket south.
Peaches coming in, dewberries

thick on the crick. How he misses her so.
Nat looks over Bernard's shoulder.
Please read it back to me.

That sounds right. That looks right, too.
Just add one more thing—
at the bottom, put this, just in case:

All mistakes are kisses.

Raymond P. Hammond

Easter at Natural Bridge

on the way home to our own church service
the reluctance to sit through a sermon,
again, was somewhat stayed by a breakfast
in the age-old natural bridge gift shop
and cafeteria, the sixties green
dining room filled with formica tables
awash in an ocean of sixties green
metal and vinyl chairs above a floor
of gray tiles with servers dressed in sixties
green swimming through the crowd filling coffee,
clearing tables to make room for the line
of people all dressed in their sunday best
which snaked along the three-foot-high railing
which separated tables and gift shop

my dad and i would only get in line
after making a stop at the rest rooms
in the basement beside the indoor pool
which always fascinated me, the stalls
required a dime to open the stall door
which, only ever knowing free bathrooms
i thought was a robbery of most cruel
intent because we had just made the climb
up the steep stairs from the creek trail that wound
its way along cedar creek which flowed under
the natural bridge it had patiently
created over eons now illuminated
by the rapidly rising morning sun
after a packed easter sunrise service

we had arrived in the still silvery
shiny morning fog and walked up the trail
past salt peter cave which was really
just a rock-shelter, past the lost river
which anybody else would call a spring,
not making it all the way to lace falls
because of time and the fact I had stopped

to see every forest floor flower
amazed at their early resurrection
into this crisp morning air of the first
flowers to flower in the spring: blood root
dutchman's breeches, columbine, trillium,
the mayapples, and jack-in-the-pulpit,
and, of course, the lily of the valley

the easter sunrise message was given
by some old country preacher who would stand
just in front of the famous gw carved
into the cliff by one george washington
cedar creek's babbling in competition
with the preacher for all but the first rows
no matter, the conceit was obvious
what i wondered was how many
of those sitting in the chairs listening
planning their noon meals, travels to get home
were shifting, struggling, and straining to hear
the preacher preach about that which he knows,
really, concretely knows—not a damn thing,
underneath the pure rush of cedar creek

Snake Proof

it is more than serpents
it is drinking poison
handling fire—all prescribed
in the new testament
for one to prove their faith
to god and the others
but foremost to yourself
but it is more than faith
it is demonstrating
a clean life in-line
with the community,
the church, proof of no sin
for faith to snake handlers
is defined concretely
a faith preached by preachers
to trusting congregants
like the founder of snake
handling George Went Hensley

who died from a snakebite
or the renowned Pastor
Mack Wolford and his son
Mark Randall "Mack" Wolford
who both died from snakebites
even a seemingly
impervious pastor
like the reality
pastor Jamie Coots
who would die from the quick,
divined-as-judgmental,
strike of a rattle snake
being a rattle snake

Cathryn Hankla

In the Belly

Earrings, like a pair of wedding gloves:

a young clerk in the old world sells me white stones
from the window display. *Amber*, she intones,

and repeats, *amber*. Neither luminescent
fault-spiked caramel nor silent,

opaque coffee grounds, these crisp stars in night
sky draw my eye, my sight

slightly marbled by desire. I'm pondering another
I thought I'd lost like an old skin, a lover

set beside me in silver, to whom I was bound
and released, as from watery deep brown.

I've climbed to err on autumn earth upon a crust
of papery leaves and spoken what I must,

yet conversations never end
when words wound inside begin

to surface through agents
like developing prints,

the way history seeps into the present hour
with purposes and meanings long turned sour.

A photograph appears darkest, tree
limbs serrating sky, where the negative is nearly

transparent. Chaos moves into form
while rigid design breaks like a maelstrom.

Beneath cathedrals, bridges, each grand structure
lies the grave of a worker,

a reversal. Where the world is torn
like a ticket, in the garden of betrayal worn

raw, I find the oldest amber
grown white and remember

the scars in the belly of love.

Twenty Minute Exposure

The risen moon, a block of polished iron.
Think of an iron after the fire is gone,
Its pyramid cooling on the silver

Board. What it meant to be a woman, wife,
I watched my mother to learn. What I
Was taught: iron the underwear, after sprinkling

It from a bottle. Iron the handkerchiefs.
This is the article I was taught first to iron,
Not a shirt. With handkerchiefs, a little girl's

Mistakes don't matter. The square is folded
And placed in your father's back pocket.
Why do men use only cloth to blow

And women use paper? What I learned:
The invisible work of women, the wrinkles
On their faces. I learned that women can spend

Their lives making the world a better place for men.

Chelsea Harlan

The Thaw

I raked the hard yard of last year's leaves
and planted radish seeds. *Onward and Upward*

in the Garden, the peacocking of the morning sun.
The apaugasma of the old and wavy window glass

in the brave young grass scattered some small
amorphous golden baths. The forecast held.

Some geese made an imperfect cursive V above me,
the little fig tree tried its best to look alive.

An exercise in finding focus is focusing on meaning,
or isn't it pretty to think so? In the lemony balm

of life returning like the emperor or the king or spring
it's also kind of sad, if it's true what they say.

Did you know there are no more wild horses?
There are no more wild horses.

Night Drive to the Dumpster

Little toupees of fog hover over the river
and from the dump on the hill you can feel
fall coming on like your favorite TV show,
re-runs of nothing but season finales
The view of the source of the smoke from the mill
is blurry and backlit by the colors of hazard,
and you wince in that way people wince when
their familiarity with distress is kind of comfortable,
like death is a high-quality goose down sleeping bag
or like déja vu of every time you've ever cried
Your eyelashes noiselessly applaud like that
in that sad way, and I, too, know what you mean
God spoke to you in the hollers, didn't he,
that day we saw his dead raccoon

Olana, Considering

I was already tinkering with the sky's wires
when starlight hit us with headshine, lo,

all the twinkle brights of Panna II Garden lit
times one thousand. I grew gloves for hands

holding so many flames up over your head,
I played hot potato with a faraway planet

proving the distance of my emotional diaphragm,
named it New Destiny, wrote in strange clay

too ra loo ra loo ra, began a civilization
then destroyed it as sacrifice to the You.

I lost sense of self in an information time-hole,
emerged resplendent in a warm ball of ice

having relearned everything, repented,
dovelike but for the most part the same

if unsure what to do about my new gloves.
My spirit suppered with dangerous horses,

I found the key, lost the key, abandoned the idea
in a river of code, surfed the frothy binary

fishing for a compromise. I was punished
for trespassing, I wasn't wearing any day-glo

so I hid in a midnight alley behind our sun,
composed a mud home from song and spit

plus what dirt I could gather in my glovehands,
until my straw memory shrine caught fire

catching also the attention of the Coast Guard
who nevertheless had better things to do,

and I was just about to star 69 you back,
had I not been plucked up by an arcane

93

wagging finger, tossed on the back of a CR5,
bucked off through a trapdoor cleverly

disguised as the green grass on this hillside,
but I hope you enjoyed the meteor shower,

and if you made a wish I hope it was good,
that is, if you believe that sort of thing.

David Havird

Molting

Before dawn even, zipping past the exit
to Myrtle Beach . . . That's where my girlfriend was
who had a summer job there singing.
But I was heading north
to see Janet. Hot and muggy, the weather
changed at Richmond to rainy,
not with a torrent of blades but a drizzle of pins,
and chilly. I had to borrow a flannel shirt
from Janet—a man's, which fit me. Janet was renting,
along with her college roommate
and one other girl, a townhouse in Georgetown.
Sometimes, while they were at work,
I'd venture afield to a gallery,
Corcoran, Phillips; mostly I browsed
the neighborhood bookstores and otherwise loitered.
I had to ask the girls, because I was getting
so many probing looks from guys,
if maybe I had an effeminate manner.
"You have," she said, the matronly one whose name
escapes me, "just a nice face." I slept
on the living-room sofa. Sunburned, itching like mad,
I'd scroll the peeling skin off my shoulders
and roll it into a little ball,
then flick it. Overhead, the women
were getting ready for bed, their heels
conveying thunder while I read by lamplight
a poem in *Harper's* by Robert Penn Warren,
whom Janet and I and her housemate Felicia had met:
"A Problem in Spatial Composition,"
in which a hawk, like something divine,
unseen above a window-framed vista
composed of a stone scarp and forest,
at sunset enters the frame as if from forever
only to go "in an eyeblink." My wife,
who was then my girlfriend, who sang at the beach
where noontide had blistered my shoulders—
my wife says it's all about sex. Not Warren's poem,
this story of mine. The thunder, having slung

flimsy bras across the shower rod,
puts up its feet—the women, nesting. Molting,
I clasp the neck of that shirt, whoever's it is,
which I'll shake out in the morning.
The weather whistles past windowsills
and under the door, and though it sings
like blades' cold steel, I picture
within the lamplight's moon on the ceiling
a hawk whose shrills are high noon's killing rays.

The Weight of a Feather

We waited at sundown,
swamp chill adhering to soles,
for ducks to show
(stragglers they looked to be, the three or four)
in the strip of sky between the snarl of treetops.

"Sure was a fine shot by one of you boys"—
a party of hunters trudging by us,
and Dan and Scott, small boys
but hunters for real already, laughing,
pointing at me, the city boy

whose shotgun wasn't his,
nor did he have a license
nor waders on for the swamp
where beavers lodged and the alligator that ate them
nor dog along to retrieve it—my one duck ever.

Reading a poem, "Mallard," by R. T. Smith,
who must be a hunter also for real—
the make of his gun? Wingmaster.
Mine? Search me—
I envied that hunter whose memory finds

a satin drake in the mouth of his hound,
sheen dimming while still in its eyes
the sunrise bleeds on the river,
who "shivers" to think of his heart's load judged
"against the weight of a feather,"

as you can see it done in the Book of the Dead
by a bird-beaked god with a balance,

behind him poised the crocodile-headed Devourer.
More than my share of ducks, which Dan and Scott
pluck and gut in the sink in the mudroom,

have I devoured—breasts marinated in what
it is their secret, bacon-wrapped
and charcoal-grilled.
More than my just portion?
I gorge to find the one in one bite more.

Prayers for a Giant

For Anthony Hecht

My mother, a girl then, was sitting on their verandah,
facing away, when a cat smacked down on her back,
locking its claws. A boy, whose only pleasure
was meanness, had sneaked around the magnolia
and pitched it. That incident preys on me, hunched at the wheel,
our daughter in back with nothing—
not even a naked giant, scored in chalk
on the hillside, wielding a wide-toothed club
and boasting a huge erection—
to make her forget she's starving.
(Remember, it's your pilgrimage, not hers.)

"Here," in Stinsford churchyard, "lies the heart
of Thomas Hardy." When *day of Judgement be come,*
Almighty, 'e'll say, 'Ere be 'eart
but where be rest of 'e? "Westminster Abbey,
Poet's Corner—remember the tablet?"
The story goes—we sit on the gravestone,
Rachel and I, amid the shade of a yew—
that when they came for the heart, they found the tin
in which the surgeon had laid it, this cookie tin
on its side, top off, the tea towel lining it
out, and Cobweb licking his bib.

Tonight her prayers include a petition
not for the smoke-colored Persian, interred in the churchyard
while still the heart's fresh grave, but for Midnight,
drowned on her grandparents' farm before she was born,
whom Rachel remembers because of one story:
still a kitten, Midnight mewed at the door

and when let in made us the gift of a bunny.
With green eyes looks at us, looks down at it,
she paws it, peers at us . . .
It went straightway, a fist-tight wad,
into the garbage can outside.

A star's reflection plunging, the well's heart thumps.
The giant tugs loose from the grass and plants himself
in the sky—*Lift up your hearts. We lift them up*
unto the Lord, whose white breath swallows
even the spires of London. I wake up numb—
I've bedded down, it seems, in my own ashes.
The comforter over me now,
my heart again declaims by rote its prayer
that its last beat may be a new star's first.
Breathing out a trumpet of fog,
I feel throughout my frame pulsations of starlight.

Habit of the Heart

I think, *How do I feel knowing she's dead?*
My habit, which my thirty years have fed
(As heartbeats have the body's—to survive
Still more), is still to feel that she's alive.
Things known by heart touch their way into bone.
My mother felt the same about her own,
Who died last year in winter, none so raw
On record. Seasons passed. A weekend saw
My parents in the mountains, as one did
Unfailingly in autumn, when leaves hid
In colors of desire (which I would read
As passion to hold fast) the heartless need
Of letting go. There they heard orchards drone
With wasps, daring tourists to pick their own
Apples. Alive, she'd still have gotten none,
Grandmother toothless in her eighties. Done
With picking, though, and with enough to dole
Out winter long to every living soul,
Her eldest daughter sighed, "Won't it surprise
Mother we picked all these!" Yet her demise—
Why, apples had been ripe since that first fall
With knowledge of it, as between heartbeats
There is a silence that repeats,
Silence is all, is all.

Jane Hicks

Night Music

I roll down windows and fly
through honeysuckle nights,
radio replays my youth,
nights WOWO came
through after midnight, oldies
a comfort of a well-worn quilt.
Breakups, meltdowns, high school
drama, dances that sent us into crisp autumn
sweat-soaked, long hair damp curtains,
songs that had dance names morphed
into protest as my senior year rolled round.
I dreamed of escape to college,
decade turned: Motown, acid rock,
protest, Jimi Hendrix, Janis Joplin,
a rough world, classmates called
to war. We thought not to survive
Cuban Missile Crisis, seed for hippies
that seized any day that might be their last.
I drive on past drowsy cows,
wary of bounding deer, stop at mountain
overlook under a blackberry sky
to watch stars herded across dark heavens—
Hercules treads on Draco,
Littlest Dipper overhead,
the Lyre of Heaven strums across the night.

Pyburn Creek

Follow sun-dabbed path to the aged and infirm
sycamore that refuses to yield to years,
across creek log, upstream to that green place,
below water-cut and weathered bank.
The flow tumbles over falls built by a brother and sister
beneath pawpaw trees, black-blossomed in spring,
fragrant-fruited by summer-end. Find the boulder

washed down by long ago torrent. Perch and listen,
draw watery breath, soak in the green, the yellow,
the blue of the season. Burbles, bird calls, distant cattle,
wind whistle or whimper in weeds and briars.
Remember dinner bell of the long afternoon called
you home to porch swing, night breeze sweetened
by white blossom and a hymn on the tongue.

Communion

Beneath crumbling shale banks, under low branches,
we dam Pyburn Creek. I stack pebbles along
shallows to pen crawdads my brother catches.
This spot, this shade, this creek, take up
the hottest hours before supper.

Blue mud at creek's edge smells
primeval and decayed. Crawdads escape
pen by morning and build their mounded
flood dams. A mulberry harbors squirrels,
birds, seen but not heard over creek rush.

Sycamores green water edge. Further back
grow poplars, straight up tall, and buckeyes,
already red-leafed in August. Dogwood
berry necklaces like blood droplets in the green.
Cold, cold creek water surges and scrambles
down mountain, carries, urges,
wears stone and tree to sand and soil.

Called to supper, we bathe in a washtub
of sun warmed creek water to cleanse our mud,
afterward douse prize dahlias in a side garden.
Tick-checked and dressed, we eat home grown
bounty, then drowse in porch swings.

II
Buffet on flat bed wagons, congregation
fills stiff paper plates with layers of favorites.
Feasters once spread through shady cemetery
on quilts or perched on stones among their departed,
now seek picnic tables in outdoor
shelter while an acoustic trio sings praise.

Dessert comes out last, a fancy after plain fare.
Coconut, apple stack, and yellow cake
clothed in caramel crowns feast.
Chocolate, cherry, chess and lemon pies,
banana puddings, meringued in brown peaks,
weep with heat.

After country communion, congregation walks
out among stones. They stroll, stop,
chat before monuments, reconnect
lines of kinship, adjust floral displays,
check for newcomers gone to ground,
unconscious nod to songs carried on faint breeze.

III
Water, stone, sand and soil—
this is where we begin and end.

Mary Crockett Hill

Backwards Ghazal and Never Again

Last week, a boy at my boys' school was beaten for 28 minutes.
The hallway empty except for a camera and the clock's shifting eyes.

Last month, a girl at my boys' school died in a way no one will talk about.
She wept the Friday before, arms cradling her smooth brown hair.

Last I spoke with my dead mother, I left the window cracked.
A bat flew in while we slept and swept cobwebs from the ceiling.

Last call is coming. Will you be ready, sir? Ma'am? Drink up!
Sure as cherry blossom—the drunk poet, lips opening...

Last night, last chance, last ditch, last dance, last word, last laugh,
last fling, last gasp, last hurdle, last hurrah, last leg, last straw.

Sky painted with a vastness we can't quite believe—painfully blue,
immortal. Open that door, slowly, Mary... make it last.

The Farmers of Good Dirt

There are seven pillars of wisdom in this world
and we can't own them all.

The Harvard Biologist, for example,
on the radio this morning

said should human kind become extinct
the loss to Life Itself would be rather slim—

a limited number of species at risk:
ourselves, and the mites

that burrow in our foreheads.
Whereas *ants*...

ants are the tillers of soil, the garbage men;
the end of ants might be the end of everything.

The radio announcer asked the man if he killed ants in his kitchen.
He said he gives them bowls of cream.

Good luck, Mr. Ant.
Good luck, Mr. Harvard Biologist.

I think I know how this story ends:
at high noon in Tennessee, you don't have to see a bird

to see the shadow of that bird
gliding like a cool hand on the hills.

Think of what you see everyday without seeing—
on the back of your eyelids, in your irises,

in your mouth's cavity and your armpit,
in the eye of the fly in the eye of your soup.

Think of the astronaut who sheds his silver suit
and climbs, naked, from the rib of his ship:

himself, an object in orbit
and nothing—I mean it, nothing—for miles.

There are places for people like that.
There are wells on the side of the universe

where no lips should drink. Teeth
turn to water, and the flesh-pulp of cheeks

turn to water, the throat, the sinuses, onward
until being water is all being; wanting water

all wanting. I've seen spots right here in Shawsville
so thick with growth and shine

it makes me wonder
my feet don't come out green.

That's one idea of heaven—we'll be strutting around
with stars on our bellies and artichoke skin

and the mouse will shit and bathe
in the dog's water dish

and the bees will gnaw and batter
the inside plaster off the walls

and the porch light will call forth
all the moths of this world

and where you are is air
and where you were is air

and the house does not dream
of being any other house

and we're all in the kitchen,
moths in our hair,

gulping ant juice
from tall silver cups.

Scott Honeycutt

Unfinished Walk to Black Point

I skim fingers through blades of marsh grass.
Here, in the shallows of the James and York Rivers
red whiskered men learned to paddle tidewater.

The first panther was shot along these banks.
Its cries were heard by lost Powhatans
as new men strung her up with braided hemp.
They crafted necklaces from her claws and bone.
Eyes were pocketed like two soft marbles,
and her tail was tailored into a belt.

At last, her lungs and stomach were tossed to pit crabs
while her polished skull was sported into the tide.

But now it's November:
The big bald cypress
presses its shadow across the James and York
and all seems so well, though it's hard to forget
the cold mud, chest deep in panther hides.

So now, in this life without ritual, who will wash my body
once the drum is broken?
Who will launch out into tide-heads pull?
Like prayer it can't hurt to ask,
and like prayer every word is a panther's scream.
Yet who—you?—will cleanse this body for the journey?

We Search for Hawks but View Only Vultures, Circling.

Along the interstate under October skies,
traces of summer hold hickory and maple leaves like torches—
the deep-rooted heat will not let them fall.
These hung leaves crib autumn, and we push north at 80 miles an hour:
Hold on, boys, don't fear.

Virginia is for Lovers I've heard,
and crossing over the oldest river, called the New, I almost believe it's true,
but love, like those doltish Herefords grazing on hillsides
often breaks off into a trot at first sight of fox tails.
So we remain, strangers passing through land—half-shadow, half-light,
Time dissolving like sugar in the springhouse.

Blue sky, true love, faces turned upward toward vultures that trailed us
from Damascus to Staunton.
Circling as they rose and fell, they floated like zeroed out lottery tickets,
but you can't scratch off luck.
Spade on Spade—Queen's Heart and Jack's Hat—detached and elevating
up the range.

How many were there above us?
Their black wings striped white or vanilla-tipped—
We know nothing, yet they shall have the last word, the final at-bat.
And where were the soaring hawks that I had hoped to count?
There was one—a broken hen looming inches from the highway,
stout as a New-Years' goose.
We could have reached out and grabbed it by the beak:
Hold on, boys, don't fear.

Ghost of summer, ghost of blue skies cantered with us along the way.
All by those ash-red mountains that neither remember nor forget,
All by those Shenandoah fields that hold the past like a lost lover.
Forgive the setting sun that black-dotted our eyes, Nobodaddy's judgment:
Goddammit, boys, hold on.

The back seat emptied, we turned and drove through owl-country,
watching day give up its feathers and turn to roost in worn branches.
Let us never forget that squash-colored moon which rose before us,
framing the road like a book jacket, signed in the soothing ink of sleep.

Fragments at Forty

For Russell James

We move from memory to image,
to a starkness that holds a bold paradise of words.

There you were at twenty, near Basque country in
Night fields that sighed north toward France.
What stars you must have seen.
Do you recall lying out on the ground in Spain
full of sardines and wine, a black moat above
and words of *Hombre, Hombre, Hombre* filling the air?
You slept there, alone in the haystacks,
not dreaming of America lost beyond the sea
but waking instead to find your tussled hair full
of this old world.

Later, you exchanged the songs of caballeros
for the high peaks of Nepal and prayer flags
that whipped to Billy Bragg's refrain:
I've fallen in love with a little time bomb;
I've fallen in love with a little time bomb.

You moved on, outward into the greeny
wonderment of Maine and Virginia.
You have seen the broken blue hills of
Smokestack and Bigelow,
Washington and Blood Mountain.
How that language of legs still informs
Your coffee dawns and morning commute.

Tell me—
Does the Black Sea howl at midnight?
How does the Steppe unfold from a train to Moscow?
Which trees tender their leaves first in a Ural spring?
How does one stare Russia in the eyes?
"Tvoi glaza krasivye," you whispered.
"You speak well," she smiled. "You speak well."

After 40 years, your body has become an orchard
of memory, bending with purple fruit
and gleaming like rhododendron leaves after a rain.

Emily Hooker

While watching purple martins dive

The back of the throat
meets the front.
The beak clicks
crooning some primal language.
Repeat the stories
As They once said.
If you drive me
to dancing
barefoot under your nest—
I promise not
to step on abandoned eggshells.
The soft pads of my feet
will bear no cuts.

Those wings are perfect triangles—
an elementary school craft
held together with
globs of Elmer's.
Yes, I made you once.
While my face was pink,
pushing golden strands of hair
from my forehead
after recess.

The Phoenicians made
your color once.
All of those shellfish baked on the coast,
crushed for your illusory hue.

Prove to me you are
more than some
imperial Mediterranean.
Any gift you bring:
a dogwood petal,
a dried sweet gum fruit,
the seed from an apple core—
This would all be more

than what they buried
with the ashes
of emperors.

John Hoppenthaler

Passing

I've just received a text that says a buddy
died last night but that doctors brought him back
to us with a shot, and so my friend is a Lazarus.

I'm in a boathouse owned by another old pal;
he is traveling for work somewhere abroad.

Mallards have lifted from the vernal pond,
and thousands of frogs are singing
because it's raining. I wish Bill was here so we could

talk about our friend who has gone and returned.
Crows call to each other across the lake. Same old

story: there's danger and it surrounds us. And now
the blue heron I'd failed to notice pulls his legs
free of mud and flies away. A small falcon skims

the shoreline. When he was raised, was Lazarus pleased?
I wonder how he lived the rest of his unforeseen days.

Were his preparations any different than they'd been before?
It's early March, and Easter will be here soon. Jesus, too,
realized how permeable the membrane is that keeps us

this side of death, and that the dead can come back
if they're summoned. The ducks, the hawk and the heron
have passed on through to somewhere else,
but the joyful frogs remain crazy
with song. A hunter's gun shots punctuate the distance,

a single crow lands in the crook of a tree, and it seems
as though the blessed rain has nearly stopped for now.

Superstition

Who has turned the jade elephant's
head from the door? That won't do

with a gunman still on the loose, herons
flapping too close to the house, so I turned

fire tongs for luck, cast table salt
into flames. I spent the whole night

pointing at the moon before I could fall
asleep, creamy light shining on my face.

But by morning, my OCD flared again.
I tapped my forehead three times, rapped

the doorframe: Father, Son, and Holy Ghost.
Mostly, I have it under control; most of the time,

I only do it once. When the third heart
attack killed my father, I knew it was a liar.

I could finally let up. All that dread
had no place, and the wound seemed to heal.

My father died doing what he'd been told
not to do. He fell to the snow he'd cleared

from his car; he died on a mattress of snow.
Not even the scar I'd scored into my chest

with a silver crucifix had the power to save him.
When the snow melted and dried, I swept

dust from the spot into an envelope. Mom
sold the house and moved away. Years later,

I mixed that dust with flour and baked
coarse bread. I put some on my tongue and let it

dissolve. I swallowed with wine and waited,
fixed the elephant's green head toward the door.

Jessica K. Hylton

Daddy's Gun

My butt smacked head sends me
Spinning to the ground
Where the grass paints
My blue jeans green

You present a barrel
Inches from my face
Long and smooth
I clasp my hands
An unwilling disciple
Worshiping its very existence

Mere prayers hardly satisfy
Your lust
Receive the body of Christ
My child
Unholy communion
Penetrates
My thoughts

Don't worry
I will not gag
On your religion
I've seen the light
You come for
My sins
Buckshot loaded with
Apostles
I want to go home
Sweet Ithaca

My creator will
Send me
Once his moment
Of divinity has passed

I touch my face
My hand wet with
Eruption
But dear Father
Is it me or is it you?

Whale Spit

"Hey sis, do you know if whales spit?'
I looked at her through the rear-view mirror
As she traced the growing bruise on her forearm
And wondered why fingermarks don't leave fingerprints
Without ever questioning whose
Thumb had purpled her skin

"Why would you ask that?"

"A girl at school said an ostrich clawed her legs
Ms. Light didn't believe her. But no one cuts
Themselves that many times on accident."

No they don't

"Why are you talking about ostriches?
I thought you wanted to know about whales?"

"Oh yeah, so you know how when you spit
You leave a white mark on something?
I figured when whales spit
They probably leave behind something blue."

I said that made sense and she proudly held
Up her arm to show me where the whale
Spit on her when Dad took her to the aquarium yesterday

He got you good

"What do you think whale spit sounds like?"
I shrugged and listened to her gurgle
Sounds around like a language poet
Or one of those puppets on Sesame Street.

"You know who else spits?" I shook my head.

113

"Kevin. He can spit a whole football field longer than I can. Do you think now that the whale spit on me, I can beat him?"

"Of course you can."

And I knew she'd have to

Luisa A. Igloria

Song of Meridians

It's spring, but in other places it's not-
        yet-spring. It's dry, or wet with

monsoon, or it is why-is-there-still-snow-
        on-the-ground. It's strange and high,

that mechanical whine in the night, coming
        from somewhere beyond the ceiling.

It's Wednesday, and in another place already
        Thursday; it's night, though here it is

still half past noon. And look at the news-
        paper: on the upper left, a woman in a pale

peach dress is smiling and waving her hand.
        On the bottom right, there's a picture

of cities burning: it's spring, or whatever
        season it is for laughter or slaughter, a

difference of one letter between one state
        of being and another. It's that time when cows

and sheep are calving, when blood is the marker
        for a life breaking away, or maybe just breaking.

The Heart's Every Heave

Say cotton, say the crease
in the sleeve of a shirt,

the plainness in a collar,
the brim of a hat. If the future

is here, whose face greets you
in the mirror as you collect

water in your hands; as you hand
your money over the counter

to pay for bread, a cup of coffee,
a ticket? A man on the train steps

in the path of someone he doesn't
even know, or trails another man

home in his truck for two
whole miles to spew insults

in his foreign-looking face. How
is this the future too? Your heart

holds its breath, lurches from platform
to crowded lobby. Say elegy, insistence,

not blank stare. Say danger and defiance.
Not shoulder shrug, not fold over.

Fatalism

after "El Flautista" ("The Flutist"), Remedios Varo; 1955

A cardinal touches down on a Japanese maple
but can't tell us where they've taken

all the children. We take turns watching,
we take turns playing songs for the mothers:

their grief, our grief, might merge
to form a thing that could unseal a stone

from the mountain. Only there is no one
walking out into the light as if resurrected.

That copper-tinged wind, that citadel
whose once beautiful blueprint is fading.

The light, too, is dismantling; or in the throes
of change. My face is the inside of a shell up-

turned to the moon. A rune, a coelacanth.
Night-blooming cereus stranded in time.

Edison Jennings

Directions to a Ruin

Follow Spoon Gap Road past the Free Will Church
and find a wide-hipped chimney stub
girdled with a snarl of berries, dark and sweet
this time of year, rooted in the fireplace,
blacksmithed pot-hook curled like a come-here finger,
but the house is gone. Lightning burned it down,
the crooked stroke still scarred across the hearth.
In easy view from where a doorway
might have been, several generations lie
beneath a hill toothed with snaggled headstones
tilted by a hundred years of freeze and thaw
where love's observance long ago succumbed
to underbrush and new-growth oak and grief's
alphabet weathered to a palimpsest
on lichen freckled slates. You might rest there,
stretch out in the chimney shade and taste
the wild blackberries, slightly tart with ash.

Connoisseur of Decline

Your rubbish strewn house, swayback and rotten
and but for ghosts, condemned and vacated,
a ramshackle chapel of the forgotten,
has collapsed on its joists as if deflated.
No well-meaning friends can now rectify
the chaotic charm of your OCD
(they loved you too well to ever dare try),
and you went to your grave with your pedigree:
a curious man, a gleaner of junk,
young wife confessor and Dear Abby reader,
dashing in used clothes, in love with a punk,
a watcher of birds, a liberal heart bleeder,
and writer of stories not enough read,
kind and peculiar and terribly dead.

Don Johnson

Isinglass

From the rubble that was my great-grandmother's
cabin, I pull a four-paned metal window
smaller than the nine of hearts I turned up
stripping thick linoleum from the loft
where seven people slept. Lifted to light
it's like looking at the place through a thumbprint.
Age and layered swirls of mica blur the logs
we've tagged and stacked, the blackened chimney
stones, the ochre clay the road smears across
the hillside following this morning's rain.

Riding out from town men called on her
to read their futures, postponing trips
or planting early, their faith in her foretelling
measured by the single coin dropped in her palm.

Weary from three days of reclamation,
all I can foreknow is work, the ache
and strain of salvage: rebuilding on my land
the home my father and grandfather were
born in, striving with each log re-notched
and lifted into place to fathom how
that tired woman, late at night,
her children aloft, her dime or nickel banked
in a leather purse, alone and staring
at the tiny window in the stove,
could divine anything beyond the fire.

Photograph of My Great-Grandmother, Nancy Bett Johnson, Circa 1923

The bleak background—bare trees, cleared field,
charred garden plot—bleeds onto the dark front porch,
the overhang held up by locust posts, slightly out
of plumb. The rough-sawn gable ends bring home
my father's claim that they were "too poor to paint,
too proud to whitewash," white being too elegant
for this Presbyterian household, fit for what
appears to be the child's baptismal gown,
the matriarch's dress, even the hat set aside
on the porch floor to reveal her face, plain black.
The sunlit trapezoid she occupies
this late winter day has coaxed out a rare smile
celebrating this legitimate son of a legitimate son.

She gave five children with three fathers
her own father's name, he dying when she
was four in a prison camp after Gettysburg,
her own mother bearing four after the surrender,
also under the dead soldier's name, the last
taking her life and carrying the given name Grief
into the next century. James Johnson gave
Nanny Bett five more children and a surname
before dying in 1900 of influenza.

In that colorless world, the small white oval
of my father's face blurs against the patch
of gray sky, pushing one's gaze up
and to the left, toward her smile that even
the slow Kodak was quick enough to capture.

Swans on Quantico Creek

for Harry Ervin

Where the creek broadens to tidal marsh,
Tundra Swans anchor themselves, head-down,
feeding in estuarial ooze deep enough
to harbor the leached bits and pieces of my life
here fifty years ago. They return each winter,
I for reunions or funerals, this seventieth birthday
for my high school best friend who owns this bluff,

the deck from which he offers as a gift for me
these swans. Not one raises its head
while we watch, making the whole flock
look decapitated. Over swamp glare, at this distance,
looked at even through binoculars, they could be
victims, unclaimed trophies of sky-busters
whose reedy, vacant blinds ring this shallow cove
like shells of blistered outbuildings.

Then one head rises, and another, and more,
until they look like miners emerging at shift's end
from the drift mouth in those hills I left
for these tides and their gifts of blue crabs, herring runs
like Bible miracles. My friend says the herring are gone,
millions vanished, and apologizes that the swans'
muck-blackened heads are inelegant. But these long
haulers out of Prudhoe Bay keep coming back,
holding on. Their dark cowls, when they let go,
shine in winter sun, alluvial grit ablaze.

One Quail, Whistling

for Dave Smith

Across the pasture, out of green-briars
at the hill's foot, one quail whistles.

My grandfather answers from a distance
of sixty years. Younger than I am now,

he doesn't echo the bird's name
or try to whistle his grown children back

with the shrill trochee even their
black neighbors knew as "Uncle Monk's

whistle." He coaxes the scattered covey in
on three soft notes, the last

almost inaudible, the way he says
my grandmother's name, "Catherine."

And they come. One scurries from berry canes
beside what used to be the outdoor kitchen,

another from the marble yard where grown men
lagged clay taws in the Depression—

another, and another, and another,
until the last two strut from khaki-colored

stalks of lespedeza to stand six inches
from his dusty wingtips, tilting their heads

like hounds at a distant train signal. No one
now sows "blessed Jesus" here or spares

edge-growing millet. So the "bobwhite"
that shears again across my fallow field

will go unanswered. With my grandfather's
warbled gift I could whistle him in to my feet

then startle him back to the nearest fencerow
with a weight shift. Or I can stand here

sharing that other old man's delight
in his homecoming, planting himself

twenty yards from the cabin his mother
had built, where he and his children

were born, those rapt birds clucking at his feet
where in thirty years almost nothing had changed.

Jeffrey N. Johnson

Particle Search in D minor

We've reached the day when Mozart is average
and Einstein a mere arranger of mathematical symbols.
Relativity has made its music and Requiem is woefully
hummed by famished school children in search
of genius in their own time. Perfection now lies
in the splendid grafting of ones and zeros in a prairie
warehouse, proof positive of our holy homogenization,
making us safe only to spend lest we be sequestered
from the masses. Hedge fund formulas frame the universe
and derivative spreadsheets provide the soundtrack,
while in a basement in Cambridge a man wearing
designer glasses will knife open the half-shells of a quark,
offering yet another extraordinary redundancy. The plates
keep grinding by, occasionally toppling a city or two
as we suck on tasteless strawberries from halfway around
the world wondering if it will all end on a complex chord
surrounded by symbols, or on a single doleful note.

Things Boys Bury

His limbs were shattered from war
games, so I buried his plastic parts
under a rock in the back yard.
Years later I showed the grave
to my son, then only a boy, and yes,
we agreed, we must dig him up.
He turned over the rock, uncovering
a pasty white lizard in hibernation
entwined in the remains of the dead GI.
We'd better let him sleep, he said,
replacing the rock over the tomb.

In Iraq my son made traveling safer
by camping on rooftops with his scope.
Young men digging by the road were
shattered by the draw of his index finger,
while families below huddled together
wondering where their children were.

Now he lives in Texas with his bride
riding through school on the GI bill.
When he is able to sleep, he dreams
only of paralysis, but in the spring
he will awaken to the birth of a son
who will bury things in the back yard,
as all boys do.

Joshua Jones

The Conference of the Birds

The latest bit of bad ecological news:
we lost one-third of our birds

since the seventies. Not *flew south*
for the winter lost, but lost forever.

Though the mechanism's still unclear,
the scientists agree we did it,

that the birds didn't decide to leave
of their own accord. Humanity's need

to occupy every habitat with pavement
or soybeans likely killed them off, though

at least one loon in front of a mic
thinks the windmills minced all the dark-eyed

juncos into pâté. Someone says congress
should do something for the woodpeckers,

turkey vultures, and finches, and someone
else says songbirds don't pay taxes.

Maybe they tried to file a complaint, failed,
gave up, and flew off after the hoopoe,

spiritual seekers fleeing industrial
and suburban life for their king

in the East. We'd likely spoil that too.
My Penguin edition of *The Conference*

of the Birds has gathered them around
their leader's charismatic crest as he explains

the path, undoes their nest of excuses
in signs and parables. But the picture's

been cropped to stay faithful
to the poem and not the painting

from centuries later. The full Persian
miniature adds birds Attar left out,

prime of the host, a white rooster.
How'd this domesticated cock

end up here anyway, perched
in the midst of the avian host near

a fig tree and winding stream, a wing's
length away from peacock, heron,

and hawk, equal at last to the raptors
and waterfowl after years of captivity?

He's got his eyes not on the hoopoe
but a hunter whose boot nestles

between the rocks to steady himself
as he chooses his target. The musket's

so long it can't be held by the picture
frame, and only the rooster knows

what an armed man signifies. Having seen
his hens' eggs eaten, having seen them

slaughtered one by one, their heads left
on a stump and pecked at by his children,

he sees the man and knows there's no use
staying at this conference. His voice

can be heard anywhere, and better
anywhere else than near a man with a gun.

Though he'd like to fly through
the seven valleys and cross deserts

with the mad flock of feathered saints,
his wattle wags as he startles,

flaps a time or two toward sanctuary
in the fig tree. He feels his clipped

wings give out but doesn't know
what else to do but scream.

M. A. Keller

Rope

I can think of few things more inexplicably pleasing than rope,
a new coil of it, the heft, the smell of a wood porch trackside hardware store,
the barn loft scratch of it, and for me, its uselessness, who has no boat,
no load to haul, no iron stake begging a barking dog and the ensuing
muddy circle, no need tie anything down. Have you ever unraveled
the ends—just so—and woven them back to finish off a fray
to a perfect nub. Or cut a rope in summer just to splice it
together amazed at how this thickened sisal weave can hold. Have you singed
stray fibers with a careful match for hours. I'll teach you how
to do it perfectly, to put two pieces together, to make a good end,
to tie a square, a timberline, a half hitch, a monkey's fist,
and the one-handed wonder that will save your life.

Jennifer Key

Winter Solstice

No neat bales tally the end of winter's ledger.
Instead, my father's dog, an arabesque
in white, whirls in the haze grown two feet tall.
The setter who always points his target
cannot find his master. Late afternoons hereafter
we'll see what we've been navigating in the dark.

Indoors, a pointer patterned in green toile's
the only thing that hunts. It holds its point
on grouse, mid-flap, aloft on curtains, walls,
or bedspread folded at my father's feet this year.
Too soon he will be scattered far from here
in another field with neither dog nor me.

But here in branching dusk his dog alights,
content to flush whatever birds bed down.
He sees no absence where none yet exists,
and so he stalks the grass as he was taught
while in my father's room small rabbits dart
and pheasants burst repeatedly to flight.

Blue Ridge

On the porch my father lies flushed
and dreaming back to boyhood
or war, when soldiers crushed heroin

with their hands and smoked it.
He refused, but now wears a patch
more potent than opium behind one ear.

Beyond the porch screens, bug-picked
and spider-laced, the hills of Virginia
march into a future we can't see,

just as birdsong insists on daylight
long after it's gone. The lilies father planted
to flower the season of my wedding

open their awful mouths—
the first just yesterday and by today
two turned trumpet. There is no silencing

their dreadful fanfare. Why must they persist
when each pink tongue only says the same thing?
The more that open the sooner he'll be gone.

Ghost Psalm

No longer will I find you
as blown ash and bone
in flattened grasses where deer bed down

but in the sun flare and flash that move
through this world as dapples
on the backs of those we number in the field.

Their bodies steam in the pre-dawn damp,
and when they rise they wear you in the mud
thatched to the v of their hooves

and in the wet slicked to their fetlocks' curl.
On the slenderest of legs, they carry you
past what blurs into bramble and branch.

Once you were the field and everything in it
that grew while the sky, pearlescent
in its making and unmaking, slid over.

Now you, who have already traveled
from one world to the next, must travel again
across lowlands on the paws of the dog, on

the hooves of the deer, docents of dirt
each divot recalls. They carry you
into the reeds at the water's edge,

silver tongue lapping the bank where they stand.
They carry you beyond my cries.
Clover fed, the deer walk through summer,

then winnowed by want, long miles,
they walk from one year into two.
You will never come back

though my blood sings your name,
and the heart, ghost of a continent,
sounds the syllables sewn to its own.

I will stand in the field clothed in silence.
Tell me, Father, where should I look
when not even the rain can find you?

Chelsea Krieg

Portrait of My Husband as the Owl of Minerva Takes Flight in the Dusk

When we married, you opened
the cabinet of your body to me,

and I placed all I did not understand
on the shelves of your ribs: the bullet

that killed my uncle, my mother's
cancer, the way the body destroys itself

from inside. I arranged it all there
beside each specimen of your own,

the bottles I had not yet come to know,
and you trembled open, glass gleaming

in the dark as I reached
my hand inside. Every night since,

I have taken the bottles out, held them
to the light, questioned the way

each specimen floats, swims
in midair. I've spent hours

considering the hue and curve
of each of those creatures—

examined every cross-section, noted
which is more flower, which, more sea

anemone. Everything with a wing,
I touched, pinned those translucent sleeves

so they glistened—each body,
a separate yearning. Every night

that passes, I observe, trace the glass
with the tips of my fingers, name them all

with the swells of my palms.
So today, when the surgeon pries

open the oak of your chest and cuts
them from their shelves, I know he does not know

how to hold them. How could he?
I want to tell him, *Look, look at this one.*

I want to tell him, *I can tell you its name.*

Anytime Firecrackers

My grandfather's favorite was the tank,
camouflaged cardboard enveloping
the explosive center, ruby paper cinched
around a thick fuse. We didn't need a holiday
or a reason to light it and we never waited
for dark. Each time, my sister and I held
our breaths and clung near to the 1982 cream Chevy,
legs vibrating in anticipation, blue eyes unblinking
as our grandfather struck the match in one
swift swipe. He bent quickly to place the tank
and pressed the flame into the string. As it caught,
his eyes fixed on the tiny engine glowing in the drive.
Fire burst through the turret, igniting the guns
and the tank popped, spinning on its wheels.
When the sparks began to sing, a grey cloud bloomed
into the sky and the neighbors rushed
to their screened-in porches. From the kitchen,
my grandmother lifted his name harshly
into the air. But he did not hear.

If he had been wearing his dog tags, I imagine
the light would have shot across the metal grooves
of his name, illuminating date of birth, next of kin. Instead,
those thin sheets of stainless steel remain buried in a shoebox,
slid back deep into the black corners beneath
his four-poster bed. As the fire glittered
in the dimming summer light, we watched.
He danced defiantly before the tank, swirled,
laughing like the teenager he had been
in 1941. And as the smoke cleared,
we saw his face. And oh, was he beautiful.

Callinectes sapidus

In summer, just before the sun drowned
        in the Chesapeake Bay, my father would pull
                the crab pot up from the pier. Twenty

or thirty blue crabs at once—their claws
        chattering against the wire. Tips
                of their pincers burning with red

horizon as they emerged, dripping
        from water. Angry glistening
                bodies clambering onto other

mud-colored backs. My father
        would shake the metal cage
                until the crabs were piled

into the white paint bucket on the dock
        and I'd watch them squirm,
                kick their legs against

the plastic. In Latin, *callinectes sapidus*
        means *savory beautiful swimmer*—
                bodies named for the way they move,

how good they taste on the tongue.
        My mother kept the water boiling
                and the first time I watched my father do it,

he lifted one from the bucket, taught me
        how to jam a knife hard into its mouth,
                rip off the shell until it was dead.

I dreamed your name was River

mouth open inside my belly,
        rushing forward into limb,
white-capped vertebrae
        held together among stone,
and I combed your seagrass hair
        until it shone, whispered your name
and knew you heard it.
                When I awoke,
I still saw you, lapping the banks

of my skin, light
glinting from the wave
of your cheek, learned
to call you *daughter*.
And already
I am grieving the hour
I will pour you from my body,
watch as you flow from one rock
to the next, sing
into unknown spaces, cracks
where not even my voice
can follow.

Postpartum as Corpse Flower

It's like this: In the rainforest,
the corpse flower grows tall, caresses

the boughs of the acacia, lifts
her wine-dark skirt to flaunt

golden garter blossoms beneath. Seven years
of waiting—then for two nights, she burns

with fever. Midnight air, heavy
with rot as carrion beetles and sweat

bees flock—tapping, humming
until—pollen-dusted—they flee

and all, for a moment, is quiet.

Nine months after, breasts—swollen
heavy fruit. T-shirt, damp with milk.

We have been at this all night. Drink, baby. Please.

Hair, unwashed. A tiny, hungry mouth
crying, crying, crying, crying

lips circling her nipple in the dark.

Jessi Lewis

Should I Draw the Mountain for You?

These will be our slate rocks, our slick frogs, our soft-
toned deer, our leaning woods, our puddle dust,
Our driveway, our reasons, our hurt, our fluid clover,
our losses,

Our cedar door chirr, our found cat with thick ticks, our
slipping youth, our wiry chicory,
Our boiled creek, our smooth-gilled creek chubs, my
dead grandmother's house, our vacancy to fill, our
birthright to fill it, our thirsty skin,

Our silver maple, our wasp nest in the tire swing, our
rain over gutters, our duct-taped door, our sonograms of
children, our purple martins returning,
Our missing streets, our grassy café, our phone calls
ringing over the field, our dull handsaw,

Our dim flashlights, our broken dolls, our forgotten
Gaelic, our invaluable curse words,
Our sailing wind children, our grown hearts, our
chopped wood, then our teenaged owls, our losses, our
cedar door chirr,

And yes, here are our offspring who go missing one
summer to find their own, our dusted books, our hurt,
our purple martins returning.

And us. That's us there, clinging.

Christopher Linforth

From a Window in Southwest Virginia

A barn spider creeps through a hole in the patched
screen and explores the travel guides on my nightstand.

Cicadas outside remind me of my childhood in the South
of France, the brittle chirping ripping the night air

as I ran up the mountain path to my grand-père's stone villa.
Every morning I woke to a view over the Massif des Maures,

and the rescue planes dropping large claws of seawater
on the charred scrubland shot with cork oak and pine.

My toes felt the cardinal points etched in the concrete patio
by my grand-père's iron chisel and his last great sweat

of independence before the roil spiraled his heart.
I sweep the barn spider into a champagne flute and carry

the glass to the backyard, freeing the spider on the linden
where I hear the last call of the cicadas.

Robert Wood Lynn

Voicemail From My Mother

for Claudia Emerson

You know, I haven't heard from you in a while. Did I tell you
          a bird flew into the house?
Found an open door on a cold day. Something small,

like a chickadee, but even more chickadee than that.
          I chased it around the house
with an upturned broom until I lost track through all that

sweeping of dirty air. This was a ways back, two cats ago.
          I didn't see it fly out,
so it's hung in my mind ever since. An unclosed parenthesis.

I've braced myself, the way the ear hears a squeal of brakes
          and begs for a thud.
Braced myself to find a tiny skeleton each time I clean

behind the curtains or rearrange the furniture. Today,
          opening the drawer
of cords that go to things I probably already threw away,

it flew out, perched briefly on my shoulder,
          then alighted hard
and I mean hard into the mirror of the closed window.

It Was Time Again for Bushhogging the Paddock

and there I was five foot four and most way old enough
to drive and so with the kind of deliberation useful
for disguising fear my father went about showing me
the stick shift on the old Ford tractor the one he bought
with his first government wages and loved so much
he even had it loaded on a lowboy and brought down
to this house when he moved off the mountain this house
where every morning he took coffee on the porch
watching two wild turkeys disappear into the woods
with the last of the dark and on this day he taught me how
the clutch engages and to keep careful on the revolutions
per minute leaving one hand on the wheel the other
steady behind me on the mower lever ready to cut it
at his hand signal and this day was a turning over of something
like an engine coughing slowly while my father walked ahead
scouting in that grass so tall only the shoulders of his blue
shirt peeked out above the greenbrown stalks that my machine
trampled and spat out behind me with the constant turning
of that heavy steel blade he explained was dull by design to whack
but not catch in the dense growth and here I was cutting clean
the swath behind me in the field scanning to my side to check
for big rocks and other unmowables and I might as well have
been Hannibal riding an elephant over an alp and I felt the earth
yielding for the first time to my adulthood as I sawed a slow
zig zag back across the paddock but then it was there the flutter
of wings alongside me and my father yelling which seen from
a tractor is all visual a mouth opening all the way and not
closing overwhelmed by the din of the engine his hands
waved a gesture what gesture the signal and we watched
two turkeys flee to the woods while we waited for the blade
to sputter stopped and there in the earned silence I climbed
down from the giant stilled tire and my father pointed me
to the dashed nest the dozen broken eggs and whatever
he'd yelled he'd already gotten it all out and now was well
past speaking he simply turned and walked the long way back
up to the house through the tall grass which closed behind
him in the buzzing air and so I followed hoping we might
both disappear and so we leave the tractor where it stops
and no one finishes mowing the paddock this year
or the next or even the one after that which is to say
this is how a field returns itself to woods.

About the Phones

Closing my car door, you always say   *Watch*
for deer and text when you get home.
I want to, I do, but I will forget.
Time moves and I forget.   *Look*
I am trying, I am, but it's not the kind
of thing that trying solves.

Once
on the side of a highway, a cop told me
about dragging a full grown buck out
the windshield of a wrecked car all by himself.
About the sounds it made, *Like the devil learning*
what regret feels like. About the woman it kicked
to death in the driver's seat. The phone call
he had to make to her grown daughter after
whose first question was, *Did the deer survive?*

Different cop, different time, different highway.
Said she keeps her phone on silent then spoke
about securing the crime scene in that classroom
in Blacksburg where the one student shot
all the others. Every single one of them
had a cell phone, she said, and for hours after
every single one rang and rang or vibrated
across the floor in the same slow way
that blood pools. No one was allowed to answer,
no one, so instead the phones rang all night
until batteries were empty, voicemails full
of a thousand *Call me when you get this so I know*
you're okays. Turns out time moves the way
blood does. Batteries too. Runs out
like a startled deer across a road.   *Listen*
I am trying to find a way to tell you this.
There are things that trying solves but this
is not one of them.

The Summer After the Winter I Taught You How to Start a Fire

You asked me what I knew about thermals—
heat's tendency to rise, cool, fall again and so
I showed you how to recognize the circle
of turkey vultures over our neighbor's field
as a clue another calf had died. Immediately
you declared yourself the Detective of All Dead
Things. *Something's dead*, you'd say, squinting
skyward. *Case closed. That'll be fifty dollars.*
It was one of your better jokes and as with all jokes
funny at first then a little less until repeated only
as an epitaph for how funny it once was.
Fifty American dollars. This debt smoldering
like your anger after I told you the words
I love you work the same way. I was careful
to say so in the joking tone reserved
for the parts of this living too disappointing
to speak plain. *Something's dead*, you'd say,
a skill precisely too late to be of any use.
Same as me here explaining the joke, the check
I'd mail if I had your new address.

Catherine MacDonald

Court and Bower

In the unkept house as sleepers
        sigh, the spider spins. The sleep
of the child is the keeper's sleep,
        the sigh of the child, her sigh.
In the unkept house the child's breath
        clots the keeper's breath.
Silk crosshairs the scope and lattices
        the eaves. We pack the wounds
with it. In the unkept house
        dragline and filament unfurl
as the keeper robs the spider
        of her silk. Keeper, child, spinner—
thralls to the thread and the spool.

Bird Study

i
        Though there were rookeries of crows to darken
the skies and robins by the thousands both

        summer and winter, Thomas Jefferson bought
his first mockingbird from a Charles City slave,

        hung its cage with moon-flowers and trumpet-vine,
fed it bits from his own lips, in thrall to this

        slow-westering stranger, *Mimus polyglottos*. Wild mocker
in that mulatto landscape, it would not on its own

        find Jefferson's mountaintop for twenty years yet,
its tidewater song pinned to eastern cedar

        and shallow-rooted shrub, to the shoreline's sure
subsidence as it receives all the waters of all the rivers.

ii

      For the first time, in her seventies, my mother,
nearly blind, sees, she says—*sees*—

      yard birds: goldfinches and hummers in August,
yellow-rumps and juncos in January, the dumb

      doves raising chicks in the hanging basket
by May's banging screen door, and the mockingbird,

      all year, on the taut clothesline. She frets,
knows this life-list is short, so I've given her

      a suet cage, field guide, binoculars,
a feeder, to see what might still come.

      Her last spring, too hot, too early, ravening
black birds descend—starlings, grackles, crows—

      devouring all she offers. Her questions then:
When to stop feeding, what to withhold?

iii

      Glossy black wing torn from a shoulder
in the tangled vetch at the yard's edge.

      Rain, wind, foraging ants—another season finally
arrives. I forget to look, and then I see that it's gone.

iv

      Just off the road to Lanexa, a hungry crow
shadows a box turtle at her shallow

      dirt nest, gulping each small egg
even as the turtle pushes them out.

      Nearby, I crouch on a ditch rim
in mud and sun, camera shuttered,

      shuttered against the crow,
crow dark as any old sorrow.

v

        Pests mobbing his feeders, crows work
without music my father says. Yet when my sister

        phones, he goes, leather gloves and towel in hand,
to a crow caught at its throat, wedged between fence-

        pickets in her yard, each wing-beat bloodying
wood, crow unable to call or rise. Approaching the bird

        from behind, he cups belly and breast, releases it,
lowers it to the ground. Free, the crow seeks

        shade in the cool dirt beneath looping boughs
of forsythia, at once its bright shield and bower.

Rousing the Machinery

                The tygers of wrath are wiser than the horses of instruction.
                    –*William Blake*, The Marriage of Heaven and Hell

i
Observe the perpetual boy, as one
with the pop- eyed crowd. He's come
to see the King's menagerie: camel, bear,
leopard, lion, *tyger*: stripe over stripe,
swinging its heavy head with each sullen
step. He notes the fixed pit of its pupil,
the eyes' bulge and slow blink. Who will extol
this captive, pacing the round tower room?
Who will grind its bones for luck, pluck
stiff whiskers for a paintbrush, rend fat
for an aphrodisiac? Who will inhale
scent of musk, tang of urine soaked
in stone, sing, *Marvelous, its assets?*
A boy.

ii

This morning in Raleigh's exurban flank,
I watch the bad boys of Selma
Alternative High School craft paper wasps.
They loft them across the bedlam
of the classroom to where the *tyger*, perfect-
bound, sleeps in my hands. With a stroke,
a stroke, a stroke, the machinery is roused
and in the corner of the classroom,
above our heads, gangly wasps disgorge wood
to make paper. Watch: the miracle
occurs in a vessel, an enclosure, in a lidded pot
on a hot stove, in a woman's body
where a child grows, or in the insect
jaw, ganglia, and lobe.

Margaret Mackinnon

Flight

Born in Fairport, Virginia, Leslie J. Payne (1907-1981), an African American, grew up on a farm in rural Northumberland County. There, he attended public school through the fourth grade...In the 1960s, he moved back home and began building an entire airfield that included an airstrip, a machine shop, a 12-foot air control tower, and a row of airplanes ready for fantasy travel.

American Folk Art: A Regional Reference

Leslie Payne called them his *imitations*—
those earthbound airplanes, brave

assemblages made of metal, wood,
canvas he decorated with wild designs.

On the Sabbath, he traveled to his runway
built amid sun-burnt fields, invited

a local girl to wear her Sunday best—
one remembered *white gloves and pearls.*

She'd hold a sign for that day's imagined
journey: Ghana or Paris. California. Montreal.

All places Airplane Payne would never see—
but we can see him, now, on the Lord's Day,

trusting in the Father to lift him high,
toward some kingdom all his own.

Safety first, Take no Chance!
his motto carved above the machine shop door.

But this *was* his chance, believing even
the oldest hurts could be displaced.

Like my father—and the one fine thing
he knew to build for us: kites.
Sticks and brown paper. A bedsheet
torn to a clumsy, straggling tail.

146

Craft he'd learned when he was a boy.
Those kites were awkward, sometimes

too heavy—but sometimes, rising, rising,
turning our Sunday sky a brilliant blue,

floating toward a burning sun,
this world's brokenness transcended.

And so, we who are their witnesses must close
our eyes and see them now—

high above their small, failed hours,
faithful, always, to those they've left behind.

Anne Spencer's Letter / Family Portrait

According to her family, the poet Anne Spencer (1882-1975) often wrote letters which she never mailed. The italicized text below was found among her papers after her death.

Dear Family—The happy thing about the sorrows of your great temporary loss

Imagine a time when nothing was lost.
And you've come back, as you have before.
It's summer, of course, season you loved
for its longest light. For the wealth of green.
For the return, always returning, of softest nights.
What I miss are the ways we filled each other's
lives: that year we watched sea turtles
come ashore, generations of females
on the same sands, building their nests, guided
by moon on the water at night. How far
the souls of those we've loved travel home!
Now, outside, I imagine curious birds call out
your name, song so clear I know it lasts.

is that as believers, we know it is but temporary. God's promise gives eternal life.

Sleep has rearranged it all.
I'm in a sad house, rooms
spare and strange. You're here,

again, but agitated, as if you can't
stay long. It's a place where nothing
changes, though you are all

change. Your eyes focus elsewhere.
How much I wish I could say!
I strain to hear the words you speak.

Hesitant, you look back
before departing—
we are figures made of longing.

Which one of us is most unmoored?
The front door's open, allowing light
from the street to enter, the way light shines

so we discern the shadows—
as if this dream were as much about the light
as about your leaving—

The line has many breaks for us, but we know that they shall all be joined.

You've come now in winter, trees
beyond my window bare and dark-limbed,

ancient and evident. From somewhere else,
you've come to show me this:

Snow begins to fall, white on white on gray.
Old light, hidden and always there, beneath the cold.

Josh Mahler

House on a Hill

Where stones once lay along the path, burnt grass
emerges. The naked windows, grimy and homesick
for human eyes and the strange music of our bodies.

It stayed that way for years. If you were to drive by
at a certain time of day, the shadows would linger
on the walls like a drunk man's beard. If you faced

the door during a storm, you would need to knock
and bow against the torrent, burdened by the sound
of footsteps. I know nothing beyond what I have seen.

Fire and Smoke

After hauling up wood
from down the hill,
I slam shut the back door.
I make breakfast—
homefries and scrambled eggs.

Spring is a dream for some,
recognition of the day
that blooms a fresh palette—
listen, the trees are alive
with whispers of true sound.

Somewhere,
he's swirling dirt in the valley,
reciting tall tales. Lust for the truth,
evening deep as a footprint
left behind on the trail.

If necessary, any rock
can serve as a tombstone.
With hope to learn why she is gone,

I take long walks, the pain
of pine needles piercing my bare feet.

I stare out the window—
snow falling from the branches,
wood smoke and coffee
turning cold. I taste all of it,
the hollowness in my bones.

Jeff Mann

Cosmos

My father is eighty-nine.
Bright flowers are what's left

of his garden this late,
mid-October. Color-

blind, I ask: *Lavender?*
Purple? Maroon?

No matter. They are
the last cosmos,

breeze-sway by
torn soil where

half-runners grew.
Bumblebees busy

themselves, supping
in the cups of central

gold. How many years
has he tilled this same

soil, brought in bushels,
filled family shelves

with stored sunlight?
The bees know nothing

of the cold
to come.

They burrow, they
quiver, sunk in

the source
of all delight.

The Gay Redneck, Hankering After Celebrities, Hikes the New River Trail

The outfit's *Brokeback* to match the aching spine—
the sort of rawhide jacket and felt cowboy hat
Ennis Del Mar might have worn—which leads me
to memories of Jake Gyllenhaal naked, on his knees,
grunting with invaded discomfort in a high
mountain tent, and that at least makes my sacro-
iliac joint feel a little better. That, and my cautious
loping along this woodland rail-to-trail, my compulsive
autumnal botanizing: pokeberries, samaras of ash
and box elder, dying wingweed, fallen mulberry leaves,
the scattered seeds of tulip trees. This blessedly far
from human beings, little sounds save the occasional
crow or woodpecker, and, in my head, the latest
truck-cab tune, Thomas Rhett's "It Goes Like This,"
his furry chest, black beard and sloppy bangs almost
worth the complications and consequences of
a kidnapping. Boys so beautiful should always be
bruised and sore in all the right places, as I find myself
today, despite my distance from cities, backed-up traffic,
condo sprawl and suburban malls, the fascinatingly
fashionable Gay Community. Thanks to ornery
defiance, appetite, and a lot of luck, I have found
in my native mountains everything I need, and so
let me take this opportunity to congratulate myself
on having the damn-fine solid sense to stay.

Gold

An *altered look*, said Dickinson.
Yes. As if morning mist

were green-gold,
or rainclouds

were chartreuse,
new leaf clinging to April

and Appalachia's
dark, long-bare limbs.

Again and again,
the earth regains its youth.

Twenty years
have gleamed and grayed

since the spring
we shared.

The color of these hills
captures that mislaid morning

in a distant city,
sleeping together

for the first time, naked,
side by side.

I woke before you,
pulled back the veil covering your body,

and stared in wonder
at your repose, the hard

and helpless muscles
of your arms, the brown hair

mossing your chest, your unconscious
cock, your breath's rise and fall.

Our beards were still glossy and dark,
though even then my hair was thinning.

There was hope for us, I thought.
If I loved you hard enough

you would leave him and choose to stay
with me. So I watched you sleep,

aching
to touch you, to top you,

but terrified,
for then you might wake

into distance and defense.
You were my son

then, my only child.
Once, however briefly,

153

this tenderness had a home,
and all my bonfire

passion was welcomed, not wasted.
I was right, I was right

in my suspicion, that when you woke,
all springs would leave with you,

and every April after
would be word, not flesh,

and I would hold nothing
so young and golden again.

Green Man

(for John)

The gifts you leave in my desk's bud vase vary—
a white rose, a sprig of rosemary, grape hyacinth
or species tulip. All summer you have labored,
and now, mid-August, the house is surrounded

with acanthus and honeysuckle, coneflower
and black-eyed Susan, geraniums, hostas,
julep mint. In the tiny garden, squash vines
refine their gold. In the fig tree, plump fruits ripen.

If I am the Lord of the Animals—their furry rut,
their hard-horned musk—vacillating wildly
between nuzzling affections and growling ferocity,

you are the Lord of the Greenwood, forest foliage
twining from your beard and callused fingertips,
swathing me in fertile and protective shade.

Hemlocks

A tiny insect,
       the woolly adelgid,
              is eating the needles.

Without boughs
       to sough, the wind
              has less and less to say.

The green dwindles,
       twigs brittle and brown,
              like black beards gone silver,

the wilderness
       leaching away.
              Inside spheres of hemlock

shade, your body turns
       to emerald. Jewels
              are shattered one by one,

the abacus of age
       tallying the black
              numerals, tallying.

Unframed by limbs,
       the vistas disappear.
              No composition now,

only stumps and vacant air.
       The forest shrivels,
              the graveyard fills.

Chestnut, hemlock, ivorybill,
       cancer, gallstone, adelgid.
              Emptied out,

my aunt's cornfield,
       my grandmother's house,
              my mother's clothes.

John Q. Mars

I am but a hollowed carcass

the kids' favorite plaything on the side
of the road, their pavement-bound

pet. they point to the flies treading
the once-whites of my eyes and ask, "are you

dead?" my only response is buzzing and decay.
they prod my tail with sticks and ask, "how

does dead feel?" the sticky, blood-spiked fur
around my gut quivering and bulging with rot.

"are you still hungry?" they gather whatever their grubby
hands can find fastest: fistfuls of litter and bugs, debris,

dirt and gravel they shove in my mouth. I cannot swallow
but it slides down anyways. inside I'm all echoes and thuds; their waste

bounces and pounds off deflated lungs, against wriggling intestine
until ribs crack and flesh splits seams—a weary torso fit to burst.

leave me behind when what joy I bring you and daylight
starts to go. when you remember and pass me by

in a few days' time I'll be gone, melted
by maggots and sun. there will be no

remains but a streak of pelt and lifeless
teeth pressed in the concrete,

waiting for the rain.

21

. . . Lol my bday was a like week ago

A friend brought me back Muse candles from the witches'
quarters in NOLA *not for my bday but still ugh* So fuckin sweet

My bf got me what I got me last year for mi bday He was so sad
ofc but Tbh it was still good I feel güd & loads more confident just cuz

I'm old enough to not be denied (like freshmen year when I forgot
I still had my mom on Snapchat & she told me to stop drinkin

but *shrug* Her bf told me I could have some moonshine It was
'apple pie' but just tasted like the stick stuck to the bttm) Like the other day

I went to Rite-Aid & bought three (3) bottles o' wine *just cuz
I could doesn't mean I should I kno* Doesn't mean much in the grand

scheme tho I mean I spent like (2 many)$$ in bday money on SPF for
the spring into summer Evryday I practicly drown my face in toner & My bf doesn't

think that can be v healthy but . . . idgaf So long as my skin is holographic-like
Alexa, play "Heavy Metal and Reflective" on Spotify A hologram or sumn

unnatural & pretty like all them eyeroll #InstaGays *ugh* I mean I obvi follow
em too but that sounds like a pickle for another poem Ya kno I lit

those candles Not feelin too mused rn but they kinda smell like cinnamon &
I fucking love cinnamon flavored/scented shit bc it's sweet w/ a lil kick

Too bad there's no such thing as cinnamon wine *lmfaooo that actually sounds
quite barfy* I'll stick to cider or that good goddamn 'apple pie' I think

I like cinnamon so much bc I know what's coming ig This bday wasn't so
shitty as bdays are want to be bc I sorta knew what was comin . . .

Irène P. Mathieu

soil

the way you say *soil* sounds
like *soul*, as in

after we walked through the woods
my feet were covered in soul

when it rains
the soul turns to mud

the soul is made of decomposed
plant and animal matter;

edaphology is the study of the soul's
influence on living things

while pedology is the study of how
soul is formed, its particular granularity.

you are rooted in a certain red patch
of soul that bled you and your

hundred cousins to life, a slow
warm river you call home.

maybe there is soul under everything,
even when we strike rock first.

the way you say *soil* you make
a poem out of every speck of dirt.

thunder's baby

for Alice Moore Dunbar-Nelson

Then comes a sudden flash of light, which gleams on shores / afar.
—Alice Moore Dunbar-Nelson

i.
here's a summer blues:
where lightning strikes deep into the flesh
in case you forgot your feeling.
the air likes to remind you
of pain where it touches you.

ii.
a woman dancing to music you can't hear
looks like a far-off kite with a key tied to it.

I'd be thunder's bastard baby
if I didn't love the rain so much,
slicked face-of-a-woman it lathers
like a lover bathing me.

I'd be a locksmith if I weren't
filled with wind.

iii.
I once had a hundred birds in my hand
and when I turned my palm up to heaven
they flew off in a feathered confusion.
my husband cried real tears;
I had no need of newborns.

iv.
the first time I loved a woman
clouds held my hair up

I was the space under a fig tree's
bark, a solemn sweet bite.

v.
a person will imitate the thumb
that pushes him until he becomes
his own double-jointed bruiser.

159

where my fingers used to be
are tiny men I bury under the pillow
when I dream.

vi.
the insistence of a bricklayer
is like a human hailstorm,
the crowd chanting with delight,
the small pieces of ice burying
each bulging tongue into a frozen wall.

they laughed when I brought a pick
        hiked up my dress
and threw salt over my shoulder.

I don't believe where the devil lives
is warm.

vii.
name any uninhabited island
and I'll give you the name
of a happy woman.

viii.
before he tried to kill me
my first husband wrote of
wearing a mask. he was not
from the city where I was born,
where women and men put on
masks once a year
and take them off again. he was
not accustomed to watching
disguises shed every spring—
a whole city of molting copperheads.

ix.
a copperhead is a man with
pennies for eyes, pennies for teeth.

a cottonmouth is a man who
can no longer speak because
he is slowly suffocating himself.

both species are common in
my home state, which is why
we don't go about with bare feet.

x.
I never set out to set anyone
in particular free, but he felt
my hammering on his skull
and feared losing his sight
if he listened too closely.

his fist told my bones over
and over to let it be, to let
his glorious, aching blindness be.

xi.
in hurricanes I hear the stories
of the dead, which I write down.
I've never lived a day of drought—
I think it would kill me.

xii.
the low brooding of the window
is why it's named after wind—
it sounds like pain where the
glass is struck, but nothing can really
hurt a manmade sheet of glass
except a fist.

xiii.
keep in mind that
I am half only in my dreams.
my living is preoccupied with
making and
making myself complete,

a (re)construction of opposing
force fields hovering near
each other but refusing to
be welded—

but I could not move as a
jointless, solid mass;
I would sink a brackish death.

xiv.
my father and mother
were neither two myths
nor two countries.

their hands were small
and mean, their hearts
were red and warm,
they gave me all my blood,
their faces I cannot
recall anymore.

xv.
when I was born
it was the calmest I
have ever been.

I had the calmest eye
until it opened.

xvi.
bold   scarlet   stubborn   bodied-without-fear   knife-tongued   heady

I presume you will say—

but I would say: opened
and then not able to be closed

never have I ever

Mother's Day I'm at work, where the hospital ward is thick with babies.
I enter room after room to look into their eyes—long-awaited or unexpected guests,
the babies stare at me, solemn and decisive: the next links in a chain of desire older
than any of us can imagine. later that day I order a hands-free breast pump,
giddy with the thought of making myself into food. I love land so much I become it.
I want more so badly I'll make it from my own body.

behind the final door, an operating room,
parents beaming under heat lamps—
the abundance of twins—my own baby swelling
against my scrubs as I congratulate them.

never have I ever wanted so much—eating ice cream at any hour, crying over the chorus of spring peepers Dopplering through the passenger window, my whole body a horde of seventeen-year cicadas wrestling their way up from the dirt. I said I wouldn't want so much the wiser I got, but Earth, forgive me: I got drunk on thick-knotted blackberry rising from the humid flank of this land, breathed a dream of ancient honeysuckle and crabapple, woke in a wetland clutching cattail & throating a swallow's nesting song—

this is the Day my mother has made   today I walk into room after room
          today I tell the babies: never have I ever known a way to be   that wasn't
velvety white on the tonguesweet salt & fat   letters curdled in the mouth,
rising from amniotic foam   at the moment of the first shout!

lesson on critical race theory for my daughter

on the night of your first election
fog clasped us all by the throat.
the copper sun in its disappearing
had been liquid enough to pull
slippery O's from my gums,
rubbing a small burn on my wrist
as I guided the four-wheel-drive
toward your waiting mouth.

the days before, there had been
so much talk about suburban moms.
and what kind of mother was I?
one who comes down from the
hills each dawn, and casts her
blood through the eye of a
wooden needle, crafting proudly
my marine mammal's howl-coo—
a mother woven of memory.

on the night of your first election
I turned on the heat, oil snaking
through the entrails of our house
while your father counted precincts
and projected with his fingers.
I bundled you in extra layers
and every hour that evening I
slunk, shadowed, crib-side, to
check and recheck your cheek
for oxygen, for warmth.

in the waiting I remembered
the dampness of a White woman's
tears, in the front row, during a
poetry reading long ago, where
I spoke a piece about the death of
a Black boy. how her loud tears
suffocated then astonished me,
almost choking out my voice
at the podium. a day like that
must lie in wait years for a
night like this, crouched on
its haunches inside the empire's
basement, licking the wet walls
to stay sentient.

that night we wavered between
frozen and ablaze—extremes
or the illusion of extremes—
while invisible beads of moisture
gathered on the porch, rolled
under the door, crept between
our teeth so silently we didn't
know we were taking on water.
in the sky seeds smoldered.
the ground was littered with sparks.
while I bathed you I sang a song
that went, *nothing ever changes,*
and I meant it as a lullaby.

Gretchen McCroskey

Cleaning the Spring

I come each year to a spring—
cloudy reservoir holding on
to dead leaves, pine needles,
and earth's soft, brown silt.

My long-handled hoe digs deep
into the rocky hollow, scraping away
winter's residue. I lift bucket
after bucket of muddy water
until I stand barefoot on the rock floor.

Bending, I wash the limestone
basin, my white sheet remnant
removing any trace of dirt as earth's
chilly stream begins to trickle about my feet.

By evening, nature's limestone cup
will overflow into the moss-lined
run to the concrete cooling trough,
refrigeration for fresh-churned butter,
cherry Jello and red, ripe watermelons.

If Mildred's well dries up, she will bring
buckets to fill. When the road men stop
for lunch under the walnut trees,
they will quench July's thirst
with nature's cool refreshment.

My husband, hot from work in the fields,
will take the tin dipper from the nail
on the door and relish water that willed
his grandfather to this hill land.

Shapes of Comfort

In a time of brush arbor
meetings, tent revivals, cottage
prayer gatherings, with no
instrument or accompanist,
eager they came to raise
four-part a cappella harmony:

farmers, tired from bent-back
labor—hoeing tobacco, loading
hay onto wagons, driving cows
to the barn for evening milking,
and women, weary after canning
peaches on a wood-burning stove
in 90-degree weather or scrubbing
clothes on The Brass King washboard
in water warmed by the sun.

Do, do, re, re, mi, mi, mi, fa, fa
so, so, la, ti rang out sweeter
than chimes from the pipe organ
in Grace Presbyterian Church.
Guided by shaped notes on a page,
they sang of white robes, crystal
fountains, a glad reunion day.

The day Thomas Kilgore's son
got killed in a Clinchfield coal mine,
neighbors gathered in Corn Valley Church,
picked up Sacred Harp Hymnals and sang—
untrained voices following shaped notes
to "Farther along we'll know all about it,
Farther along we'll understand why."

Harmony that could not be shattered
by methane gas and coal dust,
an eruption of human sound
trying to seal up sorrow.

Saving the Family Farm

Between my finger and my thumb
The squat pen rests.
I'll dig with it.
              —Seamus Heaney

Eighty acres of hilly
Virginia earth tug at me
like Scarlett O'Hara's barren
Georgia land wooed her

Crystal water once flowing
into a limestone basin
now choked
by mud and decay

Towering hemlocks
victim to chain saws
Lush green grass furrowed
by farm trucks and tractors

Yet the land endures—
opening for scattered seeds
to fall on fallow
and fertile ground

While other hands
tend this land
of my childhood
I plant poetry—

Tilling lines
winnowing words
so that my ancestral ground
remains permanently mine.

Marianne Mersereau

Sleeping with the Serpent

–For Aunt Mary Ellen

On threshing day, she said,
we emptied the straw tick mattresses
poured the old chaff into the pig sty,
washed the cotton sacks and hung them
to dry in early autumn sun.

None of us saw the black snake slither
into the pile of new straw.
He did not move when we picked up the stack
and stuffed it into the large pillow case,
sewing the prison shut.

Uncle slept atop the hibernating serpent
until spring came, the mattresses were
once again emptied for washing, and out
crawled the survivor—
well rested, resurrected.

Bees and Tobacco

We see the small cubes on stands
and they appear to us
as miniature stoves, refrigerators, sinks.
We pretend they are toys
and approach to play house.
Opening the door, angry bees fly out.
Like hot grease
they sting our skin
and we run screaming down to the field
where daddy hoes corn
while chewing King Edward tobacco.
He pulls a wad from his mouth,
and puts it on the stings:
the mix of saliva and nicotine
heals all our pain.

Jesse Millner

Each morning I wake up filled with dreams

and darkness, barely remembering the flutter
of birds, the loud clicking
of a clock in another room
that signals there is time passing
in dreams as well as the daylight
I have awakened to: Florida summer.
A light rain of mosquitoes.
My little dog eating grass because
her stomach's upset. A quarter moon
already high in the eastern sky
and sunlight burning the fringes
of cumuli. I drink coffee, feeling
the clarity that comes on like a foreign
language's beautiful shadows
speaking the past in barns and swallows,
in the brown and white cow kicking its stall
and once kicking my brother's head. He was only three

and my grandfather carried him from the barn
back to the house where the Baptist women
gathered around him, my grandmother wiping
away the blood with a kitchen towel as I wondered
at the tiny gash just above his black eyebrow,
a little quarter moon itself without the light.

This happened a long time ago before all the pine
woods were chopped down, before my grandfather
lost his farm, before the big oak in the front yard
was killed by lightning, before my grandma's favorite
Calico cat died at fifteen, before I lost my religion,
discovered Jesus was only a ghost and the Bible
its own book of the dead filled with pestilence and drought,
the sacrifices of lambs and children while
blood flowed knee deep through the streets of Jerusalem.
Fire this time the preachers promised
on Sunday mornings in another world
where cars guzzled gas and flew over

one-lane roads lined with kudzu
and honeysuckle. *Sip the horn*

of a blooming honeysuckle blossom
and you will be transformed forever,
tricked into believing in a sweetness
that fades like the memory
of the red oaks and chestnuts
flashing by in their green syllables of summer.

Leaf Becoming Ash

The earliest world I knew could be drawn
across a dirt driveway with a tobacco stick.
I used them as swords to fence
with my brother, or I'd ride them
like horses, the grey length of wood between
my legs I imagined to be Roy Roger's horse, Trigger.
Sixty years-ago my world was defined
by seven acres of tobacco and one hundred
more of pine and red oak.
I'd string tobacco on the sticks
but I was not strong enough to hang
them from the rafters of the curing
barn, where, in the heat of late August
a kerosene stove steadily burned on a dirt floor.
Even as a kid, I loved that smell, understood
why adults smoked Lucky Strikes or Camels,
taking that scent into their bodies,
becoming holy themselves amid
the smolder of leaf becoming ash.

Squirrel Hunting

Gush and silence of creek rippling
over face and shadow
of the afternoon my uncle

and I went hunting squirrel
in high Virginia woods. White oak running
toward the sky, branches revealing wind

or rodent feet, and if the latter,
my uncle would bring up the twelve gauge,
blast that sucker
into a falling grey rag. He had

a burlap sack for their broken remains,
was almost gentle
as he lowered the bloody fur
into itchy darkness. Later my grandma

or another of the women
would skin the little beasts,
bring them to a nakedness
nature had not intended, then chop

them into pieces
that cackled in the welcoming lard
of the frying pan. Browned like chicken,

served with collard greens
on my grandma's pretty china—
bone plates
bearing the freshly dead

over frail geometries of blue.

Jim Minick

Blink

Cardinal lies on porch, beak open,
wings splayed, graceless and still.
Her mate calls from the yellowbells,
but she doesn't answer.

I cup my hands to hold her, this morning
bitter cold. Her beak glows a red
lit from within, and her tail pulses
with her heart. She looks right in-
to me, her eyes so black—the membrane
no longer a separation, no longer
anything but us.

What does she see?
A world of trickery, where air
betrays with hardness, the sky
solid enough to kill,
and me, trying to unknow
my way back into the earth.
I shiver. We both blink.

My hands grow numb as I listen to her
partner sing from the frost-covered grass.
I imagine little flames traveling
my veins, blood brighter with whatever
heat and power my great-grandma could call
as she laid on hands and healed
other people, other birds. Did she
lay her hands on me, my ears
that ached through infancy?
She held me, that much I know.

My fingers tingle
cold. I pray and breathe and stroke
the bird's soft cheek and hope
my hands aren't just stealing heat.
Come back, I whisper, come back.

Geese honk down the valley.
Wren can't stop chattering
as clouds filter the rising sun.

She blinks more, lifts her beak.
Her red crest peaks. I step away
from windows, hold her to the morning light.

Is it time? I ask. She turns
her head, looks out, and launches
her yes, the air once more soft
enough to fly through, honest
enough for love.

Lasts

i.
They arrive unannounced—
       last kiss and welcome home hug
       last hiccup and "hurry up"
       last horse snort and nicker;

and all the time and every time—
       last catbird feather
       last dimpled blueberry
       last puppy wiggle and lick;

we rush through them unaware—
       last bloom of chestnut
       last bare-leafed ash
       last ice-cloaked hemlock;

our lasts trampling all over this blue marble.

ii.
Juncos: slate-black against snow
in winter, white bellies among snow-
drops in spring. They never sing
until they're gone
to their tundra home
for the summer,
and they never let you know

when they part.
Goodbye, I always say too late.

iii.
And what about those other lasts?
I have saved beechnut trees
and acorn-loaded oaks,
foods they loved;
I've waited for flocks
of passenger pigeons
to blacken the sky for days
once more. And a parakeet
in these woods—so hard
to imagine, so hard to not
look for that splash of green and red.
Goodbye, we always say too late,
or we never get a chance to say at all.

iv.
Twenty years ago, monarch butterflies
glided these fields thistle to thistle
too many to count;
now they are too few.
I save milkweed, look for eggs,
but what will remain
twenty years from now?
Goodbye doesn't have to be
the only way to say love.

To Spoon the Dark

Yesterday when we fought—
                    the knife-slice of *no* so easy—
that moment we stared
                    into each other's raw hurt,
I felt that black pit open
                    and yaw me in.

                    How do we live with such darkness?

Before the aural flower
                    the wood thrush sings
in the gray dawn waking

that eclipses the night,
he must trust the light
                will come.

                How does the darkness live with us?

And to make the flower
                the wood thrush sings,
he first must cup
                each note in his throat,
shape it with breath—
                those tiny lungs
must spoon the dark.

                Every seed, every song comes through the dark.

Those spoons we call our lungs

                can only hold so much.

Even this breath

                has to let go.

First Hard Frost

and the bear's fur glistens and rolls,
the fawn grows fat on wormy apples,
the bluestem glitters, seed dispersed.

Each crystal-covered, mitered blade
bends the light to flicker and shade.

First hard frost and the goldenrod
no longer brightens the speckled air,
wands of aster emptied of purple pulse—

both now beheaded and brown,
their roots live on underground.

First hard frost and the sunrise sparks
yellow hickories, blazing oaks,

the wine-red creeper vine that climbs,

waving in warblers to settle and sup
this blood of the earth slowly drawn up.

So tell me why, in all of this,
am I so afraid of Death's quick kiss?

Tim Slack, the Fix-It Man

Been nothing but fans this week. This makes the fourth.
Had to replace an attic fan a day ago.
Lost five pounds doing that. Can't live
without a bathroom fan, can you?
(He has the old one out, dust caked thick.
It whirs in his hands, loud and rattling.) Yep,
it's bad. Sounds like a high-pitched
machine gun, don't it? Right there. (He points
to where it broke.)
                        You say you're from Virginia?
That's where I grew up. Fauquier County,
The Plains. You hear about the double murder
last spring? Well, that was my parents,
the ones that got killed. Yep.
Fellow done it, I grew up with, lived
up the road. Needed money for drugs.
Tied them up and beat them with a bat.
Next day, they missed church. That's how
they got found.
                        First double murder
in the state in twenty-five years.

Hit that switch, will you?

Felicia Mitchell

Mother Tree, Ailanthus altissima

A paradox inhabits my woods,
a tree both ornamental and invasive.
The birds do not mind it, but I do.
Each spring, I walk these woods
looking for morels and wildflowers,
pulling garlic mustard before it goes to seed.
The sapling Trees of Heaven go too—
hacked down and even poisoned,
despite my fear of herbicides.
I wear gloves and covered shoes
as I spray the root of each hacked sapling.
I apologize to every tree, to the soil,
to myself for failing to avoid herbicides
the way I once failed to avoid chemo.
We are not always in charge of what invades.
Last year, Dutchman's Breeches emerged
where I killed a colony of Ailanthus.
This year, the Dutchman's Breeches have spread.
Violets and ferns want to flourish there too.
Maypops dancing across the hill are my offspring.
But I am nothing if not hypocritical.
I know that every year more saplings will come,
the mother root within the soil branching out
to compete for a natural habitat.
How many years has this tree grown, this tall tree
that I stand and look at every summer?
How did it end up in a grove of beeches?
What else would return to my woods if I killed it?
One year, I will chop down the mother tree
that sends its roots and chemicals out like toxins
that are as bad, I think, as cancer.
But she and I are kin, this tree.
Both of us are invasive species,
my own body a map of colonization of this country,
my own survival dependent on weeding my genes
and poisoning the cells that take up too much room.
It is hard to kill a tree: a sapling or an unborn tree.

I know I will die before the Ailanthus destroys my woods.
But I want to pass this land on, I want its flowers to come.
Bears that trek out back may one day find a pawpaw.
I want to believe anything is possible if I try.

Another Eden

When you say how you understand
why the first settlers called this place Eden,
I think of a garden before the fall too.
Mine is another sort of garden
although the people in it are just as naked
as they are in the story you believe in.
There is no apple to tempt them, though,
only blackberries and chanterelles.
Sometimes Adam hunts, sometimes Eve gathers.
Everything they need is in their hands.
Paradise in these hands, these hills, could last forever.
Eve is happy to make do with what grows here.
Adam uses deerskins for blankets.
Eve weaves pine straw to soften the ground.
A black snake is still just a black snake,
not temptation coiled around curiosity.

But across the way, across the ocean,
men are building ships to bring apples
that are bigger than any pawpaw or crabapple
ever grown in the story of these hills.
One day settlers will show up to plant them
and to build houses where they can eat them.
They will call the black snake evil
even before apple trees shade the valley
and hard cider casts a pall on paradise.
One day, this Adam and this Eve,
not unlike the couple in your story, will fall,
but only because they are pushed,
and we—you and I, before we are born—
will help them flee the garden
because we—before we are born—want it.
We want this place we will nickname Eden.
We want to name this wild place and call it home.

With Howard Finster at the Taubman Museum

It feels holy here,
the insane sane.
I could be standing
in Paradise instead of Roanoke,
my dress painted on
with angel wings—
dozens of them
fluttering over my shoulder
and under my arm
and next to my big toe.
My smile is always red here,
red and bright and big lipped
like Cheer Wine.
Everybody drinks it,
or Coca Cola with peanuts,
as all the cats I ever knew
yowl across a bottle-covered fence,
mating for eternity
so Paradise will be mine—
always as full of kittens as of hearts
broken and healed now,
healed now in Paradise,
the biggest back yard
I will every visit
where on every tree
hangs a tire by a rope.
Hope swings soft and sultry
in the celestial breeze,
like a summer in Georgia
that will never, ever, never, ever,
never, ever end. Amen.

A Love Poem for My Son at Wilburn Ridge

If you were a wild pony,
you would be wilder than I am by now—
out there on the other side of the mountain
looking for a greener pasture
and your own mare.
You might be drinking water from a creek
at this very moment.
I would no longer be following you,
nudging you away from humans
who stand with cameras and smiles,
nudging you with the weight of my belly
as I turn a corner where we will climb the ridge.
I would not be writing a poem about you,
although I think I would recognize you
if our paths crossed on the mountain.

But you are a grown man and not a wild pony,
and I am not the old gray mare.
Still, I remember your own lithesome legs
and how they galloped up this trail
even as I trudged, a little slow, behind you.
You always knew I would be there,
not so far behind.
I always knew you would be up ahead,
not so far out of reach.

Years come and years go.
I am even slower now and alone,
a hiker who seeks the company of wild animals.
I return to this meadow once a year, son,
and watch the ponies with their foals.
I remember how it was.
Those were the days when I would follow you anywhere
even if the top of the mountain
was as high as Virginia got.
You remember how it was
when there was nothing but blueberries
at the end of our hike
and dreams of even longer trails and taller mountains.

A Poem for Lost Ancestors

I wonder who they are, the missing links,
as I stare at a few small red strips on a DNA report
that reflects the history of the peopling of South Carolina
in my one genome.
All my ancestors travelled far to make me, I know,
and I know so many of them, already,
but not all of them.

There was an underground railroad.
I think there was another railroad
some of my ancestors had to travel too.
It ran not from south to north or east to west
but from generation to generation,
their lineage stitched in the pockets of genes
as invaluable as silver coins sewn into skirts.
With each child born, another coin spent,
color in South Carolina determined who went in what door
or drank at what water fountain
and who stayed home to clean house
or who married whom and who moved
to Paris, or another neighborhood, to start over.
I want somebody to take me there,
to that point of departure when
a trade was made, unfair as a fast train
spiriting away a girl colored by a society's prejudice and fear.
I close my eyes and see her waving from the metaphorical train,
waving at everyone who came before her as she passed on
and into me—so white she has become a ghost of herself.
I want to call back and call her Granny.

Thorpe Moeckel

West Fork of the Little

So flesh comes to this: hawkweed & monarch,
   sweetflag in clumps, densities of ochre,
new vowels up from cutbank's loam, some dot
   to dot the eyes trace to spell a way into
flame azalea, pink azalea, laurel buds,
   so many, about to burst. Bless, double,
the startled raccoon, the eight wood ducks
   taking off. Goldfinch, hermit thrush,
how flowering blackberries unbramble the dusk.
   And bless this breath, the next. Each rill
and mewl, cohosh's glances, trillium in fruit,
   the gash & gush of a tributary entering
under black locust, brief flurry of blossoms
   in the breeze, spring's plunder & wheeze.

On Hearing the Waterthrush Again, Jefferson

March 1794

     ordered a Nebbiolo, briskmost vintage,
to be fetched from the cellar;
        ordered Lilly, their overseer,

     to deliver the canal men
an extra whiskey ration by
        the same cart, mule-drawn, that hauled

     the grindstone, spare tools. See,
the dogwood petals were beginning
        to drop, and hickory's fires flared dusk

     wilder than the day's measures
of rain, last storm a gusty pelting
        around five, followed by blue

     in breaks like waking. Walking,
he'd heard parula, cardinal, spooked a blue winged teal
        (pale whorl of its face),

countless geese, turtles, a green heron,
wood ducks in pairs. *My fits of head-ache* that dawn he'd
        inked *have stuck some days*

    5. *hours.* Stingers, still. Yes, everything reeked of
abundance, the strafe & groan beneath
        all growth, banks a forge where blossoms

    were sparks rising from that hammer
no hand ever bears. Even the river—siltslappy Rivanna—
        seemed to have grown

    wings, a throat lusty and coarse. He heard
molt. Heard vowels, their origins, too,
        but knew only the lost could follow such

    speech, if speech, and turned for home.

Little Reed Creek

Here's about to, the prepwork,
        saprise & seepdrip. Here
is all there
        isn't to know.

*

Schisms in the soilsphere—
    toothwort, violet, cleaver.

    *

    Early April,
poplar's green shiver,
    visibility for glades.

    *

This ridge Terrapin Mountain,
        that one, White Oak Knob—
no morels yet, many ferns still curled.

    *

Plungepools & pocketwater—
    trillium there, & there, trillium.

*

Don't call it work
                    what the boulders do,
but what they don't do, the rest.

            *

The punchbowls, the hollows in every hollow.

*

            Here is lair, & the waterthrush
at evening piping up,
                    at morning, too.

            *

Still a little bite in the air,
still a little gobbler scratch, & rue.

            *

            The duff a treatise on parchment,
weather's imprint,
                notes on the future,
the last next generation all at once.

            *

    Buckrub & split trunk, a tick in your flanksteak,
deadfall, more deadfall.
                    If zest, if spritz.

            *

That it go on, the hellebore,
the black birch's shelf life,
        polypore & parasitic burls.

            *

Anemone, anemone.

Crowded Barnyard, Pretty Spring Day, One Little Goat

now sprawls against the fence. Now bends a foreleg under. Now gums a stalk, tongue so pink
the fescue seems to bleed. Look,

her head is anvil. Her ears, ridged by veins, flop & curl. Curl & quiver. I like them. Streaks
of dark, streaks of pale. Elegant frames

for an elegant neck. I like the way the long ears of these Nubians splay the ground—outriggers,
landing gear—a full inch before the lips

part, dark lips, revealing the kernels of her tiny, ancient teeth. This is graze. This is abdomen,
the fast throb. Lava tubes of her pupils:

what they see is what they see. But now her legs, four Floridas, erotic with flex, send her flying
to perch on the overturned enamel tub,

a 180 mid-air, some little skate rat. It's hard to keep up. I'm breaking in pieces. Of giggle.
Perfect. And the fence is a dulcimer, too.

Posts for frets. Wire for strings. Play it, little goat. Let the breeze. Let the sun, shadow machine.
Showy, showy & a bit spastic, her hop

from tub. Dainty, cloven toes. Now Mama's here, Miss Clementine, so doeling kneels, tail
atwitch, neck jive-pistoning for milk

to run. But not for long. Mama needs shade. So doeling prances. And then she bounds. A walnut
burning. A nimble, hazardous balance.

Elisabeth Murawski

Still Life with Timex

At last I am mad enough
to part with the boots,
surly and yellow, the laces cut.

A heavy thud when they land
in the bin. Maybe someone
at the dump will rescue them—
like soldiers in battle
who steal from the dead.
Surely he will walk again.

I'll buy him new.
Unnerving, the way his watch
still runs, the crystal

whole despite the impact,
the second hand rounding
the face in tiny jerks.

In the Meadow

There's a picture of him
in the slideshow:

a boy with bandy legs
hanging from a branch,

on his face a climber's
monkey joy. Taken years ago

when I brought him here
to see the cows, the clouds.

Now I say out loud
I don't know where you are.

A leaf drifts down
from the oak.

Kayakers in the river.
An insect, half grasshopper,
half bee, buzzes the thin
orange marker. Lands,

clings, flies off,
veers back. Again

and again. Deliberate,
persistent

as grief. Look.
A white butterfly.

Isadora
loose in the meadow.

Know, Heart

The head knows
the child who grew inside her

is no more. Between
head and heart

a tundra lies,
windswept and cold,

to be crossed on foot
without boots

or overcoat. The heart
winds itself

round and round
with silk thread,

tight enough
to hold everything

breaking. The head
consoles: in time

the miles to go
will grow shorter.

Muffled in silk, cocooned,

the heart cannot see

the houses have lights on,
can only reach back

like a blind person
to the way things were.

Waking alone on Sunday morning

The bed warm, the house cold,
the sun bold as Paul

setting out for Rome
and certain death,

I surrender to languor.
The birds have flown south.

A dog barks to be let in.
Each year, hearing

for the first time
the double coo that gave

the bird its name, Wystan Hugh
would note the moment

in his diary, calling it
holy, the return

of the ordinary
knocking him to his knees.

The two-note wonder
fortified,

like two blue clouds
in a child's drawing

of the sky, white
because it doesn't have to be.

Elegiac

I hold a funeral for the farm.
In my head, like music returning,
the mewing of the blind

kittens, my mother's mother
in a drab cotton house dress
pointing to their nursery,
a crate lined with straw.
She left Posnan and silks
to be a farmer's wife.

I didn't speak her language.
From the pump in the yard
I fill a dented cup; here

is where they drank, the horses
I shied from. I discover
artifacts: a green-black

feather in the coop,
a corncob stripped clean,
light as a hornet's nest.

It hurts to see the beam
the turkey hung from,
waiting for the ax.

Beyond the weathered fence,
row on row of blackberries
ripen, untended.

They taste of sun and rain,
her fortune in a strange land:
baptismal gowns, black arm bands.

Yvonne Nguyen

I Would've Called Her Honey

She was blonde-adjacent.
Quasi-brunette. That sun-ripened
syrup hue that made my mouth salty. Not *curly*,   just playful
like the top of a soft-serve ice cream cone.

For that wheat-field, molasses river, I sacrificed the last hair band
around my wrist. The one I hadn't lost
in three weeks, because
she probably needed it. To concentrate
on her Trig test.
      Or to play goalie in hand-ball.
         Or to tie off her unfinished bag of pretzels.

I didn't even mind when I saw her hold it between her teeth.
I just held my breath, watching
to see if the thinning elastic would hold against
her four-twist ponytail.

Even now,

even all these years since the last time
I put my hair in a high-ponytail or tried to find one girl's exact
shade in the hair dye aisle of a CVS—just to know its name.
I still wear that indented mark
on my wrist, that puckered phantom bracelet
and regret the baby hairs falling out
onto the nape of her neck.

The ones I couldn't help catch.

Mel Nichols

Bicycle Day

and then rode down into the rock-filled cave

        one among the we in the unfinished

                night of drying leaves or was it   a broken

tunnel beyond in hearing cold smoky farms of morning carry distance

        like a ceiling with sun while I sleep

                there are earthquakes   like a curtain

the window amber curtain and with nothing else to do   take the elevator

        down to the incinerator

                the elevator growing hotter in the doors & going

        down take it down

            get my earth's heart

              get my boarding pass

and we paddle out among the regal ducks and geese

        the armada after the stars have left us

            just the creek water and absent smell of pine

            holding us   frail tenants

            on temporary mosses

            in the distant yellow and orange of construction

Day Poem

earth breathing fireworks that never explode and it is hard
to walk here with the narrow dangerous riding close
and newer to the eye than light   is it true to be careless
frozen dangerous on fire   is it true to be a guitar
broken and waiting in the rain   is it true they won't let me
get on the plane   oh my rogue something-
or-other   I have worn a circle in the grass   I crumble
I am   green emerging from whitecaps   a true mute
a torso   arms gone

we are falling from the echo's wandering fires of spring
dissolving ink paper solar system   all behind a great house
scraps of text blowing in the parking lot of a condo building
scraps of text on paper blowing away scraps of text through pixels
delete them please

         let sequence pull me statue from the sea

Luxurious Time

      for Kathy Mitchell

                the leaves fall
                   and the woods fill
                     with the sound
                  of machines

         then the dream then

       comes the idea
         of distance   the broken star
              the role of   the not-knowing

           wilderness bewildering through a text

sick saved hungry

what are you writing   toward
                                        don't know

an old ghost   on a dark
            house   the air is warm

                        first spring in Iowa

                                                        stare

at a blue sky cloudless suddenly white line of an airplane appears across the window look at it
until it fades no one could refuse

                                        I don't know what anybody says

                        or why they say it

                                                I was a bit
                surprised   don't know why I was surprised

                                        a story could end

with the image of going to bed

turn out the lights   see fireflies cover the ceiling in the dark room like a multitude of stars

        a few fly by our bed in the darkness like meteors

                                        and this is how I became lost in the landscape

I felt like I was already a ghost

after I the saw the same boy on the same

street   we spoke to each other as ghosts

I think he reminded me of a ghost

made me think I was a ghost

and when we talked on the phone I felt like

a ghost trying to tell you we talked

because it was easier than looking
at a self

everyone knows

the red barn is something special when it shows up in a bleak landscape against a grey or blue

sky the plastic owl I saw at Lorine Niedecker's house

reverse reverse reverse and fold you up

like a bird on a book cover into pretty blue pixels

lack of newsprint washed away in another Walmart stampede

a leaf stuck in my pen
with all these arbitrary seasons

because what is spring but a division

a train being used again as an example

a very dead thing on the other side of the river

written into a notebook for safekeeping

a place to keep account

an unholding in the slippery fog and

one grows used the weather

but the sky is cold and still and there is the hero's dead eye

and I am terrible with transitions and this is how

I became lost in the landscape

a heart-shaped scar on a tree trunk where love's initials fade

the horizon note of a leaf blower

wrapping you into my strange grammar

and what is spring but a diversion

among the trees a man   forced her into the sky

creatures of the constellations flower staring back the falling leaves

and every time a barn collapses it belongs to me

Evan Nicholls

The Mud Doctor

lived in a trailer. He had no wife. He had no daughters, or sons. He had no mother. And no one had seen his birth certificate, if he even had one. His name was a question. He was a question. The townspeople guessed Daniel. Ethan Frome. Poodle. No one knew anything. No one ever asked him. We only spoke to him during the planting season, when we needed the soil examined. He would listen to the ground. Tell us what could grow. Then after, he'd walk to the antique store. The place with the weepy-eyed dog. He loved the weepy-eyed dog there and came more for the dog than the tchotchkes. We think. We don't know. The dog would lie on the floor and he would pat it. He died the day before yesterday, and I am the town's stone mason, and now they're having me engrave the headstone. Only no one can say what to chisel in. I stepped up into his trailer this morning and sifted through things for a name. I only found a Bird of Paradise. Walnut shrapnel. A rotten mouse fused to the baseboard. Sea of gum wrappers. And years from now, I will be dead. We will all be dead here. But our sites will be big. They will have lawns. They will be mown every day. The finish work done with barber shears. And the Mud Doctor will have a tiny plot. And it will be in the weeds. The stone will be gobbled by barberry. And the only thing read there will be:

HERE LIES DUBBLE BUBBLE.

Foxhunters

We stop for bathroom and gin breaks only. When Miss Fenny comes out of the pissing trees exclaiming *Oooweee*, the noise avalanches us all with drunken laughter. Then we clamber onto our saddles again & hurdle after the black-nosed dogs boating between icebergs of dung. We bugle all along the way. At one point in the hunt, we cut a jump through the government fence. Later our war party elopes into a neighborhood; my thoroughbred obliterates some youngster's lemonade stand, Mister Shaw tramples the entire school system. But always the fox is a stray smoke signal. The fox is an impossible baby wailing from the other room. The fox is a sputtering helium balloon. The fox is triple-doubling back. The fox is a fox.

Wildfire

Contrary to what the newsreels say I feel
cold on the inside I came West to plunge
my body into the Pacific They call me *Death
Toll Rising* This is not my first name My real
name was whispered to me by a paper-dry
leaf hopping & dragging like a flightless bird
She was my mother These are all my cousins
I am holding my breath for: domestic cats
alpacas bears pigs ponies squirrels & ashen
dogs You cannot tell the jackrabbits from the
pumas from the goats inside of me We are all
one species of smoke *Deadliest in History* Now
the people in shining jackets call for hoses &
buckets of foam over my head They send hot
cell signals through my belly & I watch them
the whole time They do not recognize a son
chock full of animals If I waited on the ridge
for the proper light would they finally see me
call me down by my first name I want to hear
the words from my fathers mouths: *Drought*
our soft child stop picking at the floor &
sweeten into the big blue ocean you were
meant to be But life is so unforgiving Say
you want the water & you become the sky

Rock Hill Mill Stable

The horse has been drinking
and I have been drinking.
I have named the horse Grief.

William Notter

Field Mice in the Garage

A week of afternoons I heard a scruffling
in the corner and finally found the nest,
a black trash bag chewed to threads.
With young, so new their eyes were not yet open.

We took the baby out to see—what I called her
though she was almost three. She squealed
in delight when the velvet-brown mother
skittered toward a hole in the threshold
and when she saw the pups, wrinkly,
squirming in their lawn-and-leaf bag nest.

Later, I put the babies under the tulip tree,
then swept out the nest and filled the hole
with expanding foam-in-a-can. Maybe the mother
would find them and build another nest outside.

Gone soft living with storybooks
and a girl who sleeps with a hand-sewn mouse,
I couldn't drown the pups or let them starve
in the trash. I remembered too late the kitten
whose hindquarters I had crushed with a tractor,
how my father stopped its suffering with pliers.

After supper the mice were all still there,
unmoving, swollen, swarmed by tiny ants.
The flesh would be gone in just a few weeks,
leaving the intricate spines exposed.

Things can turn out wrong for someone
no matter what you try to do.
There was no sense in burying the bones.

First Death

The Holstein struck by lightning doesn't count.
Long-dry, she roamed the farm like a pet,
a cow too dumb to come down off the hill.

The other was just before supper at my friend's house
whose mother served bread and butter every meal
and made sure we said *please* and *thank you*.
His great grandfather sat on a milk can
against the kitchen wall, retired farmer
in overalls and a feed-store checkerboard hat.
One moment he's talking timothy hay
with the young fathers while their wives
arrange the children and the silverware,
then he's pitching sideways to the floor.

They shuffled us kids to the paneled living room
and I forgot whatever happened next.
There was no casket, no absence in my life.
Now I know his son sped over
from the farm before the ambulance and medics
who would wheel him through the narrow door.
It took years to connect that sudden fall
with words like *heart attack or stroke*,
things that strike the body from inside.

My uncle chained the Holstein to the Allis-Chalmers,
pulled her through the pasture, left her behind the barn
to wait for the rendering truck in a cloud of flies.

Wondering About Cremation

We'll never know the difference between furnace
and the long purgatory of formaldehyde
in a sealed zinc vault the funeral people say
can keep a loved one safe for centuries.

Fire, though, conserves materials and cemetery space.
It turns you elemental right away,
the flourish out the smokestack
almost like a soul escaping.

And haven't you been on fire your entire life
for what you couldn't have,
or what you tasted just a little of?

Gregory Orr

Sugar Hollow Notes

With a twig and some
Ink you could
Paint words on bark.

It would be a start.

*

Hello, dirt. My name
Is Greg.
        Haven't we
Met somewhere before?

*

White calf following
A black cow
Down a path
Across the green meadow.

*

I don't want to float away.
I don't want to sink
In the ground.
        I want
To walk this earth
As long as I'm around.

*

Many things have been
Mentioned
Not least among them
Love.
      There was a stream.
There was a river.

Not least among them, love.

It's pretty much a consensus

It's pretty much a consensus
Among us poets:

What we humans have
In common
Is our senses.

And only an idiot
Would dispute
That they're our
Greatest source of joy.

Embodied, mortal:
What we are,
What everything we love is.

And so, grief enters
Through the portals of bliss.

The poems we love—what are they
Made of?
                    Nothing.

Yet when we recite them
Our voice climbs the lines
As if they were stairs
Made of air
In a house made of breath.

Structure invisible as death:
A house made of breath,
Stairs
That are nothing but air—

Yet each so solid we can pause
When we want to and stand there.

If the world were to end...

Yet it ends every day
For someone.
           A death
Or sudden loss
And just like that
The merry-go-round stops,
Its cheery music ceases.

You climb off the horse
You were riding;
You leave
The painted lion behind.

You see it's dark now;
The park is closing
Or has already closed.

You follow a path
You hope leads out,

A path you never noticed before.

Sort-of Sonnet for Hank Williams

When Hank Williams heard it—
The whip-poor-will's call
And then, as if in response,
The locomotive's low moan—
He knew both were echoes
Of his own lonesome soul.

But that song he wrote isn't
Stored in a college library,
Locked in some dusty archive—
He entrusted it to the beloved,
Who has it in her keeping,
Never lets it out of her sight.

It's there on every jukebox—
You could play it yourself tonight.

James Owens

Last Thoughts Cooling like an Abandoned Cup

–i.m. Jack Owens, 1936-2003

1.

I must have dozed. And found him watching day
illuminate spring's imperfect unrest
from his pillow, starlings unskeining, blown astray
over open furrows, until the fist in his chest
spasmed, the next hacking fit wrung blood
and soot from his raw throat. He spat red grief
in a cloth and winked to say he understood
what I knew, too. The end would be relief.

"Torment after this and fire forever, I guess
that's bullshit," he rasped—asking, paying breath
to ask. And I: "Bullshit. What God would bless
with one hand, while the other tortures his dead?"
He nodded, half-smiled, slept. I paced his bedside,
unquiet as hollow ground, unsure if I'd lied.

2.

He called again, just days before he died.
"I can't breathe, Jimmy," he panted, though no one
had called me Jimmy since I became a man.
"My throat feels stuffed tight with lint. I could cry
for one real breath of good air." It was late.
My wife was working. More work awaited me.
Our sleepless two-year-old crawled around my feet.
Vague wind fumbled between us in the dark states.

"That's rough. I'm sorry to hear it," I tried,
ashamed, already, for the harried note,
the awkward pause. But he chose the odd moments,
as if, long awake and stumped for words at night,
he knew the weight of unbalanced accounts
that should be righted, though impossible to right.

3.

Death was so far from upheaval, the cup
of coffee balanced on his knee did not spill.
Perhaps his final breath or failing scrap
of dream cast tremors across the little pool
of dark. Would dying then have surprised him,
his chest veined with Pall Malls and coal,
one lung left, a gray mitt, gripping the slim
shaft of air? Might he have known and let go?

His wife came into the room. She said "Jack"
and touched his shoulder, thinking him asleep,
and then she knew. She stood, suddenly calm,
as spring breathed at the window, lifted the cup
like a small animal's slain heart—again, "Jack"—
and held it, warmth soaking into her palms.

4.

As neurons failed, he lost the big plow horse
that broke his wrist when he was eight years old,
the forbidden gallop across stubble and frost
worth the hurt for the joy of that shining ride;
the first, secret and primal time he learned
the shocking gush of semen; the entire year
he and a buddy hitched to Florida; the burn
of moonshine; dogs and hunts, night and fire;

whether the cherry blossoms he cut for my mother
as she was weeping ached, too light in his embrace;
my sleepy weight, when he came stale with beer
to scoop me from bed and nuzzle my face,
spent from a bender, begging entry, and me his shield,
he deflecting her just wrath by holding his child.

5.

An ordinary grave that smelled like a ditch,
like any other. In sunlight. An April day
when new leaves already gleamed like patches
of silk that lived on the old leaves' decay.
The pain that clogged his chest with dust had died.
We sat on plastic chairs and glanced toward
the mound of dirt that would fall back in to hide

his box. Like headache, the blur of holy words.

I punched him once, in play—first he laughed,
daring me at twelve to show if I could hit,
then, shocked, my knuckles on his teeth, lip split,
he staggered back a step and rubbed his mouth,
spat blood, and hunched away. And now the sorrow
of that blow is in my fist and beats me hollow.

6.

The shrew was not his valedictory ghost.
I wanted to lie and drain myself from myself,
so hard it was to parse out spring from grief.
The wind died down and rose again, almost
as if a hand had roughed the grass and crossed
where banks of violet and renewed twinleaf
flaked light off air. I needed but damned relief,
and walked alone in woods, and walked to be lost.

Leaf litter rustled. A humble thing, the shrew,
and oddly unafraid, came straight as a herald
across the path and nosed around my shoe
but left no message and sought the weather-gnarled
roots of an oak. Too wild or wise to call it true,
I walked on, heavy, and carried this only world.

7.

If we meet, it will be in some mine's solid dark,
timbers popping as the roof settles, and I'll know
by his blackened face in the helmet light's glow
how far he has traveled since death has done its work,
how much forgotten, of life and love and work,
when he smiles vaguely, unsure. "I used to like
the high ridgetops, where you felt you could fly....
I know you...." I move to him—but the rest is dark,

so I borrow from Virgil: "Give me your hand,
father, do not draw back from my embrace."
He spoke thus, tears flooding his grateful face.
Three times there he tried to link his arms around
that neck, but the vainly held shade, every time,
fled on the empty air, a flitting dream.

8.

I was best man at my father's wedding, before
the cancer gnawed him thin. He looked like *his*
father, nervous in a new jacket, but sure.
I met his new wife, saw her sneak him a kiss,
who had softened the place with a few rugs,
woman's knickknacks. When the preacher said so,
I gave him the ring, then a rare, brief, last hug,
and we were two ordinary men, letting go.

I have a wrinkled photograph of him as a boy,
before his wives and many years before me,
where he faces the world with an uncomplicated look,
nothing to forgive. I'm old enough to be his father,
so I'd hold that yet unharrowed body, gather
him unembarassed in my arms, and rock.

Poem Ending with an Imitation of a Line from Phillipe Jaccottet

—*for Erin*

Hold this. Windows down, throwing strawberry stems
from the car, you and I drive the ruts by Cutler Lake,
moaning with pleasure as the sun-sugared berries
shiver, burst, and dissolve, the best just now starting to blet.

Hold this. A goldfinch flits and dodges. We scent woodsmoke
like foreknowledge of autumn. And swathes of the cold water,
watching wisely through birch trunks as we skirt the shore,
are as dark-sifting blue and deep-memoried as soot.

Hold this. Just as you lift a bitten berry by the stem
to praise, "It's like drinking life from a goblet,"
I ask, in the dim guard booth at the top of my spine,
some wordless question that might translate as "Why death?"

For answer, from the roadside: *vetch, trefoil, curled dock.*

Scythe

My father fought incursions of pigweed, bindweed,
and purple loosestrife. As the blades of lesser tools
thinned and snapped from use, he repaired hoes
and hatchets and spades and released them to any hand,

but the scythe was his alone, a man's deadly implement
that, swung stupidly, would open a leg to the wet bone.
It glowered from its pegs on the shed wall,
shaft crooked to ease the work, cracked from weather,

handles polished as pleasurable as skin with the oils
of labor. The dark crescent of steel glinted
along its edge in the dimness, attractive but forbidden
for boys prone to stumble in their ignorant gravity.
I remember plain work done as it should be done,
the hand's or eye's love for the angle tapped true,
the clean hole dug square, the measured cut.
He sat cross-legged at the base of a slope too steep

and rock-bound for machines and plied a file in curt
strokes that raised a new sharpness on the blade.
Then up, leaning into his own spun center, a wide-elbowed,
flow-hipped rhythm that snicked stems an inch

above the soil, the scythe seemingly as without effort
as light bending through water, he laid thistles and briers
in long swathes, to be raked in mounds and to dry
for the sweet smoke of fires that marked the cleared ground.

Lisa J. Parker

Observations of Escape

for Aunt Linda

An osprey drafts thermals
that gust across Blue Ridge peaks, up from
the pulse of Rappahannock river and rock,
bug backs and fish scale scintillate with sun strokes
and water breaks catch his eye, turn wings
to bank left, dive earthward, talons splayed.
Sunfish scatter, race for rock-shelf cover
where floor bottom is dappled,
the petal of a wild cherry blossom floats the current,
casts a shadow the fish track
as they wait in rock shade, tails
in perpetual fan motion, water over gills,
shadow-watching, all the things
that land and pass
or circle and circle.

Deployment: Homefront

On my knees beside the sunken tub,
I've sprayed a straight line of cleaner
across the porcelain base and halfway
across the tub on that first swipe, brush bearing down,
I see the faint outline
of your foot, yank the brush back and push
the bleach bare-handed from that piece of you,
phantom and unexpected.
I press my hand flat, palm to your heel,
my fingers fitting easily
to the instep not quite
to the pads of your toes,
leave it there until the slow burn
of bleach begins and I pull back,
one thin line where my forefinger rested
etched to your sole.

What We Kill to Save

Today it's tree vine around hickory,
a decade of slow choke, beautiful metastasis,
it cripples its way up the bark,
so savage its grip that Dad's swing
can sever only top from bottom,
and sweat pocks his forehead
as he runs the axe blade over
and over against the mooring veins,
the tight weave anchored so deep
pieces of bark come away as he pulls,
leaving the meat scarred with lines
like hieroglyphics or hair splayed
against a pillow, and the vine dangles
a headless snake in his hands, oozing
slow droplets that smell like oak tussin
and our foreheads touch as we sniff the stump
like animals at a fresh kill,
and I surprise us both touching
the amputated piece to my tongue,
my mouth suddenly full of alfalfa-summer.
Dad straightens himself,
lets go the vine where it stands
recalcitrant in the ground, cleaved
by only a few inches from its top half,
both ends weeping a steady flow.
Mottled brown spring peepers move in
even before we've left, buzzards
to the carnage, their bodies shiny and covered
in the wet, loamy aftermath.

Hillbilly Transplant: Bethesda Fountain, Central Park

Three hours after the towers fell,
alone at the Angel of the Waters Fountain,
no mimes play the sidewalk's edge like tightrope, no
queens from Chelsea rollerskate choreographed numbers, no
people at all, no sound but the elm leaves
twisting against each other,
metallic smoke in their tops, and the strange, rhythmic tapping
of a grackle who whips a piece of popcorn in its beak
against the fountain's edge, breaks off kerneled pieces
to gulp down, bits of white cast-off landing on the water, sinking
finally to rest on pennies and nickels,
a thousand slick wishes lying still.

I return months later, look up through the angel's wings, acid-rain-worn
and white with pigeon shit. It appears without sound, an airliner,
its wings like a goose pointed counter to the angel's.
I watch as it disappears behind one granite wing, hold my breath
the few seconds it takes to emerge past the angel's wingtip, feathered out
like saw teeth, still soaring, still airborne, moving sure
as I feel the ground beneath me, sure as this shifting wind that blows
dust and ash that settle against the back of the angel's downcast head,
and against my own.

Lynda Fleet Perry

Girl

I plucked the plump carcasses of mourning
doves, shot-riddled, sockets of eyes

empty windows, my fingers swift over
the bloodied, feathered, goose-dimpled

trophies of boy-cousins. Not allowed
to aim for more than the straw-stuffed

bulls-eye, my .22 propped on the sawhorse—
banned from stalking deer in the gully—

purely for being a girl. I scraped
rainbows of scales from brim and perch

snagged with my own barbed hook
from a boat I paddled neatly as my father

taught me—how to slit the bodies open,
to rinse and salt the purple cavities,

to dip in egg, then dredge and fry
the tender flesh I swallow.

Tracking

In the old
neighborhood, teenagers split

the bodies of toads
between saplings

of hickory, live
slingshots. Toddlers

screwed off the lids
of buried backyard oil

tanks to plop the soft
toads into their rich, oily

depths. One dropped
one into a pail full

of box turtles. I didn't know
they would tear it with their beaks

and fight over the shreds.

*

The woods encircle
and empty

into the place
entered: nowhere—

dense piles of pine
needles, the crow's shadow

—and everywhere.

*

Red clay marked
with tracks of deer,

dog, man. Deer
heads in the clearing,

then carcasses of rib

then carcasses of rib
cage, skin, and sinew.

The ground strewn
with fur, no sign

of blood. One soft
head has nubs of

antlers, another's
twisted around

a sassafras. Bent
severed hooves.

This is no standard
field dressing. No

self-respecting
huntsman would

leave this mess.

Kiki Petrosino

Farm Book

Whenever I write about Mr. Jefferson, he gallops
over. *Knock knock*, he begins in quadruplicate. It's
pretty wild, like my student's poem about a house
of skin & hair, a house that bleeds. Mr. Jefferson's
place is so dear to me, white husk my heart beats
through, until I can't write more. In my student's
poem, the house stands for womanhood, pain coiled
in the drywall. Sorrow warps the planks, pulling nails
from ribs. In Kentucky, I'm the only black teacher
some of my students have ever met, & that pulls me
somewhere. I think of Mr. Jefferson sending his field
slaves *to the ground*, a phrase for how he made them pull
tobacco & hominy from the earth, but also for how
he made of the earth an oubliette. At sixteen, they went
to the ground if Mr. Jefferson thought they couldn't learn
to make nails or spin. He forgot about them until they
grew into cash, or more land. For him, it must've seemed
like spinning. Sorrow of souls, forced *to the ground*
as a way of marking off a plot. At sixteen, I couldn't
describe the route to my own home, couldn't pilot
a vehicle, could hardly tell the hour on an analog
clock. I had to wear my house-key on a red loop
around my neck. Now, I rush to class beneath a bronze
Confederate, his dark obelisk, his silent mustache. My books
tumble past the lectern as I recite Mr. Jefferson's litany: Swan.
Loon. Nuthatch. Kingfisher. Electric web of names, yet
in the ground, I know, a deeper weave of gone-away ones
who should mean more to me than any book. I live in language
on land they left. I have no language to describe this.

Monticello House Tour

What they never say is: Jefferson's still
building. He's just using clear bricks now
for his turrets & halls, new terraces
to belt his estate in transparent loops
of dug air. After death, it's so easy
to work. No one sees him go out
from the Residence, his gloves full
of quiet mortar. Jefferson's coat is narrow
as daybreak. His long sleeves drag in the muck
as he minces his turf. You know the room
you were born in? It's part of the tour. Hundreds
of rooms unfolding for miles, orchards abloom
in the parlor. Remember that wingchair you loved, the one
with a face like a lion, especially in the dark
of late winter, when Mother sat with you
in her pink gown, humming? As it happens
Jefferson built you that lion. He drew your time
in prudent proportions. You have one job: to fit
the design he keeps spinning. Your whole life is laced
through a ring of similar finds. Just look in the binder.
It's all Mothers in pink gowns, humming.

Alex Pickens

Malaisonaisse

"Squash is an excellent conveyer of butter,"
my friend said. The strangest things go in
and come out when he opens his head,
watching fat-spackled beef bricks and spit
hit the coals as barbecue sauce drips
from ribs and wings and fingers and patties
squeal on the stove, ketchup and mustard
will spray and with a scraper and a knife
we will scoop out the jiggling white pus
and glob it onto that conveyer of greasy bliss
that society calls dinner—arteries be damned,
smear a nice veneer of the salty plaster of Paris,
Texas. Besides, meat is mostly muscle mass
so when aliens either invade or bring back Elvis
then the gyms will be buffets, and the buffer
the beef the better the feast, so to hell with this—
let's stick suckling pigs and pluck carcasses,
trim fat and pry apart ribcages and shred beef
and add sauce, that heavenly sauce, basting
in a base of sticky goo straight from the tube
that will lube it as it goes down because
a lawn chair and ice tea is where I was meant to be,
to kick back and watch the world burn,
because it's a hundred damned degrees out here
and I propped up my feet to watch the pig turn,
soon to transport the boon of sauce into
my heart and soul, soul music, soul food,
play the blues and sooth queasy unease
within the corpse that propels that soul
through this world and the flaming lattice
barbecues that it seems strangely drawn to—
be calm, be still, because this salve of pus
will either bring back Elvis or satiate us.

The Reel

On midnight shadows he floats with the loons,
pitching and casting his baited hook overboard,
a bobber twitching as catfish nibble his mind,
fiddle strung under his chin, a fishtailing grin
in the ripples, he warbles maniacally. The sky
drips moonshine into the pools in his eyes as
he casts, spinning, flying on the spool, twisting
as he loses grip and flutters away on currents,
jigging in the depths while I weigh anchor.
I smile as we laugh and reel down the river
and he winks until only a grin remains in the stars.

Matt Prater

Sensing a Thaw in My Life, if Not the Weather

I don't know what will happen next.
I cannot ledger loss or luxury. But if this
has been a kind of wintering out,

through a night so dark Orion's bow twanged ice,
what, then, is this shaking, this heat, this itch
like dry skin near the banks of a fire?

I search through bins of synapse for old records.
I search until a drop or note or passage falls down
from the forehead like lines on a wet wax seal.

To think what ease, what gifts, what grace, what station
I have been awarded for administering water
and occasionally taking a listen to new ideas!

Soon I will wake to fresh snow and branches
cracking in the canopy of wind. There will be fire,
and talk around the fire. But for now I'm here.

A Longing for Things Left Unsaid

I'm rooming with a spider now, it seems.
I do not ask their name or spider business,
but they are a better roommate than some
have had when they've had me—including myself.
Maybe I've been wrong about this virtue,
as I've held it, of not inquiring into
other people's business. I wouldn't be
the first, as it were, to confuse liberty
with selfishness. I let you go your way
to focus on mine, and by I no one
comes to learn much from the spiders. I
never asked very much about the sepia heads
on I's grandmother's cabinets, either—

now I's grandmother barely remembers.
I went where I wanted for a number
of years, asking few very interesting
questions. Eight legs, cousins' names,
minor updates, etc.
Etc.,
it seems, filled both the walls and idle hours
in the apartment of I's hollow gestures.

For Voyager, Leaving the Solar System

Owed to Nikki Giovanni

One needs the urge to go and the urge to stay,
a perfect balance of those two, and a taste for silence.
One needs a stoic intimacy with the long success
that seems like failure for a lifetime, then marks
that life in the memory of all its scoffers' children.
One needs to know about finding and being found.
One needs to know about mistaking, being mistaken,
and all the dangers on each side of that wobbling coin.
One needs to know what not to touch, and how to step
in a river where they haven't stepped before. A genius
for numbers and plasmas would be nice, of course.
But far better to know how to die before we die,
and the difference between that death and the death
of the body or soul. One needs what won't be taught
by Caltech or the branch Academies. That being this:
we will find what we bring with us. We always have.
Every monster we ever imagined was our projection.
What the conquistadors imagined they saw, they did.

Rita Sims Quillen

Garden Rite

Each spring on his postage stamp of earth the same rituals:
At the first warm breeze out came the two-by-fours
nailed together into a rectangle
where he tenderly pushed lettuce seeds into soft mud
draped the airy muslin covering over it all
like a communion table waiting for the church bell
stepped back and smiled.
Consecrate this crop.

The days had to lengthen
before the rest could join in.
The old rusty push-plow of his ancestors
a hoe he had kept from the barn of his boyhood—
lifelong tie to the gardens of the dead.
It is right to give thanks and praise.

He used the creek and tree line in April
to sight the straight line that would become
by the hot buzz of August
a choir of corn releasing soft hallelujahs.
Beans would be the kneeling women at the altar,
onions the sour deacons of the doxology,
squash women in yellow bonnets and calico of his youth,
sweet fat cabbage babies wafting and waving,
in the blinding sun's light.
We are what feeds us.

He plunged little crosses in the ground
where tomatoes, smeared with stigmata
of juicy joy, would shine over the garden.
Not a thing wrong with the bread and the wine
but a country boy had to have beans.
No communion wafer unless it was made with ground corn.
Let us keep the feast, lift up our hearts.

And my father, the high priest of the scriptural lines
of this bright dusty kingdom,

giving absolution with green garden hose in days of drought
would know precisely when to slowly lift the cloth
from that communion table, pinch tender shoots
to lay on his tongue, just the tiniest bite,

Take and eat.
This refuge, this is all—

Our salad days.

Why I Dance

It's the lifting, defying the heron's physiology
the whoosh of the heft of all that weight
leaving gravity behind on the creek's glass face
that I feel, lifted by the fiddler's hand,
weightless for that split second
when both left and right foot are off the floor.
I lift my arms out like the climbing hawk
soaring over the still world beneath
moving through pockets of hot and cool air
floating like a note on the evening's breath.
My hard heel beats like the woodpecker's beak
on the old tree bones beneath me
drumming out the tune's heartbeat
in a smiling choir of souls in motion.
The fiddler and I lock eyes and smile
wordless, weightless all at once
joyfully alive in buoyant youth
my feet and his hands together,
warbler and chickadee rising to the dusk
until the song ends
only the nightingale's song ringing long and strong.

The Gospel of Junior

The Book of Junior was economical,
only needing a half dozen commandments:
Gardening is a sacrament,
your tithe paid with hoe and bent back.
Keep everything Godly clean.

Keep the Sabbath, no matter
what the hayfield says.
In fact, go to church every time the door opens
but don't crow about it.
Your life will tell the tale.
Most of all, don't throw things away.
Everything, all of it, is a gift.

My dad's dime store dungeon of detritus
down in the dark basement was a wonder.
Nothing escaped him,
not the broken or rusty
the warped or the worn.
Dozens of nails driven in joists
held bags of treasure:
screws, nails, nuts and bolts,
belts, brackets, brushes and buckets—
anything you could ever want or need
or never want or need.
His underground hardware was a goldmine
to the tinkerer or child of the Depression.

He could've bought new
but that's heresy
in his anti-prosperity gospel.
Living cheap is living humble.
Transcendence is to be saved
by what's broken,
sanctification sent by self-sufficiency—
Grace from going without.

Junior was the camel
passing through that needle's eye
every day,
a piece of broken pipe in one hand
rusty wire in the other,
his dusty broken-down brogans
with the recycled laces
shuffling down that Redemption Road.

Something in That Winter Light

I thought of you today
when brown leaves rained from racing clouds
and the sky burned through, fierce blue.
Rushing air hummed and droned
like an organ bass pedal.
Trees jerked and bowed in amber light.
I placed you among them
a paper doll on a bright page
just beyond the fence
letting you lean
on your shovel or rake or hoe
look long and longer
at what you're missing.

I thought of you today
your back to me, head down
walking away to some other place
where light is all golden.
Just as in life,
you are somewhere else
a slow-moving figure in the garden
parting a mountain meadow far off
fixing, mending, digging
salvaging whatever you can.
You never speak in these visions.
You would think I wouldn't bother
to dream without gifting us
all those missing words.
The wind rushes along, one sound
and syllable, whispering "See."

I thought of you today.
when brown leaves rained from racing clouds.

A Woman Born to Farming

After Wendell Berry's "A Man Born to Farming"

Skin soft as morning, the mother,
the woman born to farming,
her feet bare on God's green carpet,
gathers apples and pears and eats them.
Her heart is silent, too gentle to beat.
Sometimes it hums or vibrates along a scale,
waits for the call of purpose or need,
while she cans beans, looks for calves, plants seeds.
Sometimes it sends a code
delivered by hummingbird wings.
Her children will call her blessed, the Good Book says,
but mostly they are just too busy to call at all now.
It's not their fault any more
than the leaves that fall from the tree.
They call to her thoughts every day
like the cooing of doves at gloaming,
the whippoorwill reminding us it is dark here.
The farm is a man's world.
She cannot muscle the chainsaw or sick calf,
cannot pick up the heavy hay bales.
Walking in the woods and fields is her job.
Fox bark, turkey putt, buck snort
startle her to answer with laughter.
Words are no help on a farm.
How sad to be good at something unnecessary?
Like the hens and their grit
she has dirt in her craw,
keeps hatching out barren words for others to use.
The Cherokee say Corn Mother
grew corn from her backside,
fed humankind, but the Mad Farmer's Wife
knows it all comes to nothing—
to dark, quiet vastness.
Now it's only the waiting
for the rain, the sun, the next moon change.
Accepting the briers' price,
she gathers raspberries and blackberries,
the stains' temporary tattoo
her only recognition for her work.
She has only the stains
of many things on her empty hands,
the whistled song of days passing in her head.

226

Valencia Robin

After Graduate School

Needless to say I support the forsythia's war
against the dull colored houses, the beagle
deciphering the infinitely complicated universe
at the bottom of a fence post. I should be gussying up
my resume, I should be dusting off my protestant work ethic,
not walking around the neighborhood loving the peonies
and the lilac bushes, not heading up Shamrock
and spotting Lucia coming down the train tracks. Lucia
who just sold her first story and whose rent is going up,
too, Lucia who's moving to South America to save money,
Lucia, cute twenty-something I wish wasn't walking down train tracks
alone. I tell her about my niece teaching in China, about the waiter
who built a tiny house in Hawaii, how he saved up, how
he had to call the house a garage to get a building permit.
Someone's practicing the trumpet, someone's frying bacon
and once again the wisteria across the street is trying to take over
the nation. Which could use a nice invasion, old growth trees
and sea turtles, every kind of bird marching
on Washington. If I had something in my refrigerator,
if my house didn't look like the woman who lives there
forgot to water the plants, I'd invite Lucia home,
enjoy another hour of not thinking about not having a job,
about not having a mother to move back in with.
I could pick Lucia's brain about our circadian rhythms,
about this space between sunrise and sunset,
ask if she's ever managed to get inside it, the air,
the sky ethereal as all get out—*so close*
and no ladder in sight.

Ask your grandmother

why she had six children,
your mother's mother
who was good at math and science,
but got married straight out of high school,

your *nana*, your *yaya*
who, after the first two, told her doctor
that was it, but he said *No*, the rule was six
and after the third one when she thought she would lose her mind
and after the fifth one when she did, he said *No* again,
your grandmother, who was poor
but not Mexican or Native American or Black
and so never worried about going to the state clinic
for an appendectomy and leaving without her uterus—no,
she was white and married which meant she could have as many children
as her doctor, the AMA—some guys in a room—decided,
your grandmother who's looking at you as if to say,
you've been to college,
how could you not know this.

Sometimes life feels like daytime TV

like a game show or some other excuse
for selling toothpaste. Wish I could remember who said that,
some writer describing how it feels when she can't write,
nailing it, not that I'm not guilty of a certain mindlessness,
not that I don't like the convenience of toothpaste,
of salmon already filleted in a vacuum-packed pouch,
of disposable razors and individually packaged
strawberry yogurt—of throwing it all away
whenever I feel like it. And to think—just that,
the mountains and mountains of trash—in the ocean, dumped
where we can't see it—black and brown people
living around it like company towns, working it like a 9-to-5.
And what would it take for me to try the co-op's bulk toothpaste,
to remember to bring my reusable bags,
to *own* it—the deluge of bottles and baby dolls,
of Easter baskets and string bikinis. Or little Buddhas
like the one I found the other day while vacuuming
—tiny burgundy Buddha I have no memory of buying
or being given, wondering where it came from
and then noticing my neighbor out the window
curiously hoisting his dog into the air, the twentysomething
who'd offered his shovel when my piece of crap broke,
the dog not small, some kind of retriever mix,
yet my neighbor was lifting her like a father
lifts his child to see the moon
or some particular constellation,

holding her there for a good twenty seconds
before folding the animal into his arms
and cradling her like a baby,
the dog looking around as if embarrassed,
but the guy just standing there
and me watching, still
thumbing that piece of plastic.

Late

Do movie memories even count? And why
this one—Judd Hirsch, a detective driving
down the highway with his young son on his day off,
the two of them singing *Oh What a Beautiful Morning*
as Judd notices the street of the woman who won't stop calling
the mother of the missing boy, the *crank* or so he thinks
because it's been a year and they've all been *cranks*.
In the movie, she sounds old and Black, begs the boy's mother
to come get her son, brags that she just finished having lunch
with Jesus. She's not happy when Judd shows up
at her house unannounced, barks to see his badge,
her rage biblical if not suicidal considering
she's talking to a New York City cop.
But it's the movies so Judd flinches like the rest of us,
fumbles for his wallet, some part of me trying to remember
what people used to call women like her.
And, of course, just like she said, the missing boy
is right next door, actually answers when Judd knocks,
an old white woman on a walker hurrying up behind him,
complaining *they had to take him, she needed help,
that her brother worked nights*—and did the writer
mean for us to see in her logic the same logic
that built this country? Back in Judd's car,
the missing boy—who must be old enough
to have his own kids by now, asks if he's under arrest
and aren't we glad Judd left his engineering job
at Westinghouse to try acting, aren't we happy
he gets to stare into the rearview mirror a long second
before saying, *No, honey*
and something else that doesn't matter
because apparently that's the moment I've been waiting for
—not the camera cutting to the boy's mother
turning the corner, not the boy spotting her first—no,

it's that *Honey* and those German Shepherd eyes
wishing they'd listened to that Old Battle Axe
sooner, that would give up sunsets or singing
for a chance to save the day better.
That's why I'll be late for work,
why the two-minute shower, why
I'll have to grab my make-up to put on later.

First Walk of the New Year

Little wiener dog doing his best show horse,
jumping one, two, three stumps in a row;
his boy is too busy scrolling to notice, but I smile
all the way up the hill. Bitter cold
yet this curious stand of trees with green leaves
—not magnolia, not holly. A man's walking boot
tied to a no trespassing sign, a brown kestrel
high on a branch spreading her wings,
the shock of cloud-color underneath.
I think of the conversation last night, four women
in the kitchen eating popcorn and olives,
how quick I was to roll my eyes, say who has time
—as if love was a second job, as if joy could wait,
as if my heart was the kid on the phone
and not the little dog.

Allison Seay

Thou (the well)

> It is late last night the dog was speaking of you;
> The snipe was speaking of you in her deep marsh.
>   —Isabella Augusta, Lady Gregory

I have carried everything down and am talking to you
from the inside
It is late the dogs and the snipe were speaking of you
I carried them with me
even the deep marsh I carried it and my entire life
I have carried down the city of you
the continent the fields of corn the fields of you a grove
of olive trees moon sky wind you
I have carried the entire thing my love I carried us both down
and from here the view is really of no view
only light as a pin prick
precise as my memory in the dark
I know I have what I need and all I need is the climate
of you who are the climate of well who are
the water and stone of well
the dog the snipe the marsh the echo of you who are
you who are
I carried you I carried all that speaks all that speaks of you of you

Thou (a feather)

It was not a dream.
Into the silk underdress of a country I disappeared

like a moth in fabric, a garment of God
whose hem I followed

forgetting the other world away from here
was crumbling.

I fell in love and said it aloud to no one.
It was in the late morning and I sat in a field of bright-faced poppies.

Then, in the fold of my dress
a feather.

Which meant somewhere else, I could not see,
a pretty creature was flying,

unaware anything had been lost
or anything given.

Thou (August landscape)

Like trying to describe hunger to someone
who has never been hungry. Or the feeling

of having finally unlocked the door.
Or of drawing a perfect circle.

Some desire has no language.

What I want most is to get closer to the air,
nude and lavender. Close as a cricket is close,

alive inside the ticking grass inside
sixty acres of olive trees and fields of poppies,

using its whole body to sing.

There is no language for this broad dream.
Only a record of myself in fragments:

sipping water from a clean glass,
watching light, trying to decipher

the shape of the gnats in their vortex,

fearing that something is coming for me,
fearing that nothing is coming for me.

Thou (the white moth)

From an olive tree a plastic swing in the shape of an animal
a vacant horse I think
motionless in a backyard

my memory of a hot street in Italy
a morning so still I was dying of beauty

the only movements
a honeybee levitating above a lavender bloom
the throat of a lizard

and a white moth pursuing nothing

which was how I came to understand
how desire moves or does not move
finally

      moth-like
I want what I have

Mother (of the unborn)

And yet whenever I think of the possibility of you becoming,
the entire air is different. No more of this

vichyssoise film, the color of February, this nudeness to things,
this dormancy.

The idea of you is lavender, sun-bathed and sweet. The whole world
sings to me and all the words are you.

But each time my body is useless I imagine my empty womb,
hold myself, say *my baby, my baby*, thinking you can hear me,

whoever you are,
in whatever chamber you refuse to leave.

Olivia Serio

Let's go get the shit kicked out of us by love.

Over fries and bottles of wine my best friend and I discuss
how much we wish to be in love. She says she's going to
Go home, watch a romcom, and cry. I'd die if I did that.

It's a bit melodramatic, sure, but
love feels like dying or some other bullshit like that
and so here I sit, in love with love, a spiral
of successive deaths on loop, catch-22 romance,
and they say *you have to love the person not the concept,*
so if love was a man
on the metro, I'd be in love with the memory not
the man, with his crossword filled in with pen,
and he will not offer the solutions
to the problems I assign him as I wait for the end
of a line he has already departed from.

So while she rewatches *Love Actually,* and I am not
really in love, actually I decide to go to bed,
sheets drunk against my skin as if to say
dreams are not the death you dared to crave. I'm almost cured.

Metrorail weekend reconstruction begins with service adjustments through system closing Sunday.

And here I am, four years later, still hungover,
sitting on a seat that used to be orange, nauseous
from alcohol and emotion and again
this separation between us feels like your decision.
Where summer sweat sticks to cracked vinyl
I compose all the things I will say to you when you call
to apologize, a practice we both know too well.

But three months pass and when I look up from my phone
I've missed my transfer by five stops. Still there are no messages—
not even a hello. I won't ask you to remember
my sneaking out at six a.m. to catch the first train home,
only that for once it was not you leaving.

Step back, doors closing. Please move
to the center of the car.

No matter the night, the song is always the same.

Leona Sevick

Thigmotaxis

When we sleep we are like children, moving
toward the body beside us, or away.

An unconscious or fully knowing touch
draws us closer to its heat or pushes

us to the edge to explore cooler climes,
open fields. How simple it would be if

we were only one kind of animal.
Or found ourselves lying next to someone

who's like us on any given day. It's
come to this: I'm studying the quivering

throats of birds who warble from atop my
garden pagoda, their delicate, round

bodies filling with air, contracting with
freedom, not desire. I swear I never

used to be a woman who observes birds
so closely, cold and lovely though they be.

Pedal

The gravel path is steep—a two mile slog straight
up the mountain, no switchbacks to ease the climb.

Riding my daughter's bike, the good one her dad
bought her and she doesn't use, I push past camps

littered with bottles and cans, cars whose owners
are nowhere to be found. Losing myself in

the sound of my breathing, I click through chainrings
and gears, try to shift smoothly. I scan the road

for potholes, for rocks, pray my brakes will hold on
the other side. Stomping uphill on the bike,

my heart thumping hard in my chest and in my
ears, his voice is in my head before I can

stop it. After all the lovers, the teachers,
the friends, it's still his voice I hear whenever

I'm in trouble. Now I'm ten again, straining
against the slope, his shouts pushing me uphill

from behind. We all have our mantras, the words
we repeat when we're afraid. I say *pedal*.

Leslie Shiel

Office Hours

−8 a.m.

Here in my office, I read Neruda
on sweetness, Hall on death, the bold
humility of Hopkins writing a poem
To Christ Our Lord . . . I put down the books
and drink coffee, glad it's too early for

students. *I am ordained to love you,*
a friend wrote. Time to get to
the paper about a mother, 39, with six kids.
I straighten in my chair, then
put it off. Yesterday, *my* daughter slept

in the carseat when she and my husband
picked me up at the medical building. Under
the awning crackling with rain, I
looked across Monument
at the statue of Lee on his horse,

wanting lush grasses to grow up
around him, swallowing that history
whole. In my counselor's office,
on our knees, we searched
under the black chair for a red ball

tattooed with angels, fallen
off the top shelf. When
my daughter woke, my husband
tried to get her to say *sycamore.*
Remember? We practiced. What kind

of tree did you see? At home, she shook
her head. *No sycamore!* then went back
to the breast, laughing, combining
nipple and *apple. Napple! Napple!*
Bottle of water and journals. No phone

messages. I tape Hopkins' poem
to my daughter's photo,
next to LaDuke's *Africa Birdwomen*:
(it's all that I see, these) *Keepers*
of the Peace. Davenport wrote

Christ had a *genius for compassion*.
I want it, now, before the first knock.

Maia Siegel

Wednesday at Bent Mountain

Across town,
a picture of my face burns
in a fire pit. Caecilian worm babies eat
their mother's skin. I dance and my skirt tucks
into my underwear. My belly swells
with frozen cherry pie. It's February
and hot enough for legs to pucker like strawberries.
Tomorrow, my flame-licked picture will be charcoal,
and I will know the burner. Worm babies will stop chewing skin
at sunrise. My legs will be covered and against a plastic chair.
I do not know any of this yet, and I balance
on a lime-colored line on top of a mountain,
my suede shoes dirty with dog shit and resting
next to an open can of Dr. Pepper.
The stars leak into view.

Surrogate Moon at the Roanoke Star

The metal star sculpture loomed over us like a
god. It was lit up, all in white, as if for a wedding.

We tried to get a picture but the white light blurred the edges
of our bodies, erased our heads until they looked like

door slits. Children ran underneath the star,
they grabbed at our hands. They asked us

to chase them, but I didn't want to dirty
my shoes in the grass under the star's belly.

I took their hands anyway, I obeyed their tinny voices. I
didn't look to see if you had, too. I wanted to be taken away

by the children. I wanted them to turn into
fairies once we got away from the tourists. I wanted

them to offer me cherries and vanilla-frosted cakes,
ones laced with spells or potions or at least LSD.

I hoped these children weren't human.
I wanted to take a bite that would change me,

under the belly of this star. The children never
offered me anything.

The children sat in trees
and could not get down.

The children wanted to read me the plaque
about the star, but the children could not read.

They took my hand, now my wrist,
now my arm. They ran with me over gravel.

You did not exist in that moment until
you did. Your phone's blue light was like a flare.

You needed one more picture of us, and so I left
the children under the iron bars of the star. We posed

like mutants. Afterwards, you erased
the point of my chin with Photoshop.

If you had turned your camera around,
the star's light could've been a surrogate moon.

The Kroger Car-Loading Service

The grocery boy loaded her car
with twenty free-range chicken
breasts. She did not discover this
until she was back home, after
she had cloroxed every plastic Kroger
bag he could've held. She hadn't asked
for twenty, she'd asked for two and a pack
of paper towels. He hadn't given her
the paper towels and so, she thought, he gave
her eighteen extra breasts to make up for it. She

tried to sell the breasts on Facebook, ten bucks
apiece. She said she would accept Venmo
or Paypal, so no money would have to reach
across hands. No bidders. She looked up recipes
that used inane amounts of bird meat:
a pot pie, a noodle soup, a sandwich
with breasts as bread. She couldn't eat them
fast enough, so she started padding her bra
and briefs with the defrosting cutlets,
taking mirror shots where her ass looked
a couple inches thicker. She sent these pics
to every ex in her phone, even the ones who
had grown neckbeards. The house started to stink
from the chicken strip mobile she had put up
in the kitchen. It made no sound except that of meat
knocking into itself. She called the Kroger. She said
*My grocery boy did a fabulous job. How can I tip
him?* The woman on the phone gave her
the boy's address, said *We're not supposed to
take tips but we've all almost cried and we got here
at four in the morning, so I think he'd accept.*
She hung up, she breaded the final cutlets in
money, in sanitized bills. Cutlets in parchment
stamped with the heads of presidents. She gently
dropped them into an envelope, sent them
to the boy. She thought maybe
she was in love with him. She started
making plans to paper the inside of her trunk
with nude pictures of herself, or
the photos where the cutlets made her ass
look big. She shivered every time she imagined
him opening the trunk, all of her naked meat
staring back, him placing the defrosting
chicken meat over her like a dress,
like a negligee, like a shroud.

Rod Smith

Identity is the Cause of Warts

i have a toad. its name is buber. buber the toad. buber raises rabbits. the rabbits
live in a big can named big can. or rabbit can. mostly they complain. buber
bangs the lid for them to calm down. it doesn't work. at the last annual convening
of the international monetary fund buber spoke to a packed house about toadstuff.
he talked it up good & the bankers banged their lids. sometimes buber & me smoke
pot. other times usually while banging buber has a twitch of sympathy but always
for himself & he calls the phone & it says anything so he bangs on it too & i feel
sorry for it & hang around with all these other things in the room wondering about
this banging toad in my life. buber gets a bygosh bygolly expression which on a toad
looks like all their other expressions but that toad'll sing "Little girl I don't
work in no candy kitchen / Na & I don't sell no chewin' gum." do any of you
folks have toads. can you help me through my toad difficulties. sometimes i
lie asleep all night. i just can't take it anywhere anymore. sometimes i think
i should get a frog instead but my friend jigs casey has a frog & he built a
nuclear weapon with it & i'd really appreciate it if you wouldn't call me anymore.

The Good House, etc.

> an addition
> for Peter Gizzi

the egretlike alabaster florist
in the red room
is sick—after the healing
he again
is sick—o do not be sick
egretlike alabaster florist
o do not lye ill
o do not rust
egretlike alabaster florist, fellow
helper & wielder of mums,
do not yield to fetid brethren,
the lot of us are tired, also
egretlike,

softening our loons, those of us
that have loons, or know them.

———————

what the closed inside
collapsed, asks, what the laze
lakes, our love of it, home
we have or not, how the kept
apart & the strange
layer the mis en scene, merky—

a waning pain, furthering
the excited weights & eyes, a clept
blamelessness, the kissed or etherealed
choosed & painted now—I have made

a let or will
of time or love

———————

o enlisted cleansability
to close me &
achieve or accept the good,
thunder stirs the symbolized
between & is transitory—
a downspouting, circuitous
wild—ailing the limber
stop-motions of the
expansion tank—a town
is more & more disturbed by blame, the latent
emory boards
fingering the window light dry

———————

dearest apparent
dearest well-trained

dearest
        tarantula.
It is a fair question how one
goes about cleaning such a house—

o enlisted cleansability
to close me &
achieve or accept the good,
            a confronted
good,
            the latent emory boards
            fingering the window light dry

            ———

Thunder stirs the symbolized
between & is transitory—
a downspouting, circuitous
wild—
                        the house
has a learning & the house
has a viewfinder—the best
thing in the house though
is an anklet, or a fish poacher
—they have what the skylight
has—which is not what a duct has.

the house in the lake
it is trapped & burdensome,
terrifically inert, sandbagged
& bubbling up—a blatant
causistry echoes in the
crawlspace—parietal, jipped,
plaster cast, & smarmy—

            house tells & is told
            house in the heaving
            need—woe house
            woe

            ———

it takes great courage
to visit certain homes

            ———

the house is made of would
& wonder—forty-five times

no one said it—a
former & future house,
with a dime, & definite—

the house that will save the small
animals from the ravages of inaction
the house that will impel, tiresomely,
a certain gate-kept diplomat's
bureaucratic lechery

the house that refuses the unforetold,
        stymied in the wavering, swanlike,

                —maybe a lakehouse
                w/ a horse
                on a hill,

    hmm.

        ———

some come to rub on the house & are considered weird

        ———

pronounced house
but chosen
                house which, tolerant,
                has a bias in its depth

when the painters come
all is quiet, lacking vocabulary,
when the painters come,
bravely through the pine
let them come,
those painters,
let us welcome them,
like so much harm.

        ———

in the flurry of its
unabetted finality the

unswerving focus on the faulty
good house is the making
of a meaning for the hopefully
uncoopted duration of the heartbeating
habitants & habitat-interactive
humanitarians—

        humbly it hoists
        a kind of void before it,
        housing it, w/ a temper
        of constraint & drama
        talking things over
        waiting to suffice

———

        the house is true to pagan
values without withdrawing into
morose antiquarianism—in its
youth, as trees & rubble,
among the plastic plants &
astronomers, the house kept
its council, one might say
it crept into being, displaying
an inner intensity which
was often interpreted as insensitivity—

between the columns & guided
only by the grasped true
character of the almost impossible
columns which guided the only
true character of the almost
impossible columns, between the
columns, to fit the facade, columnar,
w/out impropriety, or commentary
        shadowing what a guest
        might console, columnar,
specifically unjestlike, the
pills coming out of the clock
in the book on the house we
find this true.

———

The house the house
what of it?

247

its frescoes & privvys
its flagrant livid whiles—

say no to the house

transform its imperiled innards

unbitten, birdlike,
& hot.

———

The house has mindread
the noise of conscience
amidst the noise of
modernity, which, like
the sea, seems endless.

It has become quiet
in an attempt to escape
blame. It is a remarkable
house, here in the help
& crashing.

———

Without a tear I can leave this hut
but not w/out a grave—

It has been a good house,
hope it doesn't fall down on you,
hope you keep it up, no house
like it, no siree.

———

The good house, begun in hope,
hastened toward, has become
the destruction of desire
which is one of the things we like—

One becomes humble
before the power of the spectacle—
its saturating distrust

& abject extraterritorial
decisiveness send us bills
which we must disguise
from ourselves. These invoices
of terror & what they turn us into—
these heartless apparitions
seeping under the sill—forced
to wear masks & protective garb—
We sit next to our hearts.
Wrankled, waiting it out.

————

There are not enough particulars
in the house—
not enough soot

Did I mention the house sits
by the railroad tracks. A large
dogwood out in front—
in Virginia, above the public welfare,
below the word & deed, in Virginia,
among the golf balls & swollen books,
late into the evening, wearing Virginia
night, awake, like a house, night-
going, when he is gone.

Ron Smith

Photograph of Jesse Owens at the Gun

Beneath a puff of white gun smoke a man
the shade of cinders has risen
from between white lines
at an angle sharp with speed.
He is himself a thrust of angles:
one foot down, one hand reaching,
elbow, knee, the single bend at the waist,
all his flesh strung tight.

In the background row of pale, blurred faces
these who appear to wear his colors
must be his teammates.
We can tell only that
they do not seem to cheer.
Behind them the tiers of Berlin
mass into gray clouds.

All the races of 1936 are stopped
inside this black frame.
The man whose captured body
pulls us to the wall
cannot reach the tape, his form
caught here in the rough shape
of the swastikas that fly in the corner.

Nothing moves, nothing changes.
We stare and stare.

This poem is dedicated to Dave Smith, Terry Hummer, & Carolyn Kizer.

This Moment

You know when darkness seems to pour
from the sky, driving tense
even a mile from your own front door, two black
lanes with a centerline oh
so easy to cross—flashing lights, red in those days:
police. I think I was behind
the wheel but it could have been Royce who
pulled off Augusta Road
between the paved Ten Pin parking lot

and the mud track leading
to the Saratoga Club. We eased onto the mud side
where we'd never been before,
because that's where the crowd was, where something
had happened, cop grinning,
and more than fifty years later I can't say
whether I knew him, though we
had only four then, I think, in Garden City.
All the eyes had that look
eyes have when the ordinary hour breaks open

and shines a spotlight
of extravagance into dark routine. Headlights.
Until this moment—*this moment*—
I have not asked if my own eyes looked like that.
How can it be this moment?
Penny loafers, Wingtips, Converses arced
round a man face down
on the sludgy shoulder. Do I remember
a disappearing rivulet

of blood? I can't ask Royce. He's dead. I seem
to recall a joke about catching
a fender instead of a bus. Saturday night, right
in front of the Saratoga Club.
In my head how can there be only white faces, faces lit
with a kind of joy, jazzy
amusement—an accident, therefore, a gift. And so,
killing time, waiting for the useless
ambulance. To the south, Royce and Bobbie and I
clustered often in the parking lot,

palming a beer, sometimes going in to knock down
a few pins, but mostly circling
the nine ball table, talking trash. To the north,
the mythical, mystical
Saratoga Club, set back from the road in year-round
Christmas lights, shadowed
on the weekends with fedoras and long skirts, dark
people keeping their distance
even now, not one kneeling by this utterly still man,
dripping darkness
from black umbrellas, muted music behind them, inside.

I Always Thought I'd Die

in a nuclear wink, would not have time
to know what hit me. Or, after
distant flashes and the shock waves, slowly
of radiation sickness, combs full of hair,
bleeding from the eyes, fingernails,
nostrils, anus. After the president's head detonated,
I walked the mile home

                                   from history class,
dusty concrete along Augusta Road, scanning
the sky for the first needle-glints of Russian missiles.
But it was just Oswald, a mere ten years older
than I was, I know now, son of one Robert E. Lee,
a marine, like my father—like Lee O. himself—but dead
before the boy was born.

                           Young Oswald thought
god was a dog, a star, rats. His smiling chinstrapped
mug looks a lot like my teammates'
Wells and Strobo, who both joined the Corps right
after high school, got themselves killed
in short order. Oswald was in radar, a word
he couldn't get wrong.

                       Like my father
he qualified sharpshooter. Like my father
he was honorably discharged. Unlike my father
he didn't deserve it. He never killed anybody
until he did Kennedy and Tippet. He never

boxed, he never looked like Clark Gable.
My father believed

                                somebody on the grassy knoll
did it, even though he knew about the trip
to Moscow. He slashed his left wrist. He met
a girl with a Shakespearean handle, fathered
a kid he named after a summer month,
came home a family man, purchased
an Italian rifle

                         created within a few miles
of the Shroud of Turin. Unlike my father,
who sweated in thick Savannah air hugging
creosote poles, Lee found it hard
to hold a job. I have looked out that window.
Despite what you have heard, it was
an easy shot.

                   My father killed several men
on what he always called The Island. It wasn't easy
with an M1903, certainly not with a bayonet, never
had second thoughts about Hiroshima. They boarded
a stinking troop train for San Diego, waited
all day in the Carolina heat, were ordered
back to barracks.

                    No A-bomb, no Ronnie Smith,
he said, a million marines, soldiers, sailors, fly boys—
a million would have bought the farm
on the mainland. He figured his number was up,
but, boom, boom, the war was over. He took
his malaria to Chatham County, married an operator
with the middle name Lee,

                        and sired, as they say,
me. And though my Uncle Don, skinny and jumpy
as Lee Harvey himself, rolled hundreds of warheads
from Travis Field to Hunter Air Force Base
about the time I turned twelve—by convoy right
through the heart of my hometown, down
what is now MLK Boulevard—

                         looks like I'll make
three score years and ten. Haven't been vaporized

or particularly irradiated, far as I know. 1Y'ed out
of Vietnam, despite football. It wasn't the concussions
or the trick shoulders, knees, arthritic feet, hips, spine.
Blood pressure off the chart, the doc growled.
No Hiroshimas in my lifetime. Not yet.

R. T. Smith

Shades

When Odysseus descended to the underworld
and crossed the dark river to learn the key
to his destiny, he poured the ritual milk and honey,
the wine and barley and blood to summon the dead,
but he never expected to find his mother among
the shadows who were filled with mist and sifted
with the wind which had no source. He had thought
her alive and back in Ithaca expecting his return.
He had assumed the worst ordeals were his own.
But when he reached out, shivering as he wept,
to embrace the ghost, that wanderer found
no substance, no flesh nor blood nor bone,
and he must have felt as I did that first time home
when my mother's mind had begun to wander
and she disremembered not only the laughter,
the lightning-split chinaberry tree, the sunset
peaches and fireflies and the sharp smell
of catfish frying, but also her name and the fact
that she was sitting in her kitchen of fifty years
beside my father who stood there straining
not to wring his hands nor surrender to the tears
welling around his eyes. She gathered her purse,
her hat and wrap, then said, "Please drive me home
before strangers take evert damned thing I own."
Her eyes glaucous with terror, she was exhausted
and desperate, almost herself "an empty, flitting
shade," as Homer says it, uncertain in her haze
whether she was moving toward or away
from what might be called the Great Dream.
When she sobbed and cried, "Where is my son?"
I, too, felt bewildered, and not even a seer
from the land of night and frost and smoke
could tell me what words would amount
nor which constellation to steer by,
nor where all this heart sorrow might end.

Patsy on "Crazy"

Born country and raised it,
but I was never hick-ridiculous,
despite the red Stetson and cowgirl fringe.
I knew the big band sounds—Dorsey,
Krupa, all he wounded crooners
from Dixie Dawn to Anita O'Day,
their voices like birdsong, but singed.

Hayride tunes, hillbilly ballads? I paid
my dues, but given the chance,
I'd bend the notes blue. You've heard
about the Opry. I'd yodel okay but pick
and choose my quavers, trills
and grooves. "A natural," they'd say,
but in Vegas shows I had to stifle
those weepy tones to wilt and quaver
in ermine stoles and French perfume
under the stage prop moon. No miracle
canary or whip-poor-will cutie,
I had no time for shirking. Born
Ginny Hensley in Virginia, I married
soon and whipped up "Miss Patsy Cline"
to make the marquee's neon sizzle
and send shivers up your spine.

Some Nashville wit said talent's
just patience, grit, but I had to practice
till my raw throat whispered *quit*.
"Walking after Midnight"? That was
luck, but I learned pretty quick:
the harder I worked, the luckier I'd get.

Willie's take on "Crazy" is still the top hit
on Wurlitzers from Memphis to Timbuktu
just because I chirped it over and over
a hundred ways from dusk to dew.
I lived it, too, with Charlie, then Gerald Cline.
It was a hard stunt, sister. My advice
to showbiz chicks? "Keep the lipstick shiny,
but always be ready to scrap for your dime."

It wasn't misery that drove me crazy,
but no night of it was ever easy

or any chic shindig. Bus tours
and night owl shows, pretty boy suitors—
I was a chanteuse of the heart
song, hurt song, a torch singer
who brought life's fever
to every achy lyric. But just you listen:

first time I warbled out "Crazy"'s weepy
woeful notes, the whole sound crew
honest-to-God cried. I knew something
of a wonder was unfolding. Even if
it didn't flash like lightning, the air
in the studio was changed, scorched
for the brief sweet forever.

All gone. That last night it was foggy.
We'd killed a fifth of gin. Next gig
two puddle jumps over, we were all numb
and sleepy, too edgy to be afraid.
Our Comanche flew straight into the storm.
Ricky, the Bopper, Buddy Holly—
none of us angels. The pilot was forced
to trust "dead reckoning." Now we're gone.

They say the clocks stopped, nothing left
but March darkness and the famously
bitter price of fame, hissing wreckage
twisted around the trees. I'll sing it again:
we're born to suffer, darling,
so we cling to every possible smidgeon

of bliss. Cage lowering slow
into the last mineshaft, we get the picture
but canary on through the pain—
ice drizzle, screaming wind,
the final melody a cold hard rain.

Ghost Bird

declared officially extinct Sept, 2021

No longer endangered
but finely and precisely
extinct, the ivory-
billed woodpecker
was also called Lord
God bird because
its arresting cry of *hant
hant hant* made fearless
gator hunters exclaim
in the name
of the Almighty. Beaks
and feathers were esteemed
by dandies and ladies
for fobs or elegant hats.
Native graves held hollow
wing bones. Tough the birds
became experts at concealment,
by Audubon's time
they were perishing.

As of now, say the experts,
no more holding the breath
over forged recordings,
affidavits sworn on the Bible
or blurry snapshots
from the swamps—the White
River, the Tensa,
the Pearl. The last
specimens brought down
by a collector's gun
are stuffed now,
summoning dust
and cursory scrutiny
in a cool museum drawer.

We're left with memory
and a modest facsimile:
the pileated—smaller,
its beak black, crest scarlet—
riddling the dead
trees for diligent ants.

The larger cousins gone
deep into the marshes
seeking their preferred fare
found even celebrity
deadly. Their zealous adepts,
almost worshiping birds, were
committed to history,
and on one March day
they felled the last ivory-bill
to guarantee
no one could forget
their astonishing beauty.

Just imagine the final bird
setting out on that ordinary
morning not knowing
his feathery silhouette the last
word spoken from the throat
of that bayou oak,
the flame of his crest
extinguished, his drumming
hushed, even the echo
of his songs lost,
leaving us in envy,
wishing for the call
to unfurl our own wings
and for heaven's sake
appear to disappear.

Mockingbird

(Gettysburg: November, 1863)

That next autumn the Weaver Brothers
with their camera bigger than a hatbox
caught us at Bull's Tavern in parade dress
half-snockered on cheap oh-be-joyful.
They promised each man a half-dollar
to pose on Devil's Den where the slaughter
we'd survived in the recent summer
had been too gruesome to summon
to mind full sober. So we trooped out
into the brisk weather and reclined,

artful as a squad of studio models
tricked out as the dead, while a pair
of doctors in smart frock coats stood
over us like Satan's angels claiming
souls on the threshold. *It's all theater*,
jested the photographer's helper,
now that Lincoln and the multitudes
had remembered and cheered and gone,
but I'd be there for the big scrap—
crouching, shit-scared, firing wild.
I couldn't quit flinching, not back in July
nor in the cold and quiet. Our Corporal
Billikin, knock-kneed in his cups, kept
singing from his ghost pose a popular
ditty called "Listen to the Mockingbird,"
about the bird trilling high in the willow
by the grave of poor Halle. *We want
the look of fresh dead*, one Weaver
shouted out from under his camera hood:
*Cut out the hayseed concert, fellow
and pretend to asleep, if feigning death
seems to you reckless*. It was reckless,
but I was soused and sprawled across
the altar of the pinnacle rock to watch
empty limbs pointing out our tableau's
lie: not summer at all, but frosty season.
Fool Billikin kept warbling his somber
song, as if it was a funeral, as if we'd
not all soon head back to the tavern's fire.
Making history again, we were glad
but Sergeant Archer scolded the boy
to drop his chirping: *Secesh marched
out to that tune. It's a killer's rhythm*,
and suddenly we were all cold sober,
avoiding each others' eyes, dead solemn.
We'd had all the art a man could bear.

Mallard

Something of an arrow in him,
and something of a flower.

I brought him down just after dawn
in cold and pearly weather.

The echo from my Wingmaster
ripped blue air asunder.

In the hound's mouth his gloss was fading,
eyes still embered, amazed, reflecting

sunrise bloody on the quiet river,
wingtips sharp against my fingers.

I shiver now as I remember
reading: when you're ready to cross over

they'll judge your heart's failings
against the weight of a feather.

Lisa Russ Spaar

Oriel Theory

Study

In any story there must be waiting.
The laundry churning, my dread abating

behind three tables, arranged in fortress
beside a window facing to the west.

Light moves across my arm, the sashes,
sun more a *way* than a *thing* that casts

a shadow. My hand against this desk
evokes a gaze, sure. *Odalisque*

means "belonging to a room." And *oriel?*
A diminutive from the Latin *os*, mouth. That bell.

Room as mouth. Mouth as solar flare.
To wait without expectation is prayer.

What holds this corbeled space in air?
I sink my teeth into its lair.

Wind Wife: Power Outage

Wed to lament, brine-lashed
& barnacled, all night the smash

of sleet into needles, cones, forcing
pine temples to kneel, cuffing wires

with crippling ice as limbs large as trees
crack, gunshots, in the woods & fall

within the woolly scrim of toss & heave.
This midnight white would have held

my child-self in thrall at any window,
world erasing itself, magnificent tantrum,

dervish in magic cloister, a diamond trigger
for joy that care, age, dullness, what you will,

have now reduced to link rot. Sadness
in this, worse than the dark, cold furnace,

day's gray creep, the clench & taunt
as sun makes its late, weak return

only to sink again. Time's sepulcher.
We are what we make of weather.

Pileated

Maples erupt, busking beauty
all along the highway.

Driving, I pay, I pay, I risk
attention. Back at the desk,

I'm afraid. Why? From whence
this staccato gunfire, tree or house?

Either way, old timber's rotted,
rich with insect grapeshot.

Weird comes from "wey ward."
Do we begin as something backward,

head cresting, blood-red,
toward ground, stretcher, bed?

Like a fire storming the head
out of necessity, not dread?

Flaw

The sense of defect, of fault,
 as in, *They did that to you? That's flaw,*

comes later. First, Old Norse, a flake
(of snow), a splinter, a bit, a speck,

a winter nick, lit wick become word
spitting beneath the four-wheel's swerve,

adrift a moment over crenellated ice.
So you're not perfect? Not in paradise?

Lean into it, why not, whether inherent,
or whether, unfair or fair, a judgment.

As in spring, its colossal sleight of hand.
That mistake. Be child again,

at the piano recital, saved by one wrong note
from being anything but human.

Lush

How "flush" contains it, money enough,
money here meaning love's ample crush,

luscious as this pickled cherry pepper
drifting in an iced coup of bespoke liquor

laced with gunpowder tea and herbs. And why not,
as fuschia buds thieve trees, dissolving winter

at effing last? Soft, lax, luscious—
the thrush, two-throated, heard at dusk—

drink it down. Have another.
Only one time to live, that we know of,

though I've loved you so lavishly
I've been mythic, girl, boy, man, even me.

As we all begin: extravagant.
Impossible flesh on naked branches.

Sappho Stanley

Joseph Stanley Did You Dream of Transsexuals?

Did you yearn in your heart
to not have ghastly eyes and a beard
that covers your neck?

Did the hairline that disappeared
as you got older keep you up
at night?

What about the stars? Did you
watch them intently, drinking
the popular beer of your century, singing?

Did you rub scabs into your skin,
praying to make it softer?

Did your cat make you jealous,
strutting in a way you quite never could?

Was I born because you never were?

One night celibacy

Sometimes,

I   think
about my gravestone,
what'll the   name be?
Who'll   clean   it?
                Sometimes,

I   think   about
my   bones,   are
my   hips   shifted?
Will the anthropologist
who discovers   me tell
people I was a woman?
Will   "woman"   and
                                "man"
mean anything in the
future?
                Sometimes,

I   think   about
my   skin,   soft
and   decayed   by
fungi,   possibly
scrumptious,   sweet
fat   cells   filled
with   estrogen.
                        I've

become   ready   for
                        love.
It's been   hidden in
my vial of estradiol,
and now I find it in
the   mouth   of my
          lover,
deep   inside,
where I desire for her
                to say:
        "You look
        like a girl."

Dialectical Inversion

Oh, the allure of the chain-smoking
gender-envy-giving Double Kwik gas station clerk.
The toe of her Reebok delicately dip into
a green puddle
and her wrinkled hands
grasp a cigarette—effeminately
warped by carcinogens.
The deadends of her hair wave to me,
bleached and crunchy.
The 40 volume developer
lies, waiting in the back of her cabinet
for the roots.
Her skin hangs off her bones like
a good rack of ribs.
She was the one who made it cool to listen to vinyls again.
Her conceitedly caramelized face crinkles with
each puff of the American Spirit. She rolls the smoke
so seductively in her mouth, her wrinkles flap and fold
and whisper to me, *moisturize nightly.*
The way her breasts sag, dragged
by the weight of gravity, the suckled nipples
pointing downwards.
The sweet Walmart perfume knocks me back,
hits me like a sack
of feathers. She woke me up,
unveiled my eyes to an egg
uncracked. Only my pillows
sing me to sleep, inspiring
sonnets. Give me the meds
to turn back what was unborn. Doc,
cure me of words tonight.

Sofia M. Starnes

Butterfly Effect

It sprinkles dusk and dragonflies disperse;
a bone pulls gently home under the skin;
a lamb sleeps in her pen, while mothers nurse
their babies at their breasts. Above, a crimson
cloud brings all things close, under a risen

star. For every bleat, a ewe; hosannas—voice
on voice in daily briefs, the daily choice
of words. They nudge a needle and outlast
a wrong. And though the day withholds its noise,
our silence too is offspring of this past.

Rescue

Death in the crisp branches of a lost cypress—
Eden and sin, the initial call to build
an ossuary or a sarcophagus.
Nearby, a wolf winks at a lamb, a wild
orchid falls to soil, to seed. A fox has killed
its prey—burst of orange and flame—first cry;
first crimson. *Surely not us. We will not die.*
Against these options, we posit a tomb,
stone on stone, undo eternities. By
our side, a Wound flowers, making room.

Nova

I

Forego the body and the body's shroud;
forego the bruising, this mortality—
the beaten wood, damp linen, the low cloud
above the hill.   Forego the gravity.
Give us a cheery god instead, witty
and playful.... Waive the dark night of the soul,
the ice required for crocuses; console
the yard with glitters and the drain with leaves.
Still, how the tree misses His arms, His whole
body—cold, common—   What heaven receives.

II

Our body is a booty of disposable
cells, none meant to be free, yet emboldened
by the task of bearing a life: double
reward for the helix, hips and hardened
arteries that turn a spark from Spartaned
flint to hearth-fire, and the lowliest breath
to a homestead for words.   I saw a feath-
er last night, a young bird's, and I knew how
risky the affair, how close to the neth-
erworlds are nests,   a tiger to a sparrow.

III

Most creatures fidget daily, wonder why
sacrifice is a virtue, or how desire
touches a truth.   From every child, a cry—
not for better bones but for a higher
hour. A time when we are safe from fire
and water, fret and fall. A time for stun-
ning novas at sunset, beyond our blun-
ders.   On wiser days we wince: *forgive us*—
know the ruse of breath between ribs upon
waking: the wish as wound, waiting for caress.

Fishing

—watching a boy and his father, from the shore

1
Afloat, then further in: and I, who know nothing
of boats, think of water and spill, a hand
and a rope, a ripple and wood. Are they planning
to fish into evening, this distance from land,
with barely a crib for a vessel?
Oh, the ribs of the lake speak of toil and of miracle.

2
What is blue veers to gray in the absence of fish—
no fine, silvery flesh for the supper they'll make
on the shore, when their courage, or fetish
for courage, turns dim.   The darker the lake,
the longer they sit, as blue yields to dusk,
and dusk yields to night. And the boat turns to husk.

3
Now imagine they're gone, a boy and a man,
the ladder of sparkles behind them—
There is only the lake.   When you scan
the horizon, the water seems black, like the hem
of a woman in mourning. And you know
it is time to disown this temptation to sorrow....

4
How lovely the sight!   A boy and his dad
holding court with the hours, the waters sprung clean,
the miraculous depth. All the good they once had
and will have on this day in their laps. They lean,
and they laugh at their emptiness. *We are This,*
after all—   and the waters divide, full of fishes.

Ruth Stone

At Eighty-three She Lives Alone

Enclosure, steam-heated; a trial casket.
You are here; your name on a postal box;
entrance into another place like vapor.
No one knows you. No one speaks to you.
All of their cocks stare down their pant legs
at the ground. Their cunts are blind. They
barely let you through the check-out line.
Have a nice day. Plastic or paper?

Are you origami? A paper folded swan,
like the ones you made when you were ten?
When you saw the constellations, lying
on your back in the wet grass,
the soapy pear blossoms drifting
and wasting, and those stars, the burned out ones
whose light was still coming in waves;
your body was too slight.
How could it hold such mass?
Still on your lips the taste of something.

All night you waited for morning, all morning
for afternoon, all afternoon for night;
and still the longing sings.
Oh, paper bird with folded wings.

In the Interstices

Pleasure me not, for love's pleasure drained me
Deep as an artesian well;
The pitiless blood-letter veined me.
Long grew the parasite before its fill.
Lover, smile the other way, nor ply me with evil
Who am surfeited and taste the shadows of gray;
Nor sway me with promises to rouse my thirst
And fill me with that passion beyond lust;
Not romp my body in the wake of the mind's play.

How tired, how enervated, how becalmed I am.
That island toward which I strove in my salt tides
Has drifted out beyond the listless swell and formed
A hostile continent. I am amorphous with all deflowered brides,
Who, with their floodgates sundered, drowned when they were stormed.

Shapes

In the longer view it doesn't matter.
However, it's that having lived, it matters.
So that every death breaks you apart.
You find yourself weeping at the door
of your own kitchen, overwhelmed
by loss. And you find yourself weeping
as you pass the homeless person
head in hands resigned on a cement
step, the wire basket on wheels right there.
Like stopped film, or a line of Vallejo,
or a sketch of the mechanics of a wing
by Leonardo. All pauses in space,
a violent compression of meaning
in an instant within the meaningless.
Even staring into the dim shapes
at the farthest edge; accepting that blur.

Henry Taylor

Faulkner, Looking Up Briefly from His Desk,

catches a glimpse of a single brick column
with an iron Corinthian capital,
standing not within sight of where he is,
but near enough to see when he drives by it,

and he says to himself all over again
that the mansion on whose porch the column stood
has vanished into pasture land, that cows
can scratch their butts on the base, that anything
he turns up can be put into that house

to do whatever good or bad it wants.
What he sees next is a couple of men,
Peloponnesians deep in ancient times,
walking below a hill backlit by sunset.
Thinks of Agamemnon and Menelaus.

How their father, Atreus, killed the sons
of his brother Thyestes, served portions
of them to him at a banquet, and thus
launched generations of mortal vengeance.
And there, from that chaotic pile of stone,

he sees a broken column or a lintel
standing against the sky like a stroke of ink,
and one of those two fellows says to the other,
"That's what there is of the old Atreus place.
Hard to believe what-all went on up there."

Maul Sundial

Around a corner of your house toward the woodshed,
I saw a splitting maul parked in the top of the block,
the helve pointing about halfway up the northern sky.
I told you that since both of us had decent watches,
we could pull up a couple of chairs and a few beers
and mark the ground at each hour to make a sundial.
You gave me a curious look, trying to decide
whether or not this was something you wanted to do,
then said you'd go get the picnic chairs and a six-pack.
I went into the little shop beside the woodshed
and gathered a handful of screwdrivers and an awl
to mark the spots where the shadow of the helve would be
as we struck the coming hours. When you came back outside,

we unfolded the chairs and cracked a couple of cans,
and sat. I asked you what, roughly, our latitude was.
You said you weren't quite sure, maybe thirty-six or so
(this was years before people had GPS units).
I stood and looked closely at the helve, raised it a touch,
and tapped the heel with a wedge to make it tight again.
We drank two beers and let twenty-seven minutes pass,
and you got up and poked a screwdriver in the ground
and pronounced it four p.m. For the following hour,
or most of it, we asked each other questions about
more than latitude, and you recalled reading somewhere
a trigonometric formula for the gnomon
that includes the tangent of the angle of earth's tilt,

so we looked out at the fading landscape for a while,
talking of the astronomical distance between
our little project and how it would be carried out
if we had known enough about what we were doing.
Amid these speculations five o'clock came and went
unmarked, and we wondered how long it was till sunset,
then stood up and folded the chairs. You hooked your fingers
into the plastic loops that still held the two last beers,
and started toward the house as I gathered the tools,
pulled up the one screwdriver, and put them all away.
We parted, each to his own home and supper. Later
I lay in bed, the blank ceiling above me, snatching
scraps of coherence from stray notions about the stars.

What Was That?

It could have been a piece of framing slipping minutely
against another. It happens sometimes when the temperature
changes rapidly, as now, for instance, when the sun has gone down
and the heat withdraws from the thin, high-altitude air.
I'm used to these noises. I was fifteen before I lived in a house
that had been built in the twentieth century, and that one
was a dormitory built in 1903. So when we sit in the evening
in our accustomed corner of this adobe-style frame house
with not a single stair in it, little events behind the walls
and above the ceilings rarely interest me. Outside, though,
the driveway lights come on, prompted by motion sensors,
and the question arises whether there is enough breeze to cause
the junipers to be detected in their lazy waving to the passing air.
One of us may look out the window for the animal
that might have been there. We have been blessed by the transient
presence of coyotes, mule deer, bears, and once, a bobcat.
They pass through and go on, and some return, especially the deer
and the bears, who like to raid our bird feeders. Still, what was that?
I walk to a window, looking out and in at the same time,
catching your reflection in a corner of the pane, watching
as it slips over my shoulder and into my memory,
where some evening farther on it will make a sound
like a slippage along a fault line in my brain, or in my heart.

Dishonor Among Moonshiners

A word on a mailbox, and it comes back:
his name was Hargreave. I never saw him,
but see him now, called up from old hearsay,

farming a patch of hillside grass and woodlot
halfway up the side of Danner's Mountain,
the far end of the woodlot undisturbed

for a bootlegger's quiet use, the still
run with Hargreave's permission, then transformed
by blackmail into silent partnership,

until one day the Sheriff happened by
and asked Hargreave if he and his men might
be allowed to give the place a looking-over.

Hargreave consented. They let him ride with them,
and when the still man caught sight of the truck
he took off running before they got it parked

and started after him. Hargreave took the lead,
leaping around and in between the briars,
rocks, low-hanging tree limbs, treacherous vines

as if he could have done it blindfolded,
then caught and held the man around the waist.
The Sheriff came up and took custody,

then looked hard at Hargreave, who said if there
was anybody running a still on his place,
he meant, by God, to find out who it was.

Parcel

I lift a package from the pile of mail:
a softpack from Amazon, like a book,
and whatever's in it is heavy, but
narrower. "Feels like a pair of Vise-Grips,"
I say; you take a look at the outside,
and repeat "Vise-Grips" with a question mark,
and I recall again that our ways met
at the ends of trails that hadn't ever crossed:
you grew up in the city, and I on a farm,
and every now and then we share some bit
of worldliness that only one of us
has known before. The life we live takes on
another furnishing that we make our own,
a shard of lore to round our legend out.

Randolph Thomas

The Anniversary

In memory of Ed Disney (1962-1979)

In early August I cannot sleep.
Instead I see my friend
sitting on the hood of his orange car
trying to write a song with me.
He holds a banjo. I, a guitar.
The song turns out ridiculous
because we are too young.
He tosses a penny in the air,
catches it, and says
It is little money.
This becomes our joke.
At seventeen he climbs into a car
with two other teenagers, strangers
who drive him into unseen country,
shove him out and shoot him.
He rolls down an embankment.
In the morning he wakes,
wipes red dew from his forehead.
The blue and gold sleeves
of his band jacket
brush the grass and dirt.
I ask him to sing a song.
I am not old enough, he tells me.
His car is found beside a saloon.
The two boys are sleeping,
their white feet sticking
through the windows of the orange car.
His wallet is on the dashboard, in plain view.
The boys are stupid, my friend is dead.
Twelve years later I toss a penny.
My friend catches it, says it is little money,
and hands it to the boys who kill him.
I close my eyes in early August.
I hear crickets, the dew.
Mornings and years have slipped by.
My friend says it is little money.
He sits on the hood of his orange car
and asks me for a song
I am old enough to sing.

Fever

By autumn, crab apples tumbled
and rotted in gullies; blue jays and starlings
picked my mother's strawberries
through the plastic netting she spread.

Jaundiced, weak in blood, I watched
through the living room window
my parents raking and burning leaves.
As black smoke snaked above the trees,

behind her glass, in her oval world,
my great grandmother's lips moved
as a tiny moth's wings. I could not prove
she whispered my name, or hers or theirs,

but I watched her speak. Too weak to run,
to lift myself off the couch, too afraid
of my rough cough, of broken slivers,
to rattle my fist against the glass

I watched her brow unfurl, her shoulders
in her bulbous-shouldered black dress
turn, as she started out of the portrait
after me. Had I breath and strength to spare

I might have lowered myself to the slick
wooden floors, crawled to the doorway, across
the green and white tiled kitchen
where my mother masked the tastes of medicines

in soups and seasoned vegetables.
Had I the strength, I might have made it
to the door, stretched, unhooked the screen, drug
myself off the porch, down the red brick steps; drug

my legs, scraped my belly across the gravel driveway
where the wheels of my overturned dump truck
spun in the air. From there, I might have shook loose
the chalk in my throat, might have shouted

above the fires raging in my parents' faces
laying on their autumn tan. *She was still after me.*
Her long black dress, her wan, waxen face
pressed against the screen door. As afternoon

shadows, as the fall fell around me, my mind's
ideas crossing themselves, I found the tin-walled pool
on the hill behind the house. Hours passed.
I hid among tools, in the shed where my father

saved the horse's skull, in the woods by the fallen pen,
by the barn my father covered with tin strips
from the pool. I waited her, listened for her lips
rustling, my hand in my mouth, the sheets covering me.

The couch, damp with sweat, swaddled dreams
that moved against the autumn sky like passing nights.
Her fluttering lips blew kisses. My thinking turned
and emptied, gravel falling slowly by the glass.

When we took down the pool, my father cut
the metal for the barn roof, cut the rest
for strips to circle my mother's strawberry beds.
Rusted, those strips cut my belly, as I crawled over them,

and over the fallen gutters—sharp, with bent out
screw holes and rusted screws. I crawled
along the back wall, stained and bowed
from water rolling off the mountain.

After dark, I found the basement stairs, the door
rotted and standing open. I sat and listened to her
heavy shoes thudding through the upstairs.
I sat beside my father, his face dark and brooding;

by my mother, who claimed berries from birds,
who tended beds of rusted metals. Fall colors
seeped down into the house, into the mountain
beneath the house. As young as eight, I listened

for her, watched from my fever, waited
her coming. At night objects crashed,
fell from her groping, mystified fingers.
The past took the house. I listened

for the far away train, trucks on the new highway.
In the day, my fingers smoothed plastic
across broken windows. I replaced
broken hinges, wiped away hex signs

chalked by neighborhood vandals
on the barn's rusted walls.

Michael Trocchia

Impatiens

In 2013 a disease devastated this popular annual, also known as touch-me-nots.

Finally it felt like spring.
Night hung

back—its stars dying
to reach you

in the twilight. Rooted
indoors, you could not

wait, rising to make
way for the nearest

light, a lamp by the window.
Everything was then double-

exposed, the day found
hiding behind its residue.

Your two hands, more
than ever, looked like

they wanted to hold something

else in the pane. And that
look in your eyes still

shut into their reflection.

Verum and Factum

after Giambattista Vico

What to be made
of sparrows stuck

in the throat? What
to be made of the girl

gasping in the shed,
of dead trees holding up

sheaves of white sky,
of the hillside green

clean of human breath?

XXX of the Fatherlands

It is time, reports the city to itself, and so the city packs up and gets away from itself, to the great outdoors it goes on holiday. There it inhales the woodland winds, there it chases wild game, delights in campfire and starry nights, there it squats down on the forest floor, only the tips of its tallest buildings seen above the treetops. And on the rooftop of one such building, there lies an unclean boy in a net hung like a hammock between the roof's red brick and ironwork. The boy has trapped himself in the conceivables, captivated by the corners of his own mind. As he sways in his net, considering the nature of ends, a soft spot for the means takes shape inside him, a flowering love for algorithms and acorns. Relaxed in his reflection, he computes the certain migration of birds above, as if their flight were fixed against an endless sky through which he scrolls and scrolls. Blue and bluer still, the days go behind him and beside him a woman who could be his mother is crawling with insects, her life now a bitten thing and about to fall off. The city has overstayed its holiday, for the wilderness pushes in on its bridges and tunnels and against the glass of its skyscrapers, infesting its streets and spaces with its vermin. She has come climbing the fire escape to tell the boy as much but her mind has maddened in all the more places and instead she lies clawing at the air, babbling about other people's futures as if they were her own. Little can be made of her words but it is clear she thinks the boy is to one day have a son and that this son is herself young, full of unthinkable urges and beauty. The boy of course cannot hear her at his side, as his ears are dirtier than ever, purposely stopped up with the wax of his own head, listening solely to the pure thought of himself.

Ellen Bryant Voigt

Fox

rangy loping swiveling left then right I'm thinking
nonchalant but the doves flutter up to the roof of the barn the crickets
leap from the grass like fleas a fox is in my yard-o my yard-o
plenty of songs in my head

to sing to my child's child if she were here
she wakes in her crib and sings to herself
her brother her mother who hate to be alone laugh at this
odd happy child so like another child content in her wooden pen
with a pot a metal straw a lid a hole in the lid a glass hat
for the hole a metal basket with smaller holes
a hole the size of the straw for hours

I made the pieces fit then took them apart
then made them fit when I got tired I lay me down my little head
against the flannel chicks and ducks then slept then woke then took
the puzzle up my mother had another child sick unto death
she needed me to fall in love with solitude I fell in love
it is my toy my happiness the child of my friends
is never ever left alone asleep awake
pushing her wooden blocks around the rug they cannot bear
her least distress their eyes stay on their sparrow poor happy child

last year I startled a fox crossing the road the tail
more rust than red the head cranked forward facing me
it stopped stock-still as if deciding whether to hurry forward
or turn back it had a yellow apple in its mouth
and the little ones chew on the bones-o   .

Lost Boy

who says we aren't primarily animals for instance
you recognize at once the smell of doom and keep away unless
you're drawn by pheromones like a soldier ant or for once you worry
about your soul he reeked of doom despised by those he loved one parent
missing one parent Pentacostal disgusted by the queer parts of him
he was himself disgusted self-despising snarling sick

unto death the chronic contagious sickness of our times
a righteous judgment was what he called it the rash
erupted over and over no meds no money no readiness
for help if there'd been help no self-defense unless you count
self-sabotage the wounds were old and ugly he kept them fresh he was quick
to take offense except from me and for what for merely a kindness

that brought me letters photos poems seeds saved from his yard roses
profuse on the cards for Mother's Day on valentines because I was a surrogate
it cost me nothing until he chose oblivion the news was no surprise his gift
was always making something out of nothing

Storm

One minute a slender pine indistinguishable from the others
the next its trunk horizontal still green the jagged stump
a nest for the flickers
                              one minute high wind and rain the skies
lit up the next a few bright winking stars the lashing of the brook

one minute an exaltation in the apple trees the shadblow trees
the next white trash on the ground new birds
or the same birds crowding the feeder
one minute the children were sleeping in their beds

you got sick you got well you got sick

the lilac bush we planted is a tree the cat creeps past
with something in her mouth she's hurrying down to where

the culvert overflowed one minute bright yellow
marsh marigolds springing up the next
the farmer sweeps them into his bales of hay

G. C. Waldrep

At the George Caleb Bingham House, Arrow Rock, Missouri

You could say: this is where a people's art began.
Malaria; cicada whine. You could dress yourself up
in your wounds. You may walk in the center
of the road, as far as you like. Vanity,
to center the composition just so. You smile into it.
You wait for it to ask you a question. You could say:
the roughed-in portrait on the easel is a prop,
a mere prop. Beside the basket of vintage needlework,
pincushions, pins & needles rusted into the gay fibers.
If you are unable to walk then you might limp.
The question turns beneath your hand. It turns but it
does not break, & here you are. You could say:
marry me, pigments sprung from lead, from lapis,
from madder (a mere prop). All the blind heroes
from the past are clapping. The city is clapping, Zion
if you like. Whisper your signature into the variation:
the new bottoms through which the river once ran.
It is easy to imagine hunters here, so why not do it:
hunters. Cracks varnished over, you can see them
in this late light. The gardeners arrive & then withdraw.
You could say art sent them. You could say art
slew them. You could pioneer the use of red
underpainting, to confer a lifelike blush to human
figures, to a young nation. Overspreading
older nations, yes, the clamor sealed within the image.
You are astonishingly not alone, is the message
daybreak broke against the thighbone of a saint.
What if you pierce it. What if you make a musical
instrument of it. What then would you have waited for,
yes, I (is it time for the "I") am asking you.
Who have glimpsed this world, & possibly others.
Speak with the thread in your hands. Cicada whine
upthrust from the depths, into the plane of desire
which is to say, of representation. You, you, you,
eyes shut, eyes wide, make your decision, this stroke
versus that stroke, assisted by the glistening hairs
of an animal, some former animal. The image *alive*

alive-o as it must be. Here is the body of a pelican
stretched on a strand, here is the body of a crow
stretched on a wooden table, here is a marmot, here
is a mink (with a human hand showing, bottom left,
as if reaching for it or perhaps as if withdrawing).
You may think of the heaven of images, if there is one—
you may think there is one. An infinite plane
of perfect representations. And every fourteen years,
or every seventeen, that desperate clawing up
through the surface, that seeking. The slit
harvested just so. Uninvented because it is closed,
as all conquest is closed. Now the docent has
returned to lock the room back up, & you thank her.

Tarry

Big Spring, Arrow Rock, Mo.

The body records its absences. Water, you take water
into it—as presence, as absence, deep into the archive
of water you throw your mask. Also, your other mask.
We, being matter, are negotiated. I had not thought
to be angry, as such. But rage flexes its majestic undoing,
its sustaining negation. The reparations the body seeks
rest in time. Perhaps they *are* time. I am not insensible
to the sounds water makes flowing. Or not flowing.
Tune thy instrument, o Captor. This is the present.
I decline in it like a verb from some unknown tongue.
I knelt at the octagonal well-cap—no. Nothing
like that, not here. In this place of coming & becoming.
What did the life say to the light, runs a joke.
My blood, also running, as if in jest. I admired it
at the blurred edges. I am not unhappy, or not rigorously
so. I retain my privacies. The trees here, strange to me,
extruded. A man measures himself against such divers
entities. It is early (for me). Low musky trill of some
fledged form. As if ancient, as if an intelligence placed
its thumb just there, in morning mist. I, too, am broken
into majesties: rage; blood; lead. Cold-flow
of the soundscape around me, what chain have I forged,
this terrible vagrancy. I score it for judgment,
among the arteries my mouth has known. A new breeze
dries the sweat against my cheek, I lift my hand to it
(breeze; sweat; cheek) as if casting myself in some play.

I swing back the great bronze gate. *Tarry*, what is it,
what can it be *made* of. For surely it is constructed,
like a house, amidst this oxygen. We can step
inside & out again, tourists. Or, we can dwell. That verb,
to dwell—it hangs from the line, it flaps in the breeze,
it is not a cage because look, the cage is right here.
You may view it through polarized glass. You
may touch it (if you believe in the grammar of matter).
Make the scar tremble, yes, that's it. A small seed blows
or falls into the crook of the book, armored. Some feasts
are very small, we walk right past them, as if the moon
weren't real in daytime. It is real. In the day.
There, behind where the cage last stood, & rising.
Waters respond to it, we know this. I have been deceived
but not by matter, never. Not by the hands of princesses
or kings. I washed myself & laced myself into
a thought, a stance. Betook myself to an ancient place.
Refused memory, aside from language (itself a trace).
And now the miniature appeals, each from its petitioner.
It is too early for wonder but not too early for prayer.
—There. As cage this prayer. Touch it or else don't,
the day says, avid & prinked. There's no new distance
here. I rub my thought against it, as against the cries
from the forest which is, I am told, new in the scheme
of all things, that is, of men. A locust leaf lodges
in my beard. I was much smaller than this, I suspect,
when I had cancer, when I gnawed the red latch.
White white white of the non-sky with a moon
superimposed. These waters, unlocking for it. Both
those in my body & those at my side, those that still
bear within them the hair & spoor of the strangers' dogs,
splashing freely in the moment just before my arrival.

Canto Selah

for & after Karen An-hwei Lee

There is no identical
sculpture
of silence, night's plane
edge pressed against
the upper
lip. You dress yourself
deep in the loss

of the moment, aspiring
to smelt
a cage from a star.
The grass is praying
in the capital
of grasses, which is lit
at both ends
like a city on fire.
It does not know tides.
It buries its face
in the shadow
of justice's flat well.
I warm my hands there
even
when the mirror
repeats its only curse,
which is
Son. Son. Son. Son.

(Fountains Abbey, Pentecost)

Let's be quick to claim. Gnaw gnaw like an orchard
in the grip of an August thirst. What knowledge
took us this far, towards the intromission of tenancy.
It clings to me like a crown. A legible devotion,
the angles that bring into focus all our truest blames.
You may run your hand over them if you like.
Consider the lips of animals as one more check
signed by God, one more IOU. I present their wars
to the assembly which falls silent for a brief period
because we have so many wars, why not feast.
Early fruit of the season split and roasting on a fire
the world obscures with its ragged hem.
Strong muscles of the throat meant for wings
goes one argument, not necessarily mine but how
the scars constrict when paraphrased, by oil or wine.
This all takes some time as I'm sure you know.
I place my rage in my bag. It is not what you think.
Writing on the nature of friendship Aelred
fell deep into the archaic crush of prescriptive
fear. Of course he was drawing from nature,
what else is there to draw from, mixed pigments
sweating in their wooden bowls. Soon it will be
possible to take the life of a man you've never

seen, a form of taxidermy that relies upon the soul
as its armature, then clothes it. As with gratitude.
Glass eyes where the actual eyes had been.
It's hard to remember isn't it glass as something
new, glass as one substitute for the natural tendency
to shine a bright light, or turn away. Be sure
to record all the shadows cast by the feast, that is,
by the assembly when it settles into the posture
of appetite. Sketch every one. In the meantime
practice the management of water, as of fire.
The difference is, one can fall into water
(though of course one can also fall into fire).
Ropes tied around the perimeter to prevent any
such accident. But they are flammable too in turn.
And soluble, should they remain submerged.
I'm talking about ropes *then*. Ropes now
are made from synthetics that will last forever.
Watch for them in paintings by the Renaissance
masters, Bartolomé Bermejo perhaps, how
he manages to burn without painting actual fire
which is also something ropes can do
when they run too fast through your hands.
Or paintings of ropes through paintings of hands,
little physics experiments. It had been Lent
but that was some time ago, a spurned archive.
Little moan, disavow thirst's hollow fingers,
a foaming thread. And I said *lustral unmeasured*
skeins, or so the chronicle insists. It is possible.
I do not recall the moment clearly. It is alleged
the Victorian children's author Anne Jane Cupples
once corresponded with Darwin about a possible
position for her husband, and later Darwin
"corresponded with her about her observations
of emotions in dogs." This seems a fair trade.
There are so many more forms knowledge can take
than fire, a problem photosynthesis tries to solve.
We watch it submerging the orchard.
We watch it strip thorns from the raspberry canes.
Not like in the story where the dead man
remains dead, not like that at all. Although
that is a story each of us knows by heart, indeed
carries with us in each heart. That little parable
of where the blood flowed and where we caught it
in our various receptacles of glass, stone, wood.
This is text, it could just as well have been blade

flying through theories of parthenogenesis.
I will now stoop to sweep up the dead flies
that have collected in the forecourt. Nothing else.

On Entelechy (Montacute House)

I sit outside the great house & look straight
through the halls of it, to the other side. I am not,
evidently, meant to record this. The gale
passed in the night, it is blowing itself out now,
a great thrust. The rooks hang still in the air,
against it: form against form. Nine figures
in their niches in the second storey
whose identities I can't discern, & whom
I can't photograph. The niches, a separation
among separations. I walk right up to the lowest
niche (empty, at ground level) & place
my breath in it, leave it there. For the wind's
rope to hoist, I'm guessing. In this place
of guesses. Calendared, though the bleating
lambs do not heed it, nor the bees sunk
in their low hives. Earlier I had stricken the word
Jerusalem from a poem (another, different poem).
This is all one answer to the question,
What can we do with stone? (Subtended by:
What can we do with glass? Which is also
a form of stone.) It is not, evidently,
a pyre burning. It is not a hostel for bells.
Of all my transgressions, this is the most recent.
Lean into it, my friend advises. (I tell him,
I lean into every apocalypse, this may
be my only virtue. —Then lean away from it,
my friend emends.) The ranks of windows,
transparent stone, empty staves. Music
waits indefinitely on our infirmities. Be seated,
encourages the analogue, & so I am. I have paid
for this privilege. For this participation
in the dance of privilege. The great house settling
into an idea of itself, which time lends it.
There's no denying I covet this idea,
if not the house, if not the name. I sit before it,
as if in conference with it. It wants to tell me
a story, but it doesn't know where to begin,
so it remains silent. I feel similarly.

Perhaps the gardeners will come soon & relieve
us of our burdens. They are quite remarkable,
are they not, gardeners? With their one story,
which they step inside. I & my one story,
which is Christ. It means nothing here, & yet
its is-ness persists. The guesses, they circulate
among us, vectors in some vast blood.
I age, infinitesimally, as I consider this.
Time's convalescence within time,
which it performs by way of beings, structures,
representations, & things. The great rope
of the wind tied securely around my waist:
it replays the fault. Such wide courtesy,
bestowed by matter upon matter. Proofs I could
never fathom, geometric, trigonometric—
glints from the dire wheel. Now I raise myself
to the common signature. See, its scrawl
across the surface of the image. The greater
wealth of forbearance (within a marriage,
for instance). Any story, really—might do.
A war. A resurrection. A folk etymology. What
in innocence we then called the marriage plot.
Once, before I was alive, a man (or a woman)
fell ill here, recovered or else did not recover.
Light striking through the windows at his
or her body. We await—pretty much anything.
(The here-ness of its is-ness.) I possess
absurdly little, but it is still too much.
Parallax song of the western wind, unmasked,
you pass between, a fresh flow lengthening.
These nine figures, they can't be saints:
the house is Elizabethan. Costumed virtues
then, or else historical figures. I tell the rooks,
Plato will not save you. Relate *scion*
to *sever*, the proctor instructs. Peace be
to the proctor & to his echelon. (Be seated.)
I am bathing in the rope of the wind, in these
manacles of light. I am a body, a named thing,
facing a larger body, also a named thing.
What is broken here is the human
narrative. The recording gesture, arrested.
Lord, forgive us our names, our namelessnesses.
Is it not, is it not, is it not hiss the hives.
The life that gutters inside them, royal.
& yet we are not meant, evidently, to touch it.

Jorrell Watkins

When a Tree Falls

When a tree falls in Richmond a cloud is swept down
forming puddles and fog dense enough to be entombed.

Most of our city hears it, even if a rock concert of cicadas crash
their tymbals turned cymbals for a clamorous end.

When a tree falls in Richmond ½ of our city's grandma's
dust off kerosene lamps, a ¼ of mamas light
Family Dollar candles, while all the young folks jar
fireflies in their camera phone's eye.

Somebody hand me a lighter
for when a tree falls in Richmond it's the first time
that tree is shown in the news, our mayor gives a speech
he ain't prepared to speak—

Somebody's child goes missing.
Their school desk is packed with art projects,
math take-home tests tell me
who would dare to clear its contents?

A tree falls in Richmond, you realize that all of this
once was forest; if you knew the difference between:

Dogwood, Sugar Maple, Black Gum, Sourwood,
Yellow Poplar, River Birch, Virginia Pine,
Pignut Hickory and Post Oak trees, wouldn't
you remember their names?

Ah Bae: Blues Haibun

I don't wanna tell a story, especially one that has already been told practically worn out from the different mouths it was summoned from then bellowed. I don't wanna tell a story...came here looking for something. I don't know what it looks like, a partner of mine might say, "it is, what you ain't." I don't wanna sell a story. No good at keeping promises. Good at wandering on other's premises—oh, is this your home? My bad, wrong floor. Sure glad there ain't a shotgun propped against the wall.

alcove window fog reading the walk: lighthouse glint

Look different today that I do. Left the market brand funking new. Right away picked up a "check you out!" Did a turn-around in the middle of the boulevard. Look different today that I do! Crisscross Stacy Adams on the curb stop, tootsie roll my thighs, knee high socks showing, slacks cuffs climbing, I'm spooking out the corner of their guise. Look different today that I don't, against the wall, or on the ground.

freezing rain: asphalt still, as-fault against black ice

Hush...ah bae think a train's coming. It's running electric. That gotta be fast that gotta be that gottagotta—you know, our pulse is electric? Ain't talking about no static there's a dynamic circuit in us bae. If you take this hand my rails and your rails could make station out of prairie. Hush...ah bae think a train's coming. Got your ticket? Got your wallet? Got your—what you mean you ain't going. Why you running so fast? That ottaotta other day you know you pause...ain't talking about no stagger, there were surges in us bae. You took this hand my ails and your ails, mistakes and all prayers we whispered. Us...all day...us all—bae. Think a train's coming...gonna go lay my head. Against the wall, or on the ground. Right where you can see it.

soft cold mist close the curtain: drenched skull and nape

L. A. Weeks

Blackberries Pantoum

Silent, a few yards apart, we picked blackberries
in the wild place Dad didn't know about.
He knew this much: Men could do us harm.
Some pervert might follow our broken twigs

to wild places we shouldn't know about.
If Dad found out, icebox silence for a week.
Some pervert could have followed broken twigs
to our bare shoulders and sun-warmed berries.

We found out about ice-cold glares and silence
if we cut through the woods on the way home from school,
bared our shoulders, stained our lips with berries.
We were told bedroom doors can be removed,

that police found a schoolgirl cut up in the woods.
Frontal lobotomy, clitoridectomy—
how the wild parts of girls can be removed.
We read the news over muesli and coffee.

Frontal lobotomy, clitoridectomy—
men can do harm, kill their daughters for honor.
We read the news over muesli and coffee,
in silence. Worlds apart, girls picking blackberries.

Night Lines

What do I know of the intimate geography of the night?
—*Pablo Neruda*

All night, the slug lays down its restless lines. What do I know, but a fugue of pleasures and failures that evaporate, come morning? What do I know, but trouble left glistening? All night, the fox furrows a dream of seed and decay: Neighbor's child sent off with promise, the junkie's overpass home, the nail-bit, scab-picked, razor-writ lines that started box of Ivory Snow. In darkness, how can anyone know the why of that line's trajectory? We all know the night's business turns out rabbits without guarantee, and I know my mother's peignoir, folded blush in the attic. I still see her on her knees, praying for the next act of kindness doled out by iron. I shared her knowledge of iron—all night, pacing, jangling change in pockets. Does a joke redeem a week of silence? All I know is the fox is the end of the line for the rabbit. All night, my father lifts me to the sky—my first word, moon, called out so many times, it waxes cliché, even more distant. What good neighbor could know that line would end rusted, murmuring names of the dead and faraway, the moon too worn out to answer?

Brian Phillip Whalen

How Will I Address Him When He's Dead

I call my father during halftime when the Irish are on TV. [Family history: my father called his father from a rotary phone screwed to the wall.] It's good to hear my father's voice, to have cellular access to familiar sounds—his admonishments, his praise and anger. [Memory of bedtime songs he'd sing to me on his guitar: I sing them to my daughter now—Phil Ochs's "When I'm Gone" and Kenny Loggins's "Danny's Song."] My grandfather, who lived in Indiana, named my father James. I rarely think about it, his having a name. My father. *James.*

Dead Sister [Stories]

I'm sitting at my kitchen table in a six hundred dollar ergonomic desk chair drinking store-brand cola in a tee shirt I've been wearing since last week. I'm writing poems about my sister. In Kunderean fashion [the non-sexy kind], my body has betrayed me. Which is why the expensive chair [herniated discs will cost you]; the cola [these days coffee gives me heartburn]; the *generic* brand because my chair cost more than I make in a month [adjunct teaching]; and the dirty shirt because I watch my infant daughter all day long [I teach at night]. As for writing poems—my sister is dead. I should have written her letters instead, before she was dead, but life went on, and when she died, we hadn't written or talked in years. [A white lie: we emailed a handful of times, but nothing soulful, nothing to carry to the grave, which is why I behave this way at three AM, sitting in the dark of a rental house I hope my daughter will never call home. When I land a full-time job, one fine day, we'll move.] My sister never moved away from Richmond, Virginia. Where her boyfriend Zeb died; where her dealers and churches and service-workers were; her home the way I've never had a home, not really—a place you never quit on, a location fit for dying. [My sister had dreams before she had drugs. "I've got stories," she said to me once. "Together we could make a million dollars."]

Stephen Scott Whitaker

Privacy in a Small Town

Ask someone who lives in a small town
to swallow a Ferris wheel and they will
turn over secrets to a happy life.
Privacy? Perhaps summer, winter,
when windows are clapped shut, otherwise
Desires and fears cry out in the air
that flows and waves seaside to bayside
and channels in between. "This is why!
This is why!" parents calliope,
coming down on a son everyone
knows cheats at school and life. His grandfather
shrunk his partner's aces. Why should he
be any different? The old man
who wears blouses, his gray chest hair flowers
over lace and through gold ropes. Who loves
who and how? It is so and so and so
in the carnival open windows make
of crowned streets. Ballygirls with new coats,
mirror-bound strongmen practicing boasts,
blondes vanishing through grandstand windows,
a sour mashed pitchman for late night
money. A rabbit ringer along hedgerows.
Iron jaw work in America's backyard,
we watch, we see we are terrible neighbors.

Children Love the Dumps

Town children adore the dumps, the spent
and unspent and thrown away, the rusty hulks
dragged to the edge of a cleared field to flake.
Sea of milk white chemical, the calcium inland sea
amid a heap of red earth, like Mars come to plain.
Salt gravel, a fine pelting shift that sounds like rain
when a dumb animal stumbles beyond the lea
to the poison face that once was a lake till algae
bloomed over and raced around the banks.
The slate company down-county abandoned
their phosphorus, left rusting 100 gallon tanks
to the lake to leak. With the dead earth running into the slough
with every soaking rain, it might as well be Dante's hell
for the thirsty, for those who turned against water
in this life and the next. Now children come to throw stones
and watch the water turn pale green in summer, and listen
for the intonation of beasts that drag and die
on the mud around them. A squirrel, a wet black bird
whose wing broke left, a rat who drowned
in the poison lake on a dog's curse. A pale white body
that might be a possum, swollen and rotted away.
Children require a place to study the worst of us
the dead, the wires, the spills, the broken bikes,
the bent rebar veins from some concrete slab,
the broken, the dumped, the left and the forgotten,
in the middle of the green nowhere that used to be a lake.

Beth Oast Williams

Whelks Are Most Often Mistaken for Conchs

I'm walking in circles, opening
doors and cabinet drawers,
pulling too hard on the fridge.
You know what it's like
to binge at night. I float
with my eyes closed
trying to hear how near
the breaking wave.
Half the time it hits you
hard in the face, the other
times you ride the swell
and keep your hair
from getting wet. Some nights
aren't as certain as the ocean,
feelings come out of the blue.
I'm pulled under
by something not quite water,
the end of day never a time
to swim. Windows gasp
in film as dark as Atlantic
tide, my breath catches.
Legs kick, but this late,
there is no surfacing,
no freezer air worth a deep
inhale. Concentric circles
confuse those who hold me.
Somewhere the sea recedes.

These Stars, Now Your Mother's Eyes

The baby wears a porcelain
face, stitches on her hands.
I put her in a basket by the river

and scream before letting go.
I call this a haunting, the repeated
theme of an unwanted dream,

what turns my head at unthinkable
things. I waste most days sucking
excess pressure from my brain, fear

broken bones, heels caught
in cracks, and never seeing you again.
Giving thanks is for those who sleep

through the night, those who wake
among the living. The sun
tries to blind me, bad news bores

a hole through my heart. I blink
too long, look behind me,
and you're gone. I wish

I could tell you the stars are just stars,
and not your mother singing.

Abby Wolpert

Roadside Memorial

I never took that route to school,
so I don't know why I did that day.

There was a screech and at first,
and I could not tell if it was her,

or the man on the sidewalk,
or the tires on the bus.

I have not slept in months,
I wake by the hour hot and wet.

Sand

After the artist Teresa Ries

I am afraid
of not being an artist
of rising one morning a wife,
but a wife only,
my hair growing white
not from plaster residue
but the lack thereof,
of grays sprouting
like weeds, like men.
When I have a husband
I will have no rasp,
nor block of marble in sight.
Instead, I will be stone,
stand stone-faced
while he chisels me.
He will begin with my head,
carve sweetly, the delicate
ebb of my cupid's bow,

but forget a sliver between
my lips for my voice
to hum through.
He will clothe me, not
in my cerulean-collared
craftsman's frock,
but into a blouse like that
of a pigeon's breast,
cinch my gut
with a sash that severs
my ribs like clay wire.
When he arrives
at the bottom of the hourglass
which he has created,
he will turn me over.
But I will quickly pull
tight the laces of my corset,
before my head fills
woefully, woefully
with sand.

Karenne Wood

Jamestown Revisited

after Wendy Rose

(upon being asked to attend a gathering at the site of the Jamestown Colony,
where church people intended to apologize to Virginia Indians for everything
since 1607)

Here you come again,
asking. Do you see
we have nothing
to give, we have given
like the ground, our
mountains rubbed bare
by hybrid black poisons
concocted from tobacco.

>You would spread us on your
>platform like graven images.
>You could repent to us,
>weep into your robes an
>emotional, talk-show-like
>moment to absolve almost
>four hundred years, then
>go home to mow your lawn.

You are not the ones
who burned our cornfields,
passed infected blankets,
treatied, pilfered, raped, or
traded rum. You are not
those who ask how can I help,
offer Indians your jobs,
or even vote to save the earth.

>We are not the ones
>whose children froze in rivers,
>whose mothers wore bullets,
>whose fathers left hearts

on this ground. We are not
those about whom was said,
They haven't the rights of dogs.

We are words of tongues
no one dared speak. We are
nameless, named by others:
mulattos and *mongrel*
Virginians. We are white flints
and chips of bone, pottery
sunk in red clay, black glass

        like spearpoints found here,
        of obsidian mined among tribes
        who lived a thousand miles
        west. We are refrains of our
        grandparents' songs that drift on
        night winds with our dreams.

You call us *remnants* now:
what remains of a fabric
when most of it is gone.
You have no memory—
we sank to our scarred
knees and said there was
nothing else to give.

        You ask again, *Will we*
        come to your apology?
        A southeastern wind
        answers you. Our ears
        are not visible. Lips are not
        visible...
            0, we are the bones
        of what you forget, of what
        you thought were just lies...

Only our eyes look around.
Earth-toned eyes, forest
eyes, thunderhead eyes,
eyes flecked with gold, eyes
like obsidian, eyes that are
seeing right past you.

The Naming

Some nights we feel the furred darkness
of an ancient one's breath and are trapped
in awakening, dismembered
by events we no longer recall.
We can touch the windowsill,
where October air gathers
as hours slip past in thin robes,
the forest a concert of voices.
The last crickets let go of their songs.

The land speaks, its language arising
from its own geography—
the mountains' hulked shapes
are blue whales, remembering
when they were undersea ridges,
and rivers are serpentine strands
hammered from silver, and dark trees
talk to the wind—weaving mortal lives,
drumbeats, pillars of smoke,
voices wavering into updraft,
the storyteller shifting the present.

Diana Woodcock

Sudden Grace

A crow caws from the deck
just now, glisteningly wet
from morning rain.

I promised I wouldn't complain
when my luck ran out. But I
tell him just the same how I long
to get my charmed life back, no
breathtaking view to wake up to
these mornings in Richmond,

no rising sun singeing the edge
of the Himalayas, no South China
Sea leashed by mist to the sky,
no sound of the erhu drifting
from my neighbor's bamboo grove.

Only days ago, the dogwoods lifted
up on each blossom's cupped sail;
now Virginia's state flowers lie
scattered over the rain-soaked trail.

Lost in thought, I miss my turn-off,
circle again through the woods
along the lake. Which is why
I see her: lone doe grazing in the glade.

I've never met her there before—
            a sudden grace,
                        like the crow's caw.

Annie Woodford

Contemplating the Female in a Country Dangerous for Women

July is an ursine of stars,
a bonfire burning in a field.
July is pheromone and hay,
a heifer and her calf dappled

by laurel shade she watches
from unseen. July is a quartet
of girls just out of childhood
and born poor. Say one was born

on the seventh day
of the seventh month
in the seventh year of a new
century and today eats cake

by a manmade lake and then
somersaults slowly in water
warmed by warm Virginia hills,
her friends flowing around her.

They lift their dripping feet
and study their soles
stained orange by mud
and dive out instead of down,

just in case the water-level
has changed. July is ferrous
and full dam. It's a deaf old dog
sleeping in the road at dusk,

asphalt heat sweet on her bones.
It's ditch lilies licking flame
by the road bank and the way
I'll get lost on the way home

tonight, prophets of apocalypse
selling gold on the radio.
The fields are in flower,

all the spring babies half-

grown and where are you,
my Lord, who used to walk
barefoot over the earth, calling
all the lambs out of slaughter?

A *Flower is a Field (Poised Like Souls, Remembering)*

after Proust

My first memory of desiring
    a flower is a field
of Queen Anne's Lace
       above your ranch house.

    At the center
of the flowerhead's sequence
    was a black flower
I thought an insect.

    Heighten the whiteness.
Heighten the depths
of the dark tangled grass
    they sprang from,

umbels weedy and common,
    refuge for chiggers and ticks.
But you picked armfuls—wild
    and white, too heavy

    for their own thin stems, the froth
of their leaves dusted
    by yellow clay—and kept
them swaying on your kitchen table.

    They are half-memory, a field
of perfect tatted circles to wade,
swaying in our wake, bowed down
    by blossom weight.

    They are a type of carrot,
    useful root hidden

in dirt—the bloom
a signal, a sign, a sigh

in old cow fields still marked
by barbed wire, you
    moving through
       their wide lenses like light.

Amy Woolard

A Place Where There Isn't Any Trouble

Girl walks into a house & comes out running. Girl runs down

A neighborhood street & a pickup rolls up beside her. Storm's

Coming. Aunt says Girl you know there're monsters out there

& you never know. Aunt says Sugar this storm'll run roughshod

Over the dirt you call childhood, farm & storm spread so wide they

Each get a name. Whiskey rolls down her throat & lights the farm

On fire. Aunt says Girl, there're monsters in this world you'll call

Friends in the next, storms that'll write your name in the sky,

Clouds that roll up & announce you like a choir. A fire don't

Chase but it catches. The bells of the neighborhood church keep

Pealing on without you & do not call you home. Around here,

Ugly ain't a name for the way somebody looks, but how she talks or

Talks back. *Rotten* isn't just for apples; it's for how she acts. Girl walks

Into the woods & comes out a monster. Storm kicks up beside her.

Mongrel paces just behind her footfall. There're farms in this world,

But Girl & Mongrel are headed to the next. Around here, strip

Where a field meets the woods is called *the Invitation*. Stray piece

Of straw on her skirt like an unlit match. Stray light splintering

Through the branches like tangled hair. Oh & she is lit

With whiskey now. Now a fugue settles over the trees.

Now a path undresses itself in front of her, fingers her

Forward. On the other side of an invitation, somebody's always

Cooking up something. Trouble is a dish. A prayer: *Fill my plate*

With sugared apples. Fill my heart with discipline. Mongrel cases

Any new body might stand in her way. If you can't beat them,

Join them, the farm calls. If you can't join them, let them

Walk you to your truck but when it's time to go, it's time to go,

The bells peal. Girl peels off her Sunday skirt like a bell gone

Soft. An invitation is just another line to be crossed, after all,

All of it rinsed with a light, salted. Girl leaves the farm lit

Behind her, but takes the path with her when she goes,

Wherever she goes, pretty as you please. Full of sugared

Breath to waste on the crook of the next one's neck. The dirt

I could dish, thinks Mongrel, *I'm the one she'll miss the most.*

Well, shoot. Somebody got to be the one who stands burning

On the porch, waves Aunt, & somebody got to be the one to get lost.

Place Like Home

I was asked to show up with a side-dish. I made
A slaw of my longing. I had to keep it crisp. Nothing goes

Bad in a backyard, if you catch my drift. In a
Backyard everything is available like a catalog

World, viz.: I carried a plastic basket of fluffed
Clean clothes propped on one hip as if

A small, outdoor-fresh child. Time it takes
To smoke a 100, I'll've forgotten the second

Of three friends gone. Dry skin sky. Heartless jolt
Of a lawnmower kicking forward into gear. Wind

Punch at a pinned-up line of blue bedsheets so to
tell us about What's Coming. Porch chimes aren't

As dumb as you think they are. Oh bright laundry:
I like it when my stomach feels starved

For home. Hands trolling the dirty
Dishwater for lost forks. Facts:

Straw is to heartless body as *I lied when I said I hope*
I'll see you all again is to *Come home.* I like a lot of you

Most of the time, but I got my favorites. Don't matter
Which bricked world I thought I was living in,

The dog had his name, at least. The scarecrow was only
Ever called *Scarecrow.* Wind swing a backyard gate

Left open so to tell us about What's Gone.
Heart is to lost laundry as—Q: What if

I don't need to borrow any more boys'
T-shirts for bed. What if I'm already stuffed—

Those were the days, though, I tell you what! The way
I made a sky-blue gingham of my teenage years...

Before sleep, I like to think about all those snaking roads, &
The band geeks not wearing their seatbelts, & the prom-

Fluffed girls like sugar roses on grocery
Store sheet cakes, floating up the ladders

Of small-town watertowers to graffiti
Their triumphant 1989, sloppy in the flashlight

Moon. Oh sugar roses, I didn't even want to say that
Part about the moon, but we're all going down together.

When I didn't know what to make, I made
Breakfast. Chimes are to *sorry* as the second-hand

Smell of gasoline is to a twelve-year-old
Saturday morning. I want

To buy all the trucks parked for sale
In all the front yards in Virginia.

Neck of the Woods

Filthy as 12-bar, filthy as a stuttering key in the hazy
Doorlock at 4 a.m. Filthy as *I don't know what it means to love*

311

You. Out in the country there's no fence to speak of—there's just
The blonde path, wide enough for a truck, a truck wide enough

For two bodies to ride restlessly beside one another without
Ever touching. There's no fence to speak of, just various dusks &

I'm in love with the dust that kicks up—I'm in love with what
A dirt road does to a truck. There's no *edge of the woods*—there's just

The blonde path stretching out of the dark-green like a
Leg bone, a radio dial catching a hit of station before

Moving on past into the static. Two girls ride ruthlessly
Beside one another—one filthy as a story, the other filthy

As a storyteller. One girl might leave a trail of crumbs
Behind her. One might leave a line of poured-out gasoline.

Old evening air the way warm soda tastes like a hangover,
A long drive in July. *I got plenty of time. You got light in your eyes.*

It's all the middle of nowhere. When the music stops, everybody
Scatters, even the light—an embarrassment of a sunset, really, &

Why even talk about the stars as if we still care about them
In the off-hours, when we're not confessing to the dead?

These girls *wore* each other, is what I mean. Passed out in
Each other's shoes, passed the ends of sentences from one to

The other like taking belts of whiskey out the bottle. One
Night one girl waves goodbye to the other & the empty fifth

She leaves in my hand is where the story turns dark, is where
I stick myself against the story flush as a wheat-paste poster,

Contact-printing my body back onto itself, a decade delayed. Love,
This is where the joke begins: one girl's gotten gone. Her brother

Walks into a bar to deliver the punch line, & the other girl doubles
Over—*An inside job.* See, you got to be able to fall, for there to be

An edge—see the bar in waves, the doubled stars in waves, all just
Frosting on a cold cake. Both girls breathless in their own bodies now.

Now, it's a ruthless thing, to know what's about to happen to
Someone who does not know what's about to happen. One girl might

See years go by in waves of roadside signs, a trail of vein rise up
On the back of her hand before it begins to wind down the twin

Bones of her forearm. Two girls trailed each other, delivered one
Another from one year to the next, twinned until they wound down

To just one night. One girl might leave a line of salt in the dirt,
One a flush of dust, sifted into a river. What is there left to leave

When there's no body to speak of? This is where the storyteller
Begins: I am trying to know what it means to love anyone

Else the way I meant to love her, the way a sweet tooth
Loves salt. Sugar, I used to know this place like the back

Of my papery hand. Now there's just the blonde past,
A river oversaturated with roses & ash, a back way

Home, a way back to what there ever is to leave behind.
I am trying. The smell of fresh pine, the small task of rain

On a windshield, a drift like the bow of a single fiddle
Drawing itself across my collarbone, my lungs sinking & rising

Slow like sloppy keys in a deep octave, my heart resting dark
Like a gun in a glovebox whenever I might need to lean for it.

I've paid some hush-money to the unpaved path, the paved-
Over past, plucked up the door lock & parked two loose cigarettes

In the useless tapedeck, then that small piece of quiet—after the click
Of the ignition but before the radio cuts on, the quarterglass

Coaxing in the scalene country air, yellowing its passengerless slant
Over half the truck's bench seat, the angles catching nobody, missing it all

—What any girl with half a mind wanders out this way for, to take
As much of it in over & over & sure enough breathe it all the way out.

Wage

One by one as they burned out we
Triaged the lightbulbs to priority slots

Around the house. The bedroom still
Held a candle for us. The walls stayed

Rented white. I can take almost
Anything at this point. The waking

Wince of morning, which is afternoon, which
Is like someone holding tightly your hand

While you're wearing a ring. The kitchen litigates
Our unreturned dishes. The birds have not yet

Learned to mimic our phones, but coolly master
Car alarms & the dog's longing. Baby, paradise

Will be a house without linoleum floors, edges
Puckered up like an open carton of milk,

Its origami lip. All I need to know is
The time of day & the names of

The regulars. Not their names, but what
They drank: *old fashioned, car bomb, purple rain, dirty*

Skyy. Showing up is a full-time job where the
Paycheck is a paper ghost tendering the wrong

Kind of zeroes. It was the year of the drought.
Our stacked cash never laid flat. We pulled

One bright twenty & kept it rolled like
A rumor. A season fleshed out by what fell:

Ice into a glass, a dress onto a floor, a girl
Into a grind. Once, a boy off a fourth-story roof.

What you get is to be changed. Nothing
From the sky for weeks & then—; I poured

Everyone & myself a drink. All of us were taken
With leaving town. By which I mean:

We were taken with not leaving. The town took
As fact we'd be back. It'd all be here waiting

To step into, like a dress, or a downpour: the house,
The glass, the time of day. Even the boy, come

Back as a bird, thin beak tilting at every
Wind-felled scrap: *what-was-That, what-was-That.*

The night downtown blacked out, we walked
Out of the bars, unbanked, as if it were the first

Snow, arms raised to catch—what—on our skin. I felt it
Melt into me anyway. I've trained my wrists to carry more

Than I can carry. A malfunction of lightning bugs, the tight
Fists of peonies demanding their rights, the delinquent

Quiet, the lip-bitten memory of when we first learned
To lie, brick by brick. What was the time. That hour

Slipping itself up under my shirt. I can take anything.
Our currency is we stood outside of everyone else.

I open all the windows & doors because I do, in fact,
Want to air condition the whole neighborhood. I want

To bring it all down a dozen degrees until even the churches
Of our enfolded hands are cooled & congregationless & still

Possible. My sleep put each next day on layaway until
The once-too-many: I came back & you did not.

How could I even touch it. Your love like
An orange wedge breaking apart in my mouth.

The sky touches the birds & the birds keep
Their distance, faking thirst & emergency. How

It's no stretch for us to see how anybody—in the right
Light—surely will confess to something they didn't do.

Amy Wright

Full Snow Moon

Last season's tomato vines
         by the red barn, a dun knot

you carry to low ground—
                  crunch underfoot.

                  As almanacs predicted,
         this morning after the Full Snow Moon

                           waxed full,
                  fog clotted the Blue Ridge,

                           a prophecy of attention
            to patterns recurrent as mourning

dove's coo intervals. Given time and
         actinomycetes, dead roots will mulch,

                  though not redress
      topsoil stripped by erosion, tires, gas lines.

                           Startled doves resettle.
                           Each stamp threatens

            to breach the thatch,
                  meet a muscle of earth

you can pulp red-juiced and salted,
                  candied into sauce.

Dry stems crack
         open a body

                           of lost names the Tutelo
                           gave this land,

                  minosa moon,
         ērutāoñe warrior, *etā'hni* first,

the record lost for mountains, vines,

mourning, song.

From the pines, the doves resume
their four notes;

throats thickening before each
coo-OOoo-coo-coo

a tremolo of tissues
that clot the air

like clouds,
maqōsi.

Calf

Big as a Doberman,
dead,

black hoof to snout.

His dam nudged his jaw.   Vultures
dove
the waft.
She had not let them
at him or eaten,
to stand guard.

All night   and day
beneath a canopy of ice,

we left her to mourn.

A scarlet garland
swung from her
as she paced.

Not worth the risk, J worried
on the drive,   but I unchained the gate,
a recent escapee
escorted from the sward
where an incensed
Number Ninety-Eight
had hidden
her newborn.

317

Number Twenty was not ready

        to relinquish

     sentinel when R forced her back
     with the truck.   He circled the grove
       until she gave enough
       ground.
           He leapt out.

J stood by the wheel
      with a cane she brought.

        The calf's

              head
          lolled
     when R raised
      his chest.

The cow piqued and rankled
        with discontent.

     I helped lift the lithe body
        into the bed.

We drove out of sight,
        lay the calf in hay
    behind our house,

     to give his mother rest,
         if not peace.

       Let the buzzards,
    unseen, eat.

Where my brother—
     nineteen years gone—

picked blackberries with me as a kid,
        I knelt

   and washed my gloves

 against   each other
        with snow.

Reprise

> *They sold everything else. Only the farmers are left.*
> –Ajay Veer Singh

Locked down, Punjabi farmers burned
in the field sugarcane could not wait.

Food, once,
a public good.

A twenty-something lay on railroad tracks
beside his cotton acre. His father helped

torch Cargill's plant, thirty years prior,
rather than sow seed he could not save

indentured to a company says how.
Modi should fear God, a Sikh protestor said,

before his government silenced the press,
cut water to camps in a country owes

its independence to protest, fearing fallout
from the more than half the Indian population that farms.

Enough farmers to darken skies burning contracts,
like century-old throngs of passenger pigeons.

Enough farmers, they used to say,
to last.

*Have you ever heard of a politician
committing suicide?* Nirmal Singh asks,

as if telling a surrealist joke.
His father drank a bottle of pesticide.

The punchline is *Fish.*
Just not the kind you can eat.

319

Fieldhand

After six steers trampled my father, I moved
back to my hometown to help feed cattle he knew,
even in the hospital, meant no harm.
A neighbor, Mouse, unspooled bales
across each pasture, until he fell at work,
broke his rib. We weighed our options in the den.
At seventy-two, a shattered femur takes a year to heal.
Not the first time we went against medical advice,
but a farm cannot stop.
Dad pulled himself into the tractor cab, right leg
bearing his weight. I hovered, ready to grab his belt,
left his walker in the barn propped on cedar posts,
climbed beside him, took the training seat.
Winter light dropped sapphires in the grass.
Mom sliced silage wrap with a boxcutter, fingers up
to ask *How many?* It was almost a relief to let weather
dictate everything. At forty, the fermented bales dripped
green. Below thirty, their blue nets, veiled with ice,
scattered chips when we tugged them off.
Thawed, topsoil squandered, our tires gouged
gullies too deep for spring to seam. One morning,
Dad remembered his brother's
best friend from high school also died of suicide.
He reckoned with the implication, as years ago,
he considered the odds small the pistol
his brother used would succeed
in one shot. The chain pealed when I opened the gate.
To reassure me he would be alright
when the air seat bounced,
my father turned up the radio
and pretended to dance.

Cherokeea attakullakulla

Because we can
keep legends better than treaties, we name

Swain and Macon and Rabun County hill-cane
feeders after First Beloved Men, pin

forewings like hides
flown over lost battles,

commemorate ancients
who uniform the Southern Appalachians

and shirk light
with their own genus

to honor a people ripped
from ridges their wingtips mimic.

Now that they're dust, we dare
prick Attakullakulla's ears

cut with silver, banded
lobes almost to his shoulders,

bones scattered far from his estranged son
who knew better than negotiate with palefaces.

Past shame,
the lab floor laced with scales.

Charles Wright

from Sestets

"Well, Get Up, Rounder, Let a Working Man Lay Down"

The kingdom of minutiae,
                              that tight place where most of us live,
Is the kingdom of the saved,
Those who exist between the cracks,
                              those just under the details.

When the hand comes down, the wing-white hand,
We are the heads of hair
                              and finger bones yanked out of their shoes,
We are the Rapture's children.

The Light at the Root of All Things

Splendor surrounds us, as Kafka says,
                              invisible, and far away.
Will the right word reveal it?
Will the right name enter its ear and bring it forth like a sun?

He says you have to call, and not wait—
It's not hostile, it's not deaf.
I'd guess, if you got them right,
                              it's like, when it appears, just what's in front of you,

Something inveterate, something indestructible.

Celestial Waters

May 30th, early evening,
                              one duck on the narrow water, pond
Stocked with clouds,
The world reflected and windless, full of grace, tiny, tiny.

Osiris has shown us the way to cross the coming night sky,
The route, the currents, the necessary magic words.
Stick to your business, boys,
                              and forget the down-below.

The Song from the Other Side of the World

We haven't heard from the void lately.

Such *a wonderful spot,*
There's coffee and bananas and the temperature's hot.
So lush a voice, so lambent a tune.

Must be a bad frequency.
Our astral music, however, will come back, and harbor us
As we go gliding, lashed to the mast,

into its sensual waters.

Anniversary II

Dun-colored moth past the windowpane.

Now, he's got the right idea,
Fuzzy and herky-jerky,
little Manichaean
Pulled by invisible strings toward light wherever it is.

On the 5th of June, the mother is like a shining,
Blue raindrop the sunlight refracts

on the tip of the spruce tree,
Crack in the bulbous sky the moth is yo-yoed up to.

Outscape

There's no way to describe how the light splays

after the storm, under the clouds
Still piled like Armageddon
Back to the west, the northwest,

intent on incursion.

There's no way to picture it,

though others have often tried to.
Here in the mountains it's like a ricochet from a sea surge,
Meadowgrass moving like sea stalks

in the depths of its brilliance.

History Is a Burning Chariot

It is a good looking evening, stomped and chained.
The clouds sit like majesties in their blue chairs,
                                                                as though doing their nails.
The creek, tripartite and unreserved, sniddles along
Under its bald and blow-down bridges.
It is a grace to be a watcher on such a scene.
So balance me with these words—
Have I said them before, I have,
                                        have I said them the same way, I have
Will you say them again, who knows
                                        what darkness snips at our hearts.

I've done the full moon, I've done the half moon and the quarter moon.
I've even done the Patrick Spens moon
As seen by one of his drowned sailors.
Tonight is the full moon again, and I won't watch it.
These things have a starting place, and they have an ending.
Render the balance, Lord,
                                        send it back up to the beginning.

Lullaby

I've said what I had to say
As melodiously as it was given to me.

I've said what I had to say
As far down as I could go.
                                I've been everywhere

I've wanted to but Jerusalem,
Which doesn't exist, so I guess it's time to depart,

Time to go,
Time to meet those you've never met,
                                        time to say goodnight.

Grant us silence, grant us no reply,
Grant us shadows and their cohorts
                                        stealth across the sky.

324

"What Becomes of the Broken Hearted..."

Up where the narrow bodies lie, suffused in sundown,
The children of God are stretched out
                              under the mountain,
Halfway up which the holy city stands, lights darkened.
Above the city, the nimbus of nowhere nods and retracts.

How is it that everyone seems to want
                              either one or the other?
Down here the birds leap like little chipmunks out of the long grasses.
Wind piddles about, and "God knows" is the difficult answer.

The children of Heaven, snug in their tiny pockets,
Asleep, cold,
Under the Purgatorial hill.
Soon they'll awake and find their allotted track
                              up to the upside down.

Or not. The gravetree estuaries against the winds of Paradise.
Unutterable names are unpinned from its branches.
                              A couple
Float down to this pocket, and others float down to that pocket.
Star shadow settles upon them,
                              the star shine so far away.

"Things Have Ends and Beginnings"

Cloud mountains rise over mountain range.
Silence and quietness,
            sky bright as water, sky bright as lake water.
Grace is the instinct for knowing when to stop. And where.

THE POETS

APRIL J. ASBURY teaches writing and literature at Radford University in Virginia. She holds an MFA. from Spalding University and an MA from Hollins University, where she also worked as a visiting assistant professor. Her work has appeared in *Artemis, Still: The Journal, Floyd County Moonshine, The Anthology of Appalachian Writers,* and other publications. Her first poetry chapbook, *Woman with Crows,* was published by Finishing Line Press in 2021.

DARNELL ARNOULT is prize-winning author of *Galaxie Wagon: Poems* and *What Travels With Us: Poems* (LSU Press) and the novel *Sufficient Grace* (Free Press/Simon & Schuster, Inc.). Her shorter works have appeared in a variety of journals, including *Appalachian Heritage, Asheville Poetry Review, Nantahala Review, Now and Then, Sandhills Review, Southern Cultures, Southern Exposure,* and *Southwest Review.* She has received the Weatherford Award for Appalachian Literature, SIBA Poetry Book of the Year Award, Mary Frances Hobson Medal for Arts and Letters, and in 2007 was named Tennessee Writer of the Year by the Tennessee Writers Alliance.

EMMA AYLOR'S poems have appeared in *32 Poems, New Ohio Review, Pleiades, Colorado Review,* and the *Cincinnati Review,* among other journals, and she received *Shenandoah's* 2020 Graybeal-Gowen Prize for Virginia Poets. She grew up in Bedford County, Virginia, and lives in Lubbock, Texas.

ZEINA AZZAM is a Palestinian American poet, writer, editor, and community activist. She is the Poet Laureate of the City of Alexandria, Virginia, for 2022-25. Her chapbook, *Bayna Bayna, In-Between,* was published in 2021 by The Poetry Box. Azzam's poetry also appears in over forty literary journals, anthologies, and edited volumes. She earned MA degrees in Arabic literature (Georgetown University) and sociology (George Mason University) and a BA in psychology (Vassar College).

JEFF BAGATO produces poetry and prose as well as electronic music and glitch video. He has published nineteen books, all available in the usual online markets, including *And the Trillions* (poetry) and *Computing Angels* (fiction).

GEORGE BANDY'S publications include *War, Literature & the Arts* (USAF), *New Millennium Writings, Subprimal Art Poetry, The Baltimore Review, Blue Unicorn, The Saturday Evening Post,* and *The Dead Mule School of Southern Literature.* His poem "Return from War" won the Hart Crane Memorial Poetry Award and was published in *Icon.*

CHRISTINA BEASLEY is a writer, poetry editor for *Barrelhouse,* civil servant, and amateur cryptozoologist. Her work has appeared in *Copper Nickel, Hobart, Split Lip, Atlanta Review, The Pinch, The Southampton Review,* and elsewhere. She is pursuing her MFA with the Bennington Writing Seminars and lives in Falls Church, Virginia.

JOHN BERRY is a native Virginian living in the beautiful Shenandoah Valley. A self-taught woodworker and carpentry tradesman, he has been building 'things' since he was fifteen years old. John hosts a monthly spoken word event at The River House in Capon Bridge, West Virginia, where he is a regular volunteer and at-large member of the Board. His third book of poetry, *The Lawnmower Poems,* was released in 2019 by Foothills Publishing.

DAVID BLACK has published in more than 40 magazines and anthologies such as *Now & Then, Zone 3, Tar River Poetry, Hampden-Sydney Poetry Review, Appalachian Journal,* and *The Random House Treasury of Light Verse.* He is the former poetry editor of *English Journal* and author of four volumes of poetry.

Born in Roanoke, Virginia, TERRY HALL BODINE is a graduate of the College of William & Mary and the University of Mary Washington. Recent publication credits include *Common Ground Review, Lucky Jefferson, Heirlock,* and *The Raw Art Review.* Terry lives in Lynchburg with her husband, Bill, and works with student life at the University of Lynchburg.

TARA BRAY is the author of *Small Mothers of Fright* (LSU Press, 2015) and *Mistaken For Song* (Persea Books, 2009). Her recent poems have appeared in *Poetry, Crazyhorse, Agni, The Southern Review, Shenandoah, New England Review,* and *The Hudson Review* and have been featured by *Verse Daily, Poetry Daily,* and Ted

Kooser's *American Life in Poetry*. She grew up in Georgia, and now lives in Richmond, Virginia, where she teaches at Virginia Commonwealth University.

ROBERT BRICKHOUSE worked for many years as a reporter for Virginia newspapers and as a writer and editor for publications at the University of Virginia. His poems and stories have appeared in the *Virginia Quarterly Review*, *The Southern Poetry Review*, *Poet Lore*, *Pleiades*, *Hollins Critic*, *Chattahoochee Review*, *Louisiana Literature*, *Atlanta Review*, the *American Journal of Poetry*, and the *Texas Review*. He lives in Charlottesville, Virginia.

CANDACE BUTLER is a poet, songwriter, and graphic designer who lives in the Appalachian Mountains of southern Virginia. She holds an MFA in Creative Writing from Antioch University of Los Angeles. Butler is Editor-in-Chief of Wild Leek Press, an independent literary press, and an adjunct professor at Emory & Henry College and King University. She has two chapbooks of poetry, *Royal Crown* (Wild Leek Press, 2014) and *Nothing Is So Lovely* (Finishing Line Press, 2016), and her poems appear in print and online journals and anthologies.

BEN E. CAMPBELL'S Scottish ancestors were some of the first European settlers of Virginia's Appalachian mountains, having engaged the wilderness of Amherst County for multiple generations. Ben's poems, stories, and essays have appeared in more than forty literary venues, including *New Plains Review*, *Yemassee*, and *Floyd County Moonshine*. For the last thirteen years he has served as professor of English at New River Community College in Dublin, Virginia. He is the author of a chapbook of poems (*Darker Still*) and a collection of short stories (*A Welcome Walk into the Dark*).

JOHN CASTEEN is the author of *Free Union* (2009) and *For the Mountain Laurel* (2011), both from the University of Georgia Press's VQR Poetry Series. A third collection, *Rhythm and Blues*, was a 2019 finalist for the National Poetry Series. His poems have appeared in *Ploughshares*, *Fence*, *The Southern Review*, *The Paris Review*, *The Kenyon Review*, *VQR*, and other magazines, and in *Best American Poetry* and *The Rumpus Poetry Anthology*. He teaches at the University of Virginia.

MICHAEL CHITWOOD'S most recent book, *Search & Rescue*, received the L.E. Phillabaum Award from LSU Press and the 2019 Library of Virginia Literary Prize in Poetry.

KATHY DAVIS is a poet and nonfiction writer from the Richmond, Virginia area. Her poetry manuscript, *Passiflora*, was selected by Judge Lesley Wheeler as the winner of the 2019 Cider Press Review Book Award. She is also the author of the chapbook *Holding for the Farrier* (Finishing Line Press). Her work has appeared in *Alaska Quarterly Review*, *Barrow Street*, *Blackbird*, *Nashville Review*, *Oxford American*, *The Southern Review*, *storySouth* and other journals. Honors include a Weinstein Fellowship to the Virginia Center for the Creative Arts. Her MFA in creative writing is from Virginia Commonwealth University. She has been nominated for a Pushcart Prize and been a finalist for Best of the Net.

R. H. W. DILLARD is Editor of *The Hollins Critic* and author of *The Day I Stopped Dreaming About Barbara Steele and Other Poems*, *News of the Nile*, *After Borges*, *The Greeting: New & Selected Poems*, *The Book of Changes*, *Horror Films*, *The First Man on the Sun*, *Understanding George Garrett*, *Just Here*, *Just Now*, *Omniphobia*, *Sallies*, *What Is Owed the Dead*, and *Not Ideas: Philosophical Poems*. He is also the author of many stories, poems, essays, and literary translations. Professor Dillard has received both the O. B. Hardison and Hanes poetry prizes, is a member of the Fellowship of Southern Writers, and was named the 2007 winner of the Association of Writers George Garrett Award, given to an individual who has demonstrated exceptional generosity to writers.

RITA DOVE won the Pulitzer Prize for her third book of poetry, *Thomas and Beulah*, in 1987 and was U.S. Poet Laureate 1993-95. Her many honors include a 2017 NAACP Image Award (for *Collected Poems 1974-2004*), the Heinz Award in the Arts and Humanities, and the Academy of American Poets' Wallace Stevens Award. She is the Henry Hoyns Professor of Creative Writing at the University of Virginia.

MICHAEL DOWDY is a poet, critic, essayist, and editor. His books include a collection of poems, *Urbilly* (Main Street Rag Poetry Book Award, 2017); a study of Latinx poetry, *Broken Souths: Latina/o Poetic Responses to Neoliberalism and Globalization* (University of Arizona Press, 2013); and, as coeditor with Claudia Rankine, a critical anthology, *American Poets in the 21st Century: Poetics of Social Engagement* (Wesleyan University Press, 2018). Born and raised in Blacksburg, Virginia, he taught at Hunter College/CUNY for a decade before moving to the University of South Carolina, where he teaches poetry and Latinx literature.

HILDA DOWNER has worked as a nurse in a state psychiatric hospital outside of Roanoke for the past three years. She has an MFA from Vermont College and is retired from teaching English at Appalachian State University. She is the author of three books of poetry: *Bandana Creek, Sky Under the Roof,* and *When Light Waits for Us.* Her new book, *Wiley's Last Resort,* was released in July, 2022. Her work has been included in several anthologies.

ANGIE DRIBBEN'S poetry, essays, and reviews can be found or are forthcoming in *Deep South, San Pedro River Review, Crab Creek Review, Crack the Spine, New Southern Fugitive,* and others. Recently she joined *Cider Press Review* as Contributing Reviews Editor. *Everygirl,* a finalist for the 2020 Dogfish Head Prize, is out with Main Street Rag.

CLAUDIA EMERSON was born in Chatham, Virginia and is the author of eight books of poetry including *Late Wife* (LSUP, 2005) which was awarded the Pulitzer Prize. Emerson was Poet Laurate of Virginia from 2008-2010.

J. INDIGO ERIKSEN teaches writing at Northern Virginia Community College. Her creative work has appeared in *District Fray, The Northern Virginia Review, Scratching Against the Fabric, Endlessly Rocking,* and *TYCA-SE Journal.* Indigo is a dedicated whiskey drinker.

LATORIAL FAISON, a native of Courtland, Virginia of Southampton County, is the author of *Mother to Son, 28 Days of Poetry Celebrating Black History Volumes 1-3, Love Poems, I Am Woman, flesh, Secrets of My Soul, Immaculate Perceptions, 100 Poems You Can Write: a Journal for Poetry Lovers of All Ages,* and *Kendall's Golf Lesson.* Faison's poetry has been chosen as semi-finalist and finalist for the Gwendolyn Brooks Poetry Prize, the Wheeler Poetry Prize, and the North Street Book Prize. Faison, a Furious Flower Poetry fellow and recipient of the Tom Howard Poetry Prize, is a military spouse of over 26 years who has lived across the U.S. and abroad. She teaches on the faculty at Virginia State University and is a doctoral fellow.

FORREST GANDER was born in the Mojave Desert and grew up, for the most part, in Virginia. Trenchant periods of his life were spent in San Francisco, Dolores Hidalgo (Mexico), and Eureka Springs, Arkansas. With degrees in both geology and English literature, Gander is the author of numerous books of poetry, translation, fiction, and essays. A U.S. Artists Rockefeller fellow, Gander has been recipient of grants from the NEA, the Guggenheim, Howard, Witter Bynner and Whiting foundations. His 2011 collection *Core Samples from the World* was an NBCC and Pulitzer Prize finalist for poetry, and his 2018 collection *Be With* won the Pulitzer Prize for poetry and was longlisted for the National Book Award.

MATTHEW GILBERT is a co-founder and poetry editor of *Black Moon Magazine.* He reads for Orison Books and serves as a poetry editor at *Great Lakes Review.* He also edits the newsletter for Poetry Society of Tennessee—Northeast Chapter. His works have previously appeared in *Mockingbird, Delta Poetry Review, The Castle, Eunoia Review, Jimsonweed,* and *Mildred Haun Review,* among others.

CHARLES GILLISPIE was born and raised in Lynchburg, Virginia. Currently, he works as a counselor in Tucson, Arizona. He has published articles describing his work with poetry and counseling in *Addiction Professional, Journal of Poetry Therapy,* and the *Therapeutic Recreation Journal.* Charles has received grants and fellowships from the Arizona Commission on the Arts in support of his work with writing and therapy. His first collection of poems, *The Way We Go On,* was published by the Backwaters Press. Most recently, his poems have appeared in *December, Firewords, Nature 20/20, Oberon,* and *Psychological Perspectives.*

LEAH NAOMI GREEN is the author of *The More Extravagant Feast* (Graywolf Press, 2020), winner of the Walt Whitman Award of The Academy of American Poets. She received the 2021 Lucille Clifton Legacy Award and an AAP 2021 Treehouse Climate Action Poetry Prize. Green teaches environmental studies and English at Washington & Lee University. She lives in Rockbridge County, Virginia where she and her family homestead and grow much of their food for the year.

Happiest on a tractor named Mabel (a muse of 55 horsepower) LUCY FOWLKES GRIFFITH lives on a ranch beside the Guadalupe River near Comfort, Texas. Her first collection of poems *We Make a Tiny Herd* was published by Main Street Rag as a finalist in their poetry book contest. *Tiny Herd* was recently awarded the Wrangler Prize for Poetry by the Cowboy Hall of Fame as well as the 2020 Willa Literary Award for Poetry. She was the Returning Contributor Scholar in Poetry for the Bread Loaf Writers' Conference.

RAYMOND P. HAMMOND is the Editor-in-Chief of both the *New York Quarterly* and NYQ Books. He holds an MA in American Poetry from NYU's Gallatin School and is the author of *Poetic Amusement*, a book of literary criticism. He lives in Beacon, New York with his wife, the poet Amanda J. Bradley, and their dog Hank.

Born in southwest Virginia, CATHRYN HANKLA is the author of over a dozen books of poetry, fiction, and nonfiction, including *Not Xanadu, Lost Places: On Losing and Finding Home, Galaxies*, and *Great Bear*. She is professor emerita, Hollins University, and Poetry Editor of *The Hollins Critic*. She writes and paints in Roanoke, Virginia.

CHELSEA HARLAN grew up in the wilds of Appalachian Virginia, on the side of a mountain called No Business. She holds a BA in Literature from Bennington College and an MFA in Poetry from Brooklyn College, where she was a Truman Capote Fellow. Her poems are forthcoming or have appeared in *Sixth Finch, Hobart, Cold Mountain Review, The Greensboro Review, The American Poetry Review*, and elsewhere. She is the co-author of the chapbook *Mummy* (Montez Press, 2019), and the recipient of the 2019-2020 Mikrokosmos Poetry Prize. She lives in Brooklyn.

A native South Carolinian, DAVID HAVIRD completed his graduate education at the University of Virginia with a doctoral dissertation on Thomas Hardy. He is the author of three collections of poetry: *Weathering: Poems and Recollections* (2020), *Map Home* (2013), and *Penelope's Design* (2010). His poems and essays have appeared in many periodicals, including *Agni, The Hopkins Review, Literary Imagination*, and *The Yale Review*. He taught English for thirty years at Centenary College of Louisiana.

MARY CROCKETT HILL is the author of *A Theory of Everything*, winner of the Autumn House Prize, and *If You Return Home with Food*, winner of the Bluestem Poetry Award. Her work has been featured in *The Paris Review, The Southern Review, Poetry Daily*, and *Best of the Net*. As Mary Crockett, she writes fiction for children and young adults—most recently the novel *How She Died, How I Lived*, from Little Brown Books for Young Readers. Mary teaches creative writing at Roanoke College and edits *Roanoke Review*.

A native of upper East Tennessee, JANE HICKS is an award-winning poet, teacher, and quilter. Her poetry appears in both journals and numerous anthologies, including *The Southern Poetry Anthology: Contemporary Appalachia* and *The Southern Poetry Anthology: Tennessee*. Her first book, *Blood and Bone Remember*, was nominated for and won several awards. The University Press of Kentucky published her latest poetry book, *Driving with the Dead*, in the fall of 2014. It won the Appalachian Writers Association Poetry Book of the Year Award.

SCOTT HONEYCUTT'S maternal lineage has been traced back to the Jamestown colony, and he himself was born in Williamsburg. Scott spent his formative years in Bath County, Virginia, before moving to Knoxville, Tennessee. He has published numerous poems including two chapbooks, *This Diet of Flesh* (2016), and *Twelve North of the Kentucky River* (2018). When Scott is not teaching, he enjoys hiking the hills of Appalachia and spending time with his daughters.

EMILY HOOKER grew up in Smithfield, Virginia, a town in the Tidewater area of the state. She attended the University of Virginia where she earned a BA in English ('19) and an MT in Secondary Education ('20). She currently teaches 8th grade Language Arts. This is her first work to be published.

JOHN HOPPENTHALER'S books of poetry are *Lives of Water* (2003), *Anticipate the Coming Reservoir* (2008), and *Domestic Garden* (2015), all with Carnegie Mellon University Press. With Kazim Ali, he has co-edited a volume of essays and interviews on the poetry of Jean Valentine, *This-World Company* (U Michigan P, 2012). For the cultural journal *Connotation Press: An Online Artifact*, he edits "A Poetry Congeries," and he is on the advisory board for Backbone Press, a press dedicated to marginalized voices. He received his MFA from Virginia Commonwealth University and, for nine years, served as Personal Assistant to Toni Morrison. He is a Professor of Creative Writing and Literature at East Carolina University.

JESSICA K. HYLTON received her Ph.D. from the University of Louisiana at Lafayette and her MA from Radford University. Her collection of erasure poetry, *Gag Order*, was released by ankinoga press in September 2020. *The Great Scissor Hunt* was published by Headmistress Press in 2016. In her free time, Hylton reads for *Shenandoah* and enjoys the company of her rescue dogs.

LUISA A. IGLORIA is the author of *Maps for Migrants and Ghosts* (Co-Winner, 2019 Crab Orchard Open Poetry Prize), *The Buddha Wonders if She is Having a Mid-Life Crisis* (2018), 12 other books, and 4 chapbooks. Originally from Baguio City, she makes her home in Norfolk, Virginia where she teaches in Old Dominion University's MFA Creative Writing Program; and at The Muse Writers Center. In July 2020, she was appointed Poet Laureate of the Commonwealth of Virginia. The Academy of American Poets awarded her a 2021 Poet Laureate Fellowship in April 2021.

EDISON JENNINGS works as a Head Start bus monitor/driver in the southern Appalachian region of Virginia. He holds a Virginia Commission for the Arts Fellowship in Poetry. His poetry has appeared in several journals including *Kenyon Review, Poetry Daily, Slate,* and *TriQuarterly.* He is the author of three chapbooks, *Reckoning* (Jacar Press), *A Letter to Greta* (Plan B Press), and *Small Measures* (Wild Leek Press). His collection of poems, *Intentional Fallacies,* is available through Broadstone Press.

DON JOHNSON lived in Virginia for three years, graduating from Gar-field High School in Woodbridge, Virginia, in 1960. Until recently he owned acreage in the Tightsqueeze community of Chatham, Virginia, where his father's family had lived in a log cabin.

JEFFREY N. JOHNSON'S poetry has appeared in *Birmingham Poetry Review, The Carolina Quarterly, Dos Passos Review, Gargoyle, Red Rock Review, Roanoke Review, South Carolina Review,* and *War, Literature and the Arts.* His short story collection *Other Fine Gifts* won an Ippy Award for Best Regional Fiction/Mid-Atlantic, and included the Andrew Lytle Fiction Prize winner from *The Sewanee Review,* as well as stories previously published in *Aethlon, Clackamas Literary Review, Connecticut Review, The Evansville Review, Lake Effect, Potomac Review, South Dakota Review,* and *Wisconsin Review.* His novel *The Hunger Artist* was a finalist for the Library of Virginia's People's Choice Award, and his stage play *Affair at the Hotel Opal* had a full production at the Potomac Playmaker's 4th Annual One-Act Play Festival. He was also awarded a fellowship at the Virginia Center for the Creative Arts (VCCA) and a Creative Fellow grant from the Mid-Atlantic Arts Foundation.

Born in Waynesboro, Virginia, JOSHUA JONES received his MFA from UMass Boston and is a Ph.D. candidate at the University of North Texas. His poems and essays have appeared in *Image, Southwest Review,* and *Salamander,* among other journals.

M. A. KELLER, online editor for *Blackbird: an online journal of literature and the arts,* is a technologist, web coordinator, and writing instructor for Virginia Commonwealth University's Department of English. His poetry has appeared in the *New Virginia Review, Runes,* and *The Southern Review,* among others. He has taught poetry and advanced writing workshops as well as courses in hypertext and new media. Keller earned his MFA in creative writing from Virginia Commonwealth University.

JENNIFER KEY was born and raised in Roanoke, Virginia, and was educated at the University of Virginia. She received writing fellowships from the University of Virginia, the University of Wisconsin, and the University of Mississippi. Jennifer lives in Oxford, Mississippi, and is the author of *The Old Dominion* (U. Tampa Press).

CHELSEA KRIEG was born and raised in southeastern Virginia. She received an MFA in poetry from North Carolina State University. Her work may be found in *Tinderbox Poetry Journal, Greensboro Review, Poet Lore, Bellevue Literary Review, The McNeese Review,* and elsewhere. She teaches writing at North Carolina State University.

JESSI LEWIS grew up on a blueberry farm in rural Virginia. She was *Oxford American's* Debut Fiction Prize winner in 2018. In addition, her essays, short stories, and poems have been published in *The Hopkins Review, Sonora Review, The Pinch, Yemassee, Appalachian Heritage,* and *Flyway,* among others. Jessi's novel manuscript, *She Spoke Wire,* was a finalist for the PEN/Bellwether Prize for Socially Engaged Fiction.

CHRISTOPHER LINFORTH lived in Virginia for several years. He has work published in *Epiphany, Notre Dame Review, Southern Humanities Review, Gargoyle,* and other magazines. He has been awarded fellowships and scholarships to the Sewanee Writers' Conference, Vermont Studio Center, and the Virginia Center for the Creative Arts.

ROBERT WOOD LYNN is a writer from Virginia. His debut collection, *Mothman Apologia* (Yale University Press), was selected by Rae Armantrout as the winner of the 2021 Yale Series of Younger Poets prize. He is also the author of the poetry chapbook *How to Maintain Eye Contact*, from Button Poetry. He lives in the Shenandoah Valley.

CATHERINE MACDONALD is the author of *Rousing the Machinery*, winner of the 2012 Miller Williams Arkansas Poetry Prize (University of Arkansas Press). Her work has been published in *Prairie Schooner, Sou'wester, Washington Square, Louisville Review, Crab Orchard Review, Blackbird, Cortland Review*, and other journals. She is a Virginia native, currently living and teaching in Richmond, Virginia.

MARGARET MACKINNON'S poems have appeared in many journals including *Poetry, Image, Hampden-Sydney Poetry Review*, and *Alaska Quarterly Review*. She received her MFA in creative writing from the University of Florida. Her first book, *The Invented Child*, won the 2011 Gerald Cable Book Award and the 2014 Literary Award in Poetry given by the Library of Virginia. *Naming the Natural World* received the 2017 *Sow's Ear Poetry Review* chapbook award. She lives in Richmond, Virginia.

JOSH MAHLER lives and writes in Virginia, where he was educated at George Mason University. His poems have appeared in *The Carolina Quarterly, Puerto del Sol, Plainsongs, The Evansville Review, Exit 7, Chiron Review, Red Earth Review, San Pedro River Review*, and elsewhere.

JEFF MANN has published six books of poetry, *Bones Washed with Wine, On the Tongue, Ash, A Romantic Mann, Rebels*, and *Redneck Bouquet*; three collections of essays, *Edge, Binding the God, and Endangered Species*; a book of poetry and memoir, *Loving Mountains, Loving Men*; six novels, *Fog, Purgatory, Cub, Salvation, Country*, and *Insatiable*; and three volumes of short fiction, *A History of Barbed Wire, Desire and Devour*, and *Consent*. With Julia Watts, he co-edited *LGBTQ Fiction and Poetry from Appalachia*. The winner of two Lambda Literary Awards and four National Leather Association-International literary awards, he teaches creative writing at Virginia Tech.

JOHN Q. MARS is a Black and Queer writer, with works present in Indolent Books' *What Rough Beast, Appalachian Review*, and Damaged Goods Publications' *The Impossible Beast: Poems of Queer Eroticism*. He/They has a B.A. in Linguistics from New York University, where they also studied poetry and foreign languages. They are 22-years-old, born and raised in Winchester, Virginia, now living in Houston, Texas.

DR. IRÈNE P. MATHIEU is a pediatrician and writer. She is the author of *milk tongue* (Deep Vellum Press, 2023), *Grand Marronage* (Switchback Books, 2019), *orogeny* (Trembling Pillow Press, 2017), and *the galaxy of origins* (dancing girl press, 2014). Her poems have appeared in *American Poetry Review, Narrative, Boston Review, Virginia Quarterly Review, Callaloo, TriQuarterly*, and elsewhere. The recipient of fellowships from Fulbright, Callaloo, and the Virginia Center for the Creative Arts, she works as an Assistant Professor of Pediatrics at the University of Virginia.

A retired educator, GRETCHEN McCROSKEY grew up on a farm near Abingdon, Virginia. Her teaching career included 19 years in the Bristol, Virginia, school system and 22 years at Northeast State Community College in Blountville, Tennessee. Gretchen's poems have been published in a number of regional journals, and her chapbook *Finding My Way Home* was published by Finishing Line Press in 2009. She was named Poet Laureate of the Poetry Society of Tennessee for 2020-2021.

MARIANNE MERSEREAU grew up along Virginia's Crooked Road in the Southwest corner of the state. She is the author of the chapbook, *Timbrel* (Finishing Line Press, 2013). Her writing has appeared in *The Hollins Critic, Bella Grace, Entropy, The Dead Mule School of Southern Literature, Still Point Arts Quarterly, Deep South Magazine, Seattle's Poetry on Buses, Remington Review*, and elsewhere, and is published in several anthologies. She was awarded a Second Place Prize in Artists Embassy International's Dancing Poetry Contest in 2018. She currently resides in the Pacific Northwest.

JESSE MILLNER'S poems and prose have appeared in *Manzano Mountain Review, River Styx, Pearl, The Prose Poem Project, The Florida Review, Pithead Chapel, The Best American Poetry 2013*, and other literary magazines. He has published seven poetry chapbooks and two full-length collections, *The Neighborhoods of My Past Sorrow* (winner of bronze medal in 2010 Florida Book Awards) and *Dispatches from the Department of Supernatural Explanation* (Kitsune Books, 2012). His latest book, *Memory's Blue Sedan*, was released in March 2020 by Hysterical Books of Tallahassee, Florida. He currently teaches writing courses at Florida Gulf Coast University in Fort Myers, Florida.

JIM MINICK is the author of five books, the most recent, *Fire Is Your Water*, a novel. *The Blueberry Years*, his memoir, won the Best Nonfiction Book of the Year from Southern Independent Booksellers Association. His work has appeared in many publications including the *New York Times*, *Poets & Writers*, *Tampa Review*, *Shenandoah*, *Orion*, *Oxford American*, and *The Sun*. His newest book is *Spin: Three Tornados and a Pair of Ruby Slippers*, forthcoming from University of Nebraska Press.

FELICIA MITCHELL, whose deep family roots include Virginia and South Carolina, has made her home in rural southwestern Virginia since 1987. She taught English and creative writing for many years at Emory & Henry College before retiring with emeritus status. Her poems have appeared in journals and anthologies such as the recent *Mountains Piled Upon Mountains: Appalachian Nature Writing of the Anthropocene* (edited by Jessica Cory for West Virginia University Press). Poetry collections include *A Mother Speaks, a Daughter Listens: Journeying Together through Dementia* (Wising Up Press) and *Waltzing with Horses* (Press 53). Scholarly work includes *Her Words: Diverse Voices in Contemporary Appalachian Women's Poetry* (University of Tennessee Press).

THORPE MOECKEL has taught in the writing program at Hollins University since 2005. He is the author of several books. His work has been recipient of NEA, Javits, Hoyns, Sustainable Arts, and Kenan Fellowships. His middle grade novel, *True as True Can Be*, along with a collection of poems, *According to Sand*, will be published in 2022.

ELISABETH MURAWSKI is the author of *Heiress*, which received the Poetry Society of Virginia Award, *Zorba's Daughter*, which won the May Swenson Poetry Award, *Moon and Mercury*, and *Still Life with Timex*. Nearly three hundred poems have been published in journals or online. Prizes for individual poems include, among others: The Ledbury Poetry Festival Poetry Competition (2019), the University of Canberra's International Poetry Prize (2015), Shenandoah's Graybeal-Gowen Award (2011), and the Ann Stanford Poetry Prize (2006). She currently resides in Alexandria, Virginia.

YVONNE NGUYEN is a recent graduate at the University of Virginia, currently residing in Richmond, Virginia. As a full-time English teacher, she takes pride in nurturing creative instincts in her students. Recently, her poem "I Would've Called Her Honey" was shortlisted for the Brain Mill Press Poetry Month Award. Other works of hers can be read in *The Roadrunner Review* and *Call Me [Brackets]*.

MEL NICHOLS is the author of four collections of poetry, including *Catalytic Exteriorization Phenomenon* (National Poetry Series Finalist) and *Bicycle Day*. Her work can also be found at *The Huffington Post*, *Poetry*, *The Brooklyn Rail*, *Jacket2*, *PennSound*, and *HTML Giant*. She has been a visiting artist at the Corcoran College of Art & Design, the Museum of Contemporary Art in Detroit, and elsewhere, and she teaches digital poetry and other writing courses at George Mason University. New books are forthcoming from Flowers & Cream Press and Edge Books.

EVAN NICHOLLS is a poet from the peach and wine country of Fauquier County, Virginia. His chapbook, *Holy Smokes*, is forthcoming from Ghost City Press.

WILLIAM NOTTER is the author of *Holding Everything Down* (Southern Illinois University Press), which received the High Plains Book Award for Poetry and was a finalist for the Colorado Book Award, and the chapbook *More Space Than Anyone Can Stand* (Texas Review Press). He is an NEA fellowship recipient and a graduate of the University of Arkansas Program in Creative Writing and Translation. His poems have appeared in journals including *About Place*, *Alaska Quarterly*, *AGNI Online*, *Crab Orchard Review*, *The Hollins Critic*, *Cimarron Review*, *Southern Poetry Review*, and *Terrain.org*. He teaches at Virginia Commonwealth University.

GREGORY ORR is the author of over a dozen books of poetry including *Selected Books of the Beloved* (Copper Canyon, 2022). He has received fellowships from the Guggenheim Foundation and the National Endowment for the Arts, and an Award in Literature from the American Academy of Arts and Letters. Professor Emeritus at the University of Virginia, Orr taught there from 1975–2019 and was founder and first director of its MFA Program in Writing. He lives with his wife, the painter Trisha Orr, in Charlottesville, Virginia.

JAMES OWENS'S newest book is *Family Portrait with Scythe* (Bottom Dog Press, 2020). His poems and translations appear widely in literary journals, including recent or upcoming publications in *Atlanta Review*, *Chestnut Review*, *The Windhover*, and *Southword*. He grew up in Appalachian Southwest Virginia and worked on newspapers in the region, before earning an MFA at the University of Alabama. He now lives in a small town in northern Ontario.

LISA J. PARKER is a native Virginian, a poet, musician, and photographer. Her first book, *This Gone Place*, won the 2010 ASA Weatherford Award, her second book, *The Parting Glass*, won the 2021 Arthur Smith Poetry Prize, and her work is widely published in literary journals and anthologies. Her photography has been on exhibit in NYC and published in several arts journals and anthologies. She has worked in the Department of Defense for nearly 20 years, worked as a first responder for 15 years, and currently serves as a crisis and disaster response volunteer with Team Rubicon.

LYNDA FLEET PERRY is the author of a chapbook of poems, *At Winter Light Farm*. Her work has appeared in *Blackbird, defunct, New Zoo Poetry Review, qarrtsiluni*, and *Streetlight*. She manages advancement communications for a botanical garden in Richmond, Virginia, where she lives with her husband and daughter.

KIKI PETROSINO is the author of four books of poetry: *White Blood: a Lyric of Virginia* (2020), *Witch Wife* (2017), *Hymn for the Black Terrific* (2013), and *Fort Red Border* (2009), all from Sarabande Books. She holds graduate degrees from the University of Chicago and the University of Iowa Writer's Workshop. Her poems and essays have appeared in *Poetry, Best American Poetry, The Nation, The New York Times, FENCE, Gulf Coast, Jubilat, Tin House*, and online at *Ploughshares*. She teaches at the University of Virginia as a Professor of Poetry. Petrosino is the recipient of a Pushcart Prize, a Fellowship in Creative Writing from the National Endowment for the Arts, and an Al Smith Fellowship Award from the Kentucky Arts Council.

ALEX PICKENS lived in the Virginia Appalachian mountains for over twenty years, where he befriended bears and alienated neighbors. Recently his poetry has been accepted by *Crab Orchard, South 85, Tipton, Hawaii Pacific, New Southern Fugitives*, and *Constellations*, as well as being nominated for Best of the Net and the Pushcart. He is a direct descendant of a Revolutionary War general nicknamed "The Wizard Owl."

MATT PRATER is a writer from Saltville, Virginia. His work has appeared in *The Hollins Critic, Still: The Journal, Hampden-Sydney Poetry Review, Spillway*, and elsewhere. He has taught undergraduate composition and English at Virginia Tech and Emory & Henry, among other colleges.

RITA SIMS QUILLEN'S new novel *Wayland*, a sequel to *Hiding Ezra*, was published by Iris Press in fall, 2019, and her new poetry collection *Some Notes You Hold*, was published by Madville Press in 2020. Her full-length poetry collection, *The Mad Farmer's Wife*, published in 2016 by Texas Review Press was a finalist for the Weatherford Award in Appalachian Literature from Berea College. One of six semi-finalists for the 2012-14 Poet Laureate of Virginia, she received three Pushcart nominations, and a Best of the Net nomination in 2012. She lives, farms, writes songs, and takes photographs at Early Autumn Farm in southwestern Virginia.

VALENCIA ROBIN'S debut poetry collection, *Ridiculous Light*, won Persea Books' Lexi Rudnitsky First Book Prize, was a finalist for the Kate Tufts Discovery Award and was named one of *Library Journal's* Best Poetry Books of 2019. A Cave Canem Fellow, Robin's honors include a 2021 National Endowment for the Arts Fellowship. Robin lives in Charlottesville, Virginia where she is a co-director of the University of Virginia Young Writers Workshop.

ALLISON SEAY is the recipient of fellowships from the Ruth Lilly Foundation, the National Endowment for the Arts, and the Civitella Rainieri Foundation. She is the author of a book of poems, *To See the Queen*, and has placed work in such journals as *Image, Crazyhorse, Field*, and *Poetry*. She lives in Richmond, Virginia.

OLIVIA SERIO earned a BA in English and Creative Writing from Washington College in 2017 and is looking forward to pursuing her Ph.D. in English Literature. Her work has appeared in or is forthcoming in *THAT Literary Review, Prometheus Dreaming*, and *Funicular Magazine*, among others. She currently resides in the Virginia suburbs of Washington, D.C. with her two cats Jane and Lizzie.

LEONA SEVICK is the 2017 Press 53 Poetry Award Winner for her first full-length book of poems, *Lion Brothers*. Her recent work appears in *Crab Orchard Review, The Southeast Review, The Arkansas International, Rhino Poetry, The Cortland Review, Birmingham Poetry Review, Four Way Review, Seneca Review, Blackbird*, and

Spillway. Her work also appears in *The Golden Shovel Anthology: New Poems Honoring Gwendolyn Brooks*. Sevick was named a 2019 Walter E. Dakin Fellow for the Sewanee Writers' Conference, and her work has been nominated for two Pushcart Prizes. She serves as advisory board member of the Furious Flower Black Poetry Center and is provost at Bridgewater College in Virginia, where she teaches Asian American literature.

LESLIE SHIEL is the author of two chapbooks, *Braided* and *Self-Portrait as a New Name* (Finishing Line Press, 2017, 2015), and has published poems in *The Southern Review, Crab Orchard Review, The Sun, Poetry International, Christianity and Literature*, and other journals. Her essay "The Deep Hold"—about poet Claudia Emerson—appears in *Blackbird* (19.1, Spring 2020). She teaches at Virginia Commonwealth University, where she received the College of Humanities and Sciences 2014 Distinguished Adjunct Award, and the Visual Arts Center of Richmond, where she received the 2014 Shelly Betchel Master Teacher Award. She has received an Individual Artist's Grant from the Virginia Commission for the Fine Arts, and was twice a Fellow at the Virginia Center for the Arts.

MAIA SIEGEL is based in Roanoke, Virginia. Her poetry is forthcoming or published at *Poetry London, The Saranac Review, Cargoes*, and elsewhere. She has been recognized by organizations such as The Poetry Society and The Hippocrates Society.

ROD SMITH's latest book is *Touché* (Wave, 2015). His other books include *Deed* (U. Iowa, 2007), *Music or Honesty* (Roof, 2003), and *The Good House* (Spectacular Books, 2001). He has taught at the The Iowa Writers' Workshop, The Maryland Institute College of Art, and The Corcoran College of Art + Design. Smith edited *The Selected Letters of Robert Creeley* (U. Cal Press, 2014) with Kaplan Harris and Peter Baker.

RON SMITH, Poet Laureate of Virginia 2014-2016, is the author of five books, four from LSU Press, including *That Beauty in the Trees*.

R. T. SMITH was raised and educated in Georgia and North Carolina, and has lived in Alabama and Virginia. His nineteen books of poems include two Library of Virginia Books of the Year (*Messenger* and *Outlaw Style*) and he has published six collections of stories, notably *Uke Rivers* and *Chinquapins. In the Night Orchard: New and Selected Poems* was published by Texas Review Press in 2014. Smith has been writer-in-Residence at Washington and Lee, Appalachian State, Auburn, Converse, VMI, and others. In 2014 he received the Carole Weinstein Award for Contribution to Virginia Poetry, and he has received a Virginia Governor's Award for Achievement in the Arts, along with Ralph Stanley, Lee Smith, and others. Rod has edited six journals and retired from *Shenandoah* after twenty-three years as editor. He and his wife, writer Sarah Kennedy, live on Timber Ridge in Rockbridge County, Virginia.

LISA RUSS SPAAR is the author/editor of over ten books of poetry and criticism, most recently *Madrigalia: New & Selected Poems* (Persea, 2021) and a debut novel, *Paradise Close* (Persea Books, May 2022). Her honors include a Rona Jaffe Award, a Guggenheim Fellowship, the Library of Virginia Prize for Poetry, the Carole Weinstein Poetry Prize, and a Pushcart Prize. She writes a regular column about second books of poetry at the *Los Angeles Review of Books*. Spaar is a professor of English at the University of Virginia, where she founded the Area Program in Poetry Writing and for many years directed the Creative Writing Program.

SAPPHO STANLEY is a transsexual poet who grew up in Pound, Virginia. She recently graduated with her BA in English at East Tennessee State University. She is currently in the first year of her program at The Ohio State University's Creative Writing MFA program. You can find her work in other journals: *Novus Literary Arts Journal, The Mockingbird, Warning Lines*, and *the lickety˜split*. She uses she/they pronouns.

SOFIA M. STARNES, D.Litt. (hon.), Virginia Poet Laureate, Emerita, is the author of six poetry collections, most recently *The Consequence of Moonlight* (Paraclete Press, 2018). Her work has appeared widely in such journals as *Poetry, Notre Dame Review, Bellevue Literary Review, Laurel Review*, and *Hayden's Ferry*, as well as in various anthologies, including the Best of the Decade edition of the *Hawai'i Pacific Review*. She currently serves on the editorial board of several publications.

RUTH STONE was born in Roanoke, Virginia and was the author of thirteen books of poetry. A National Book Award Winner, National Book Critics Circle Award Winner, and a finalist for the Pulitzer Prize, Stone died in 2011.

HENRY TAYLOR is the author of over fifteen books of poems including *The Flying Change* (LSUP, 1986) which was awarded the Pulitzer Prize.

RANDOLPH THOMAS is the author of the poetry collection *The Deepest Rooms*, winner of the George Cable Award from Silverfish Review Press. His poems have appeared in *New Letters, Southern Poetry Review, The Common, Pleiades, Poetry, Poetry Daily, Verse Daily*, and many other journals. He is also the author of a short story collection *Dispensations*. A native of southwestern Virginia, he received a BA from Radford University and an MFA from the University of Arkansas. He teaches at Louisiana State University.

MICHAEL TROCCHIA'S poems have appeared in *Baltimore Review, Black Sun Lit, Colorado Review, Fourteen Hills, New Orleans Review, The Worcester Review, UCity Review*, and elsewhere. Work is forthcoming in *Arion* and *The Chattahoochee Review*. In 2014 *The Fatherlands*, a chapbook of prose poems, surfaced with Monkey Puzzle Press. He's lived in the Shenandoah Valley since 2007.

ELLEN BRYANT VOIGT grew up on her family's farm in rural Virginia. She earned a BA from Converse College and an MFA from the Iowa Writers' Workshop. Her many poetry collections include *Headwaters* (2013), *Messenger: New and Selected Poems 1976–2006*, and *Shadow of Heaven* (2002).

G. C. WALDREP was born in 1968 in South Boston, Virginia. He is the author of seven collections of poetry, most recently *feast gently* (Tupelo, 2018), winner of the William Carlos Williams Award from the Poetry Society of America, and *The Earliest Witnesses* (Tupelo/Carcanet, 2021). Since 2007 Waldrep has lived in Lewisburg, Pennsylvania, where he teaches at Bucknell University.

JORRELL WATKINS is an educator, writer, and martial artist from Richmond, Virginia. He is an alum of Hampshire College, and current MFA Poetry student at the University of Iowa, Writer's Workshop. He has received awards from the VQR Writer's Conference, and Echo Theater Company and fellowships from the Association of University Centers on Disabilities and Smithsonian Institution. His disability inclusive play, *Meet us at the Horizon*, was produced by Combined Efforts Co. for its 2019 world premiere. His chapbook, *If Only the Sharks Would Bite*, was selected by Aimee Nezhukumatathil as the winner of the inaugural Desert Pavilion Chapbook Series in Poetry. His poetry is published in *Obsidian, The Amistad Journal, Juke Joint Magazine*, and elsewhere.

L. A. WEEKS spent most of her life in coastal Virginia. Her work can be found or is forthcoming in *Green Mountains Review Online, Colorado Review, Smartish Pace, The Chattahoochee Review*, and elsewhere.

BRIAN PHILLIP WHALEN'S debut collection of fiction, *Semiotic Love [Stories]*, was published by Awst Press in 2021. His work can be found in *The Southern Review, Creative Nonfiction, Copper Nickel, North American Review*, the *Flash Nonfiction Food* anthology, and elsewhere. Brian has a Ph.D. from the State University of New York at Albany and is the recipient of a Vermont Studio Center residency. He also has a Masters degree from James Madison University in Virginia (his parents, and his heart, still reside in the Shenandoah Valley). Brian teaches creative and first-year writing at The University of Alabama, in Tuscaloosa.

STEPHEN SCOTT WHITAKER is a member of the National Book Critics Circle and the co-editor of *The Broadkill Review*. Whitaker is a teaching artist with the Virginia Commission for the Arts, an educator, and a grant writer. His poems have appeared in *Fourteen Hills, The Shore, Crab Creek Review*, and *River Heron Review*, and other journals. He is the author of four chapbooks of poetry and a broadside from Broadsided Press. *Mulch*, his novel of weird fiction was published by Montag Press in 2021.

BETH OAST WILLIAMS'S poetry has appeared in *West Texas Literary Review, Wisconsin Review, Glass Mountain, GASHER Journal, Poetry South, Fjords Review*, and *Rattle's Poets Respond*, among others. Her poems have been nominated twice for the Pushcart Prize. Her first chapbook, *Riding Horses in the Harbor*, was published in 2020.

ABBY WOLPERT is an emerging writer and artist from Roanoke, Virginia. Her work has appeared or is forthcoming in *86 Logic, The Cardiff Review, The Dewdrop, Levee Magazine, Pwatem Literary Journal*, and *Soft Punk Magazine*.

KARENNE WOOD was a member of the Monacan Indian tribe and served as the director of the Virginia Indian Programs at Virginia Humanities. In 2015 she was named one of the Library of Virginia's "Virginia Women in History."

DIANA WOODCOCK is the author of seven chapbooks and three poetry collections, most recently *Tread Softly* (FutureCycle Press, 2018) and *Near the Arctic Circle* (Tiger's Eye Press, 2018). She has two books out in 2021: *Facing Aridity* (a finalist for the 2020 Prism Prize for Climate Literature, Homebound Publications); and *Holy Sparks* (Paraclete Press). Recipient of the 2011 Vernice Quebodeaux Poetry Prize for Women for her debut collection, *Swaying on the Elephant's Shoulders*, her work appears in *Best New Poets 2008*. Currently teaching in Qatar at Virginia Commonwealth University's branch campus, she holds a Ph.D. in Creative Writing from Lancaster University.

ANNIE WOODFORD—originally from Henry County, Virginia—is the author of *Bootleg* (Groundhog Poetry Press, 2019). Her poetry has appeared or is forthcoming in *The Anthology of Appalachian Writers, Epoch, Southern Humanities Review, Blackbird, The Southern Review, The Sewanee Review,* and *Prairie Schooner.* A graduate of the creative writing program at Hollins College, she has also been awarded scholarships from the Bread Loaf and Sewanee writers' conferences as well as Barbara Deming Fund and Jean Ritchie fellowships. In 2017 she won the Graybeal-Gowen Prize for Virginia Poets. After living in Roanoke, Virginia until 2018, she now teaches community college English in Wilkesboro, North Carolina.

AMY WOOLARD is a legal aid attorney working on civil rights policy and legislation in Virginia. Her debut poetry collection, *Neck of the Woods*, received the 2018 Alice James Award and was published by Alice James Books in 2020. Her poems have appeared in *The New Yorker, The Paris Review, Poetry, Boston Review, Ploughshares, Fence,* and elsewhere, while her essays and reporting have been featured in publications such as *Slate, The Guardian, Pacific Standard,* and *The Rumpus,* as well as *Virginia Quarterly Review,* which awarded her the Staige D. Blackford Prize for Nonfiction in 2016. She has received fellowships from the National Endowment for the Arts, the Vermont Studio Center, and the Breadloaf Writers' Conference. She lives in Charlottesville, Virginia.

AMY WRIGHT is the current Wayne G. Basler Chair of Excellence at East Tennessee State University. Her nonfiction debut, *Paper Concert: A Conversation in the Round,* was published in 2021 with Sarabande Books. She has also authored three poetry books, six chapbooks, and received two Peter Taylor Fellowships to the *Kenyon Review* Writers Workshop, an Individual Artist Grant from the Tennessee Arts Commission, and a fellowship to the Virginia Center for the Creative Arts. Her essays and poems appear in *Georgia Review, Fourth Genre, Ninth Letter, Brevity,* and elsewhere.

CHARLES WRIGHT was born in Pickwick Dam, Tennessee, in 1935 and was educated at Davidson College and the University of Iowa. His books include *Sestets: Poems* (Farrar, Straus and Giroux, 2010); *Littlefoot: A Poem* (2008); *Scar Tissue* (2007), which was the international winner for the Griffin Poetry Prize; *Buffalo Yoga* (Farrar, Straus & Giroux, 2004); *Negative Blue* (2000); *Appalachia* (1998); *Black Zodiac* (1997), which won the Pulitzer Prize and the *Los Angeles Times* Book Prize, *Chickamauga* (1995), which won the 1996 Lenore Marshall Poetry Prize; *The World of the Ten Thousand Things: Poems 1980-1990; Zone Journals* (1988); *Country Music: Selected Early Poems* (1983), which won the National Book Award; *Hard Freight* (1973), which was nominated for the National Book Award, among others. He has also written two volumes of criticism and has translated the work of Dino Campana in *Orphic Songs* as well as Eugenio Montale's *The Storms and Other Poems,* which was awarded the PEN Translation Prize. He was Souder Family Professor of English at the University of Virginia in Charlottesville.

ACKNOWLEGMENTS

The editors wish to thank Tanner Linkous for assistance with proofing and editorial, and Miranda Ramírez for assistance with design and layout.

For contributors who supplied publication information, details are listed below. All poem copyrights have reverted back to respective authors, listed or otherwise, and Texas Review Press has permission to reprint poems included herein.

APRIL J. ASBURY: "Canning Time" originally appeared in *Anthology of Appalachian Writers*, Volume XII (Shepherd University, 2020). **DARNELL ARNOULT**: "Learning Strategy at English Field" originally appeared in *What Travels With Us* (LSU Press, 2005). "Ode to the Dixie Pig–Business 220" originally appeared in *Galaxie Wagon* (LSU Press, 2016). "The Gorilla Story" originally appeared in *Southern Cultures*, Vol. 21, No. 2, Summer 2015. **EMMA AYLOR**: "Saltern" originally appeared in *Sixth Finch*, Summer 2019. It uses information and some found text from "A Brief History of Salt" (*TIME*, 1982), Mike Hanback's "Mineral Licks: What You Need to Know" (*Bowhunting World*, 2016), and Larry D. Thacker's *Mountain Mysteries: Investigating the Mystic Traditions of Appalachia* (Overmountain Press, 2006). "Hydronym" originally appeared in *New Limestone Review*, November 2019. The italicized text in section 2 and the rain signs in section 3 come from Patrick W. Gainer's *Witches, Ghosts and Signs: Folklore of the Southern Appalachians* (Seneca Books, 1975). **ZEINA AZZAM**: "Like the Trees in Alexandria" was written and read by the poet for the City of Alexandria's 273rd Birthday Celebration, July 9th, 2022. "A Grammar for Fleeing" and "A Language for Colors" originally appeared in *Cutleaf Journal*, Issue 2.5, March 2022. "A Refugee Grows Old" originally appeared in *Cordite Poetry Review*, December 2019. "To Bring Justice Near" was written as Poet Laureate of the City of Alexandria, VA, April 23rd, 2022. **TARA BRAY**: "Bird on Knee" originally appeared in *Image*, vol. 97, 2018, p. 71. "Owl Prayer" originally appeared in *Tar River Poetry Review*, vol. 59, no. 2, 2020, p. 28. **ROBERT BRICKHOUSE**: "Crossing the Inlet" originally appeared in *Southern Poetry Review*, 50:1, 2012. "Days at the Store" originally appeared in the *Texas Review*, Fall/Winter 2007. **CANDACE BUTLER**: "Still Life" originally appeared in *The Pikeville Review*, Spring 2015. "White Wire" originally appeared in *Prime Number Magazine*, Issue 67. "Still Life" and "White Wire" appeared in *Nothing Is So Lovely* (Finishing Line Press, 2016). "The Kiss" originally appeared in *In Gilded Frame Anthology* (Kind of a Hurricane Press, 2013) and *Anthology of Appalachian Writers*, Nikki Giovanni *Volume VIII* (2016). **BEN E. CAMPBELL**: "Soup Bean Supper" originally appeared in *Broad River Review*, Volume 51. **JOHN CASTEEN**: "Incomplete Stranger" originally appeared in *The Southern Review*. "Dining Alone" originally appeared in *The Hampden-Sydney Poetry Review*. "My Time Among the Swells" originally appeared in *Blackbird*. "Bird-Teasing After the Hurricane" originally appeared in *The Missouri Review Online*. "For the Mountain Laurel" originally appeared in *Prairie Schooner*. **MICHAEL CHITWOOD**: "The Great Wagon Road, or How History Knocked the Professor Cold, or a Storyteller's Story, or Why Appalachians Are Mountains and a People" originally appeared in *Gospel Road Going* (Tryon Publishing Co., 2002). **KATHY DAVIS**: "Undone" and "Eve: After the Fall" are from *Passiflora* (Cider Press Review, 2021). "Undone" originally appeared in *The Southern Review* (Volume 52:4) Autumn 2016. "Eve: After the Fall" originally appeared in *The Southern Review* (Volume 47:3) Summer 2011. **RITA DOVE**: "Declaration of Interdependence", from PLAYLIST FOR THE APOCALYPSE: POEMS by Rita Dove. Copyright © 2021 by Rita Dove. Used by permission of W. W. Norton & Company, Inc. **MICHAEL DOWDY**: "The Urbilly's Field Guide" originally appeared in *Urbilly* (Main Street Rag Publishing, 2017), and is a cento made with language from Muriel Rukeyser's "The Road" (1938). "The Urbilly's Family Tree, As Seen Through Binoculars" originally appeared in *drafthorse*, 2015. **HILDA DOWNER**: "Clothespins" and "Buttons" originally appeared in *When Light Waits for Us* (Main Street Rag, 2021). **CLAUDIA EMERSON**: Emerson, Claudia. "Bee." *Claude before Time and Space*, Louisiana State University Press, 2018. **J. INDIGO ERIKSEN**: "Clint" originally appeared in *TYCA-Se Journal*, Spring & Fall 2019, Vol. 52, Number 1 & 2. **LATORIAL FAISON**: "Mama was a Negro Spiritual" first appeared in *Winning Writers* as winner of the 2018 Tom Howard Poetry Prize. "Mama Sang the Blues" first appeared in *Penumbra Online*, Fall 2020 issue. **FORREST GANDER**: "Moving Around for the Light: a Madrigal" By Forrest Gander, from CORE SAMPLES FROM THE WORLD, copyright ©2004, 2006, 2007, 2008, 2009, 2011 by Forrest Gander. Reprinted by permission of New Directions Publishing Corp. **LEAH NAOMI GREEN**: "The Transitive Property of Song" and "Jacob Have I Loved" originally appeared in *VQR*, Spring 2022. "Origin" originally appeared in *Poem-a-Day*, May 1, 2021, by the Academy of American Poets. "The More Extravagant Feast" originally appeared in *Tin House*, Spring 2018. **CATHRYN HANKLA**: "In the Belly" originally appeared in *Poems for the Pardoned* (LSU, 2002). "Twenty Minute Exposure" originally appeared in *Last Exposures* (LSU, 2004), reprinted with permission of the publisher. **DAVID HAVIRD**: "Molting," "The Weight of a Feather," and "Prayers for a Giant" originally appeared in *Weathering: Poems and Recollections* (Mercer UP, 2020). "Habit of the Heart" originally appeared in *Map Home* (TRP, 2010). **JANE HICKS**: "Night Music" and "Pyburn Creek" originally appeared in *Appalachian Places*, October 2021. **MARY CROCKETT HILL**: "Backwards Ghazal and Never Again" originally appeared in *storySouth*, Fall 2017. "The Farmers of Good Dirt" originally appeared in *Boston Review*, October 1998, and *If You Return Home with Food* (Bluestem Press, 1999). **JOHN HOPPENTHALER**: "Superstition" originally appeared in *Great River Review*, 2015. "Passing" is from Domestic Garden (Carnegie Mellon, 2015). **JESSICA K. HYLTON**: "Daddy's Gun" originally appeared in *East Coast Literary Review*, July 2014. **LUISA A. IGLORIA**: "Song of Meridians," "The Heart's Every Heave," and "Fatalism" originally appeared in *Maps for Migrants and Ghosts* (Southern Illinois UP, 2020). **EDISON JENNINGS**: "Directions to a Ruin" originally appeared in *Sow's Ear Poetry Review*. "Connoisseur of Decline" originally appeared in *American Journal of Poetry*. **DON JOHNSON**: "Isinglass," "Photograph of My Great-Grandmother, Nancy Bett Johnson, Circa 1923," "Swans on Quantico Creek," and "One Quail, Whistling" originally appeared in *More Than Heavy Rain* (TRP, 2014). **JEFFREY N. JOHNSON**: "Particle Search in D Minor" originally appeared in *Birmingham Poetry Review*, spring 2017, No. 44. "Things Boys Bury" originally appeared in *Oxford Magazine*, spring 2016, Issue 37. **JENNIFER KEY**: "Winter Solstice" first appeared in *Tupelo Quarterly*, 14 Jun. 2018. "Blue Ridge" first appeared in *Failbetter*, 5 Mar. 2014. "Ghost Palm" first appeared in *The Nashville Review*, 1 Aug. 2018. **CHELSEA KRIEG**: "*Callinectes sapidus*" originally appeared in *Greensboro Review* 106, October 2019. **JESSI LEWIS**: "Should I Draw the Mountain for You?" originally appeared in *Naugatuck River Review*, vol. 8, no. 17, 2016, Annual Poetry Contest Finalist. **ROBERT WOOD LYNN**: "Voicemail From My Mother" originally appeared in *The Greensboro Review*, Fall 2020. "It Was Time Again for Bushhogging the Paddock" originally appeared in *Narrative Magazine*, December 2021. "About the Phones" originally appeared in *Poetry Daily*, May 24, 2022. "The Summer After the Winter I Taught You How to Start a Fire" originally appeared in *Columbia Journal*, March 2022. All poems appeared in *Mothman Apologia* (Yale UP, 2022). **CATHERINE MACDONALD**: "Court and Bower" originally appeared in *Prairie Schooner*, vol. 89, no. 1, 2015, p. 45. "Bird Study" originally appeared in *Blackbird: an online journal of literature and the arts*, Vol. 18, no. 1, Spring 2018. "Rousing the Machinery" Credit: Catherine MacDonald. "Rousing the Machinery" from *Rousing the Machinery*. Copyright © 2012 by the University of Arkansas Press. Reprinted with the permission of the publisher, www.uapress.com. **MARGARET MACKINNON**: "Anne Spencer's Letter / Family Portrait" first appeared in *Fledgling Rag*, Issue 20, Spring 2020, Iris G. Press. "Flight" first appeared in *The Delmarva Review*, Issue 14, Fall 2021. **JEFF MANN**: All poems originally appeared in *Redneck Bouquet* (Lethe Press, 2020). "Cosmos" appeared in *Pine Mountain Sand & Gravel* 23 (2020). "Green Man" appeared in *Impossible Archetype* 7 (March 2020). "Gold" appeared in *Hibernation and Other Poems by Bear Bards*, edited by Ron J. Suresha (Lethe Press, 2014). "Hemlocks" appeared in *Appalachian Heritage* 33.1 (Winter 2005). **IRÈNE P. MATHIEU**: "Soil" originally appeared in *orogeny* (Trembling Pillow Press, 2017). "Thunder's baby" was selected by Jericho Brown as the 2017 winner of *Yemassee Journal*'s annual poetry prize and originally appeared in the journal as well as in *Grand Marronage* (Switchback Books, 2019). **GRETCHEN MCCROSKEY**: "Shapes of Comfort" originally appeared in *Fresh Breath*. **MARIANNE MERSEREAU**: "Sleeping with the Serpent" originally appeared in *The Hollins Critic*, Vol. LVI, no. 2, April 2019. "Bees and Tobacco" originally appeared in *The Dead Mule School of Southern Literature*, April 2020. **JIM MINICK**: "First Hard Frost" originally appeared in *Appalachian Journal*. "Tim Slack" originally appeared in *Tampa Review*. **FELICIA MITCHELL**: "Mother Tree, *Ailanthus altissima*" originally appeared in *Cheat River Review*, Issue 14, Fall/Winter 2020. "Another Eden" originally appeared in *Kestrel*. "With Howard Finster at the Taubman Museum" originally appeared in *The James Dickey Review*. "A Love Poem for My Son at Wilburn Ridge" originally appeared in *Pendora*. "A Poem for Lost

Ancestors" originally appeared in *Amsterdam Quarterly*. **THORPE MOECKEL**: "West Fork of the Little" and "Little Red Creek" originally appeared in *Hampden-Sydney Poetry Review*, Fall 2018. "Crowded Barnyard, Pretty Spring Day, One Little Goat" originally appeared in *Field*, Fall 2011. "On Hearing the Waterthrush Again, Jefferson" originally appeared in *Monticello in Mind: 50 Contemporary Poems on Jefferson* (UVA Press, 2016). **ELISABETH MURAWSKI**: "Still Life With Timex" first appeared in *Tar River Poetry*, Vol. 54, No. 2, Spring, 2015, *Heiress* (TRP, 2018), and *Still Life with Timex* (TRP, 2021). "In the Meadow" first appeared in *Southword*, Issue 28, July 2015, *Heiress* (TRP, 2018), and *Still Life with Timex* (TRP, 2021). "Know, Heart" first appeared in *Cumberland River Review*, Issue 9-2, 2020, and *Still Life with Timex* (TRP, 2021). "Waking Alone on Sunday Morning" first appeared in *Mudfish*, No. 18, 2014, and *Heiress* (TRP, 2018). "Elegiac" first appeared in *The Southern Review*, Vol. 51:1, Winter, 2015, and *Heiress* (TRP, 2018). **YVONNE NGUYEN**: "I Would've Called her Honey" originally appeared in *West Trade Review*, Spring 2021. **EVAN NICHOLLS**: "The Mud Doctor" originally appeared in *Passages North* (online, 'Bonus Content'), April 24, 2018. "Wildfire" originally appeared in "The Take" (Fall 2019) at *Mud Season Review* (online), December 4, 2019. "Rock Hill Mill Stable" originally appeared in *GASHER* (online), May 2, 2019. **WILLIAM NOTTER**: "Wondering About Cremation" originally appeared in *Lake Effect* no. 16, 2012. "Field Mice in the Garage" originally appeared in *North American Review* vol. 304 no. 3, 2019. "First Death" originally appeared in *Tar River Poetry* vol. 59 no. 2, Spring 2020. **GREGORY ORR**: "If the world were to end..." originally appeared in *PLUME*, 2022. All poems reprinted with permission of the author. **JAMES OWENS**: "Last Thoughts Cooling Like an Abandoned Cup" first appeared in *James Dickey Review*, Vol. 33, 2017. "Scythe" first appeared in *West Texas Literary Review*, Issue 6, June 2018. "Poem Ending with an Imitation of a Line from Phillippe Jaccottet" first appeared in *Southword*, no. 35, August 2018. All three poems appear in *Family Portrait with Scythe* (Bottom Dog Press, 2020). **LISA J. PARKER**: "Deployment: Homefront" originally appeared in *Drafthorse Literary Journal*, 2013. **LYNDA FLEET PERRY**: "Tracking" first appeared in *At Winter Light Farm*, (Finishing Line Press, 2011), reprinted with permission of The Permissions Company LLC on behalf of Finishing Line Press. **KIKI PETROSINO**: "Farm Book" and "Monticello House Tour" originally appeared in *White Blood: A Lyric of Virginia* (Sarabande Books, 2020). Reprinted with permission of the publisher. **ALEX PICKENS**: "The Reel" originally appeared in *Silver Blade*, Issue 42, 30 May 2019. "Malaisonaisse" originally appeared in *New Southern Fugitives*, Vol. 2 Issue 16, 19 June 2019. **RITA SIMS QUILLEN**: "The Gospel of Junior" and "Something in that Winter Light" originally appeared in *Some Notes You Hold* (Madville Publishing, 2020). "A Woman Born to Farming" originally appeared in *The Mad Farmer's Wife* (TRP, 2016). **VALENCIA ROBIN**: "After Graduate School" originally appeared in *Poem-a-Day* (Academy of American Poets) and *Emerging Form*. "Ask your grandmother," "Sometimes life feels like daytime TV," and "First Walk of the Year" originally appeared in *Virginia Quarterly Review*. "Late" originally appeared in *Forum Magazine*. **ALLISON SEAY**: "*Thou (the well)*" and "*Thou (a feather)*," originally appeared in *Image* 111, December 2021. "*Thou (August landscape)*" originally appeared in *Cave Wall*, Fall 2018. "*Thou (the white moth)*" and "Mother *(of the unborn)*," originally appeared in *Eco Theo Review*, June 2020. **OLIVIA SERIO**: The title "Let's go get the shit kicked out of us for love." is a line spoken by Sam in the movie *Love Actually*. The title "Metrorail weekend reconstruction begins with service adjustments through system closing Sunday." comes from an announcement regarding the Washington D.C. Metrorail system via the WMATA Twitter account @Metrorailinfo in 2017. **LESLIE SHIEL**: "Office Hours" originally appeared in *What Canst Thou Say*, 2005. "Office Hours" appeared in *Self-Portrait as a New Name* (Finishing Line Press, 2015), reprinted with permission of The Permissions Company LLC on behalf of Finishing Line Press. **MAIA SIEGEL**: "The Kroger Car-Loading Service" first appeared in *The Dennington Review*, Issue 8. **ROD SMITH**: "Identity is the Cause of Warts" originally appeared in *Deed* (U of Iowa Press, 2007). "The Good House, etc." originally appeared in *Touché* (Wave Books, 2015). **RON SMITH**: "Photograph of Jesse Owns at the Gun" originally appeared in *Running Again in Hollywood Cemetery* (2nd Edition), (MadHat Press, 2020). "This Moment" originally appeared in *Plume*, 1 December 2020, https://plumepoetry.com/this-moment/. "I Always Thought I'd Die" originally appeared in *Arts of War & Peace*, Université Paris Diderot, Vol. II, May 2019. **R. T. SMITH**: "Shades" originally appeared in *Sewanee Review* and *Summoning Shades* (Mercer UP, 2019). "Mockingbird" and "Mallard" originally appeared in *In the Night Orchard: New and Selected Poems* (TRP, 2014). **SAPPHO STANLEY**: "Joseph Stanley Did You Dream of Transsexuals?" originally appeared in *The Lickety Split*. "One night celibacy" originally appeared in *Novus Literary Arts Journal*. **RUTH STONE**: Ruth Stone, "In the Interstices" and "At Eighty-three She Lives Alone" from

CPSIA information can be obtained
at www.ICGtesting.com
Printed in the USA
LVHW101723221022
730997LV00010B/12